Augsburg College
George Sverdrup Library
Minneapolis, Minnesota 55404

WITHDRAWN

D1622916

STEPCHILD IN THE FAMILY

STEPCHILD
IN THE FAMILY
A View of Children in Remarriage

by

Anne W. Simon

 THE ODYSSEY PRESS,
NEW YORK

Copyright © 1964 by Anne W. Simon

All rights reserved

Published by Odyssey Press, Inc.

850 Third Avenue, New York 22, N.Y.

Printed in USA by

Western Printing & Lithographing Co., Inc.

Library of Congress Catalog Card Number: 64-14669

HQ
784
S7
S5

TO

THE HOUSE

THAT

BOB

BUILT

57711

CONTENTS

ILLUSTRATIONS

INTRODUCTION

Suddenly the stepchild state has changed, suddenly, that is, in the ages of man. In this twentieth century, the modern stepchild jumps out of folklore clamoring for recognition. One child in nine is a stepchild; a goodly number of Americans alive today have grown up in the stepchild state, perhaps 20 million in all. Parents and stepparents swell the numbers of people who have lived in a step family to more than a fifth of our citizenry by conservative guess. Each year there are more parental divorces, more remarriages; in the 1960's —for the first time ever—more stepchildren are the product of divorce than of bereavement. The softly read bedtime story tells that stepchildren are desolate, stepparents cruel. Until now there has been no compelling reason to challenge its message, and successive generations have passed it along, comforted enough by its partial truth to accept it as the whole truth.

Today, there is every reason to know more about the complicated human condition of the stepchild. He is an exponent of the modern idea of marriage.

Each stepchild need not suffer as if he were the first, and stepparents do not have to muddle through the complexities of the new family life unilluminated. As man has applied his mind to the puzzle of human behaviour, a great storehouse of knowledge has accumulated. It is fragmented, to be sure; a piece of wisdom is in the folk tales, another in the Greek tragedy *Oedipus Rex,* and the Elizabethan tragedy *Hamlet.* A handful of psychiatrists explained something of stepchild and stepmother's emotional base in the 1920's and '30's, a renowned pediatrician gave his views in a magazine of the 1960's. Raking over the well-documented subject of divorce and its consequences, sociologists discovered the step family and have made a bare start in studying it. From one such academician comes the only book known to me on the stepchild.

Rumblings from restless stepparents, no longer docile under the weight of misconceptions, began to be heard before World War II. A few articles appeared here and there in magazines; they were more frequent after the war (although one avant-garde lady wrote a spirited defense of stepmothers in a 1911 journal). Often too fearful, still, to sign their own names, the anonymous authors relate firsthand experience in the modern step family. Almost always, they attempt to toss off the old condemnation, to tell the world that all stepchildren are not Cinderellas, all stepparents not ogres and witches in disguise.

The stepchild has the fascination of the irregular, the appeal of the oppressed innocent. He has attracted the inquiring mind of great creative writers; Shakespeare, Dickens, Ibsen, Eugene O'Neill, John Steinbeck are a few who have looked at him and written what they saw and what they understood. Work in tangential but crucially connected subjects—society and its customs, laws, family structure; the individual and his emotions concerned with growing up, marriage, divorce, death—contributes to understanding the stepchild state.

Fragments of knowledge exist on library shelves, unwritten in the minds of some experienced men and women, even unperceived by some others. No one expert knows the whole picture any more than any one stepchild or stepparent, pouring out his troubles in magazine article or doctor's office, can encompass all the problems or even the pleasures of step family life. But each knows something important.

This book puts the pieces together. It is, to my knowledge, the first comprehensive book for general readers about the modern stepchild. Its aim is to press forward understanding of one of the most intriguing segments of contemporary life.

I have lived in a step family since I was born. My grandmother horrified her society in the '90's by leaving my grandfather for an enchanting Frenchman with a neat goatee. Their visits were filled with vivacity; he insisted that we small stepgrandchildren sing French ditties along with him while his lively bride, my grandmother, played the piano. Later I had a stepfather and stepmother and lived in the remarriages of my parents. The heritage is vivid, both joyous and painful. I too have remarried and am a stepmother as well as a mother.

My personal experience has convinced me that the more you know about the phenomenon, the better life can be. My journalist's training added the conviction that no single fragment—even my own—could contain the whole, that this virgin field demands more than a single mind's application. However tempting the prospect of self-revelation (and what could more delight an author than an excellent reason to tell his own story?) the subject had an urgency about it—and a seriousness—that insisted that its first comprehensive book *be* comprehensive.

This aim ruled out a one-man survey of stepchildren and parents whom I know, or could have met, as being a superficial and necessarily limited approach. Although my book does not presume to be either encyclopedic or exhaustive, it is based on considerable research of professional, literary and philosophical opinion, made more adventurous, difficult and always more compelling by the surprising blank where information was logically to be expected. In the immense number of works on The Child—from every discipline—I rarely found a reference to the stepchild. Nor did I find it in more than one or two books of advice to parents, nor in the detailed guides to child development; their value to the subject has had to be by inference. In the mass of literature on marriage, there is one book on remarriage; the how-to-do-it writers take the widowed and divorced as far as achieving another marriage and there they stop. Written exploration and explanation of the psyche—male and female—rarely examines the particular emotions of stepparents.

Even more unexpected was a remark I learned to anticipate in interviews with startled if cooperative experts; without exception, doctors, teachers, churchmen, psychiatrists, social workers, lawyers opened our talk with "I have never given the stepchild much thought . . ." or words to that effect. An hour or two later, wisdom still flowed toward the subject and not infrequently the closing comment was: "Come back in a week after I've had time to think about it."

Many of these men and women contributed information never before recorded and, in some instances, never before even thought of. I am grateful for their immediate and generous response; it brought me new understanding as well as an ever-increasing respect for the extraordinary vitality of a subject able to arouse high-caliber interest in such a variety of people. Their names are listed in the next pages as are others who have helped by painstakingly reading, criticizing, discussing or typing the manuscript. Two specialists made particular contributions: Dr. Paul H. Jacobson, demographer with the Metropolitan Life Insurance Company and author of the statistical *American Marriage and Divorce,* did a special study for this book to provide the only reliable stepchild statistics extant. His work is the basis of all statistical information herein except where otherwise noted. It has been given clear visual design by Philip Bonn. The asset of their careful professional contribution is measured in the book, where it speaks, eloquently, for itself.

My most valued, indeed treasured, colleagues are not listed with the bare thanks space allows to less intimate connections. For the highest compliment of candor unadorned, affection unwavering, and considerable personal sacrifice during the months of this effort, my gratitude and abiding love to Tom, Betsy, Lynn and Debby who are my four children. And to my stepchildren, Paul and Margo, who have helped too, in the short time we have known each other. Because their father envelops us all with his enormous capacity for loving support, my ultimate gratitude is for Robert E. Simon, Jr., perceptive critic and husband-father-stepfather extraordinary.

The stepchild is significant in the modern world. My journalistic interest in this little-explored, immensely compelling subject is increased by the experience of being and having a stepchild myself . . . and goes beyond it. In this attempt to tell readers what I have found is a certainty that the stepchild state touches the life of every man, woman and child and, in one aspect or another, reflects them.

Summer, 1963
Martha's Vineyard

ACKNOWLEDGMENTS

My thanks to these professional people who discussed the stepchild in the family with me from their own particular field of competence.

Sylvia D. Bauman
  Child Analyst, Albert Einstein College of Medicine.

Frances L. Beatman
  Executive Director, Jewish Family Service, New York.

Mary C. Clancy
  Social Worker, Catholic Charities of the Archdiocese of New York.

Reverend William H. Genne
  Director, Department of Family Life, National Council of the Churches of Christ in the U.S.A.

Dora Hartmannn, M.D.
  Psychoanalyst.

Monsignor George A. Kelly
  Director, Family Life Bureau, Archdiocese of New York.

Jack E. Kittell
  Headmaster, The Dalton Schools, New York.

Mirra Komarovsky
  Professor of Sociology, Barnard College, Columbia University.

Toby K. Kurzband
  Principal, P.S. 1, New York.

Milton I. Levine, M.D.
  Pediatrician, Cornell University Medical College.

David M. Levy, M.D.
  Child Psychiatrist.

Charles H. Lieb
  Member, New York Bar.

Rabbi Bernard Mandelbaum
  Director, Religio-Psychiatric Center, Jewish Theological Seminary, New York.

Peter B. Neubauer, M.D.
Child Psychiatrist and Psychoanalyst, Director, Child Development Center, New York.

Benjamin O'Sullivan
Member, New York Bar.

Monrad G. Paulsen
Professor of Law, Columbia University Law School.

Harriet F. Pilpel
Member, New York Bar.

Shad Polier
Member, New York Bar.

Robert D. Seely, M.D.
Internist, Mount Sinai Hospital, New York.

Thanks to my friends and associates for their advice, assistance and encouragement: Sybil Taylor, editor; my agents Martha Winston and Emily Jacobson of Curtis Brown, Ltd.; Arthur Bernkrant and Sonya O'Sullivan, editorial critics; Irene Movshon, who prepared the manuscript; Grace Bermingham, Librarian, Columbia University School of Social Work.

Thanks, finally, to Albert R. Leventhal, publisher and friend, who had the confidence to make this book a reality; and to my friend Herbert R. Mayes, who endorsed its concept by publishing some of it in *McCall's*.

Part One

BECOMING A STEPCHILD

Chapter One

FRIDAY'S CHILD

There is a short-cut in our language which goes straight from the idea of misery, unjustly inflicted, to the word stepchild. Every time the word is used to tell of neglect and deprivation, it reinforces this meaning. A week's word-watching finds a slum described as the stepchild of the city, Alaska the stepchild of the Union, psychiatry the stepchild of medicine. If you want to indicate neglect, say stepchild, and everyone will know what you mean.

The literal meaning is simply a child of one's husband or wife by a former marriage. A powerful force has made this state of being a symbol of deprivation. The symbol may apply to every stepchild and may not; nevertheless, state and symbol are so firmly welded that one has come to mean the other. The stereotype thus created thunders each day at hundreds of weddings where bride or groom or both are parents; it buffets the thousands of children who become stepchildren by virtue of these weddings, the millions now living in a step family. The same force makes stepmother, often stepfather too, a word for wicked, evil, cruel. It preordains what step relations will be. Although the modern design for marriage endorses, indeed encourages, the formation of step families, the stereotype of its children and stepparents is accepted, unquestioned, and the force which has made it is still wild and untrammeled, wreaking damage where it will.

If this devastating force cannot be harnessed, a parent's remarriage should be immediately and forever outlawed. But there may be wisdom enough, now, to repudiate the concept it has formed, knowledge enough to lay its ghost, understanding enough deftly to excise its malignancy. The stepchild and his family can achieve sturdy good health which will radiate out to society.

Parent and stepparent have a practical reason to search for

understanding of the step relation. They want their new marriage to work, they want to be happy within it, and have suffered considerable pain and stress to give themselves this opportunity. The stepchild in the family complicates their intent; at the first sign of trouble—and it is bound to come to even the most knowledgeable—the child appears to prevent the achievement of happiness all around.

There is a moral reason, too, for the search. The child-centered ethic insists that personal parental whim be tempered with responsibility. An unhappy child makes a worried parent; a stepchild who feels deprived and neglected makes a stepparent who feels and is thought to be wicked and an atmosphere that hardly promotes happiness for the family.

Men, women and children in the step relationship strive as earnestly for the good life as anyone else. Perhaps they try harder; they are advance troops for the new idea of marriage created by the present era, pioneers of logical response to the enormous social revolutions of our time. There is a gap between the response and its comprehension; the modern stepchild asks that the gap be closed. His request to parent and stepparent reverberates to every person who marries, has children, or holds attitudes about marriage, children, divorce, remarriage and expresses them in word or deed. And that is everybody.

Step relations are everybody's business because they are every family's relations magnified and exaggerated, so more clearly to be seen and understood. A parent's new marriage has the elements of every marriage and the particular ability to expose them, primitive and raw. There is not a mother who has not felt like a cruel stepmother toward her own child, not a child who has not felt himself mistreated and deprived, not a marriage unshaken by the intrusion of children's needs or immune to the pull of opposing loyalties. The modern step family, together with the society that has brought it into being, has an opportunity to find new knowledge in step relations. Responsibility urges understanding, intelligence, spiked with curiosity, argues for learning. "The unexamined life," Socrates said, "is not worth living." Now that stepchild life has been deemed worthy, it deserves to be examined.

The first clue to wisdom is in the very invention of the

word stepchild; the ancient Anglo-Saxon "āstēpan" meant
to deprive or bereave and "steopcild" from this root was a
bereaved child, an orphan, or, the dictionary says "anything
likened to a stepchild, especially as not receiving solicitous
attention." The early Anglo-Saxons may well have failed to
give the orphan solicitous attention; there are dozens of examples of earlier cultures wherein a child, handicapped by
bereavement or other disadvantage, was left to perish, exposed
to travail or made a slave. Today, the stepchild often suffers
too much solicitude; he may have two living parents and two
stepparents who vie with each other to court his fancy. Yet
the old reality clings to the new; stepchild means deprived.

It clings with such tenacity that a professor of sociology,
who as recently as 1956 wrote the first and only book to date
about remarriage, makes this comment in its beginning pages:

> "Because of the emotional connotations of the terms
> *stepchild, stepmother,* and *stepfather,* they are avoided
> whenever possible in the present study. For they are, in
> effect, smear words."

One is impelled to wonder why the child of one's husband or
wife by a former marriage has become a smear word, what
characteristic, what tone of voice or shape of mind or body
imparts the smear to him and to every woman who marries a
father, every man who marries a mother. The professor substi-
tuted "acquired" children and parents. Unless "step" has
special black magic, "acquired," should it become accepted
parlance, will be a smear word too. If symbolic logic holds,
even the largest thesaurus has no hiding place for emotion,
out to find a word for its expression.*

---

* For this reason, the words *stepchild, stepmother, stepfather, stepbrother*
and *stepsister* are used throughout this book to describe family relations
formed by a parent's remarriage. A child or adult discussed with specific reference to the step relation is identified by the prefix *step*. A degree of trail-
blazing is in the determination to simplify spelling and to make it uniform;
if *stepchild* is one word, there would seem to be no reason to give *stepparent*
or any other stepperson a hyphen.

A newer problem of lexicography is in describing the family created by
remarriage. Because it is a family as well as a setting for the step relations,
step family is logically two words as is *step relationship* and *step relation.*

Another innovation, following the above logic, is the streamlined spelling of
halfsibling, halfbrother, halfsister, newly important relatives of today's combination families.

Emotion searches out the orphan and catches him in the pious soft embrace of pity, left over from Good Samaritan visits to orphan asylums. Orphan means a child bereaved of one parent as well as two. It is more usual today that one parent survives and his "orphan" knows no institutional setting. The child is likely to become a stepchild, regarded as neglected and deprived although his tragic loss has been at least in part mitigated by his parent's remarriage.

Language expresses emotion even more emphatically when it comes to divorce. For the children involved there is silence, no word at all to describe them, no substitute for the clumsy "children of divorce" or its inaccurate, inept alternative "divorced children." The sky-rocketing numbers of children whose parents have been divorced surely deserve a noun of their own, at least equally with youngsters whose parents' marital status is told by words which call them orphans or bastards. New words evolve constantly for the discoveries of this atomic age, for the new mathematics, the new Madison Avenue culture, new art, music, poetry. But no one has titled the new state of children whose parents have been divorced. Even before they become stepchildren, language ties them to their parents' marital past and to its general tinge of impropriety, which may or may not apply to every parent, and certainly does not belong to their offspring. A neutral, factual word of their own would serve the children better.

Talk about the stepchild's two mothers, four parents, new father, is another clue to the force that gives the devastating extra meaning to stepchild, stepmother, stepfather. To avoid these words, people go to such lengths of circumlocution that they ignore the primal facts of life. Four parents, or any other biological impossibility, is acceptable usage now, forwarded every day by those who say it, write it and print it although they know, as does the first-grader, that parenthood is exclusive to the man and woman whose reproductive cells have joined in creation.*

---

* There is a valid exception in the legal process of adoption which does create a "new" father or mother or both; for good reasons, refutation of biology is acceptable in this instance, but even this does not allow for more than one mother and father at a time.

The force makes the child whose parent has married again Friday's child who is full of woe by definition. It makes stepchild an unhappy word. An uninhibited reaction is to recoil from it, to look for a way around it in language and in life. There is little recognition of what the woes are and why, little written about them, little said or even known about them. Is it possible that there is nothing to say or know, that the meanings synonymous with stepchild and stepparent were created in a vacuum for no good reason and have hung there, without sustenance, for centuries? Some professionals give their views:

> Concerning stepchildren and stepparents, a well-known pediatrician says, "There is no excessive number of them coming to child guidance clinics and other agencies that cope with family problems. So we must assume that the majority of them do a good job in solving a difficult situation."

> "I have no stepchild in my practice," a psychoanalyst remarks. "There is a tremendous denial of the step relationship. Too much guilt about it stops people from coming for help."

> "The step family is not a specific cause for disorders," a child psychiatrist states. "If it was, there would be papers written about it. Our profession writes papers about every identifiable cause of specific problems."

> A social case worker, high in the hierarchy of her profession, takes the thought a step further. "Maybe the stepchild stereotype serves more purposes than we know. Maybe unconsciously it protects the sanctity of marriage. If the stereotype is removed, if it's too easy to make a going concern of the step family, it will threaten. A man will wonder then, 'How safe is the society I know, how safe is my home, my wife, children, my marriage?' Could this be a reason for our continuing ignorance?"

These comments whet the appetite for wisdom. The informed men and women, well-qualified representatives of current thought, do not discourage the search for understanding, but invigorate it by restating its challenge. One expert assumes that the majority of step families are doing a good job in solving their problems because they do not ask for help, another suggests that the nature of their problems stops them from asking. One says the step family is not a specific cause of specific trouble, another that exactly this general nature may be the reason to avoid scrutiny. They have not defined the force that characterizes the step relation, but each from his own view questions what it is that gives the little prefix its gigantic power to change language, to cause family disruption, admitted or hidden, and universal discomfort in its presence.

Knowledge of the stepchild in the family can reveal the powerful force in its multitude of parts. The modern stepchild has come far from his Anglo-Saxon ancestor who was deprived of solicitous attention. Although today's child of remarried parents has the passions of every human born in the long chain of man, their expression has changed as society has changed. Now, the child and his family are making relations with each other unique to this particular moment in history. The force is evident when the infant starts growing toward maturity in the present climate; insights, fresh sprung from the behavioral sciences, expose its roots. Becoming a modern stepchild means being a modern child of modern parents, it means living through a parent's death or divorce, knowing the new kind of one-parent family, approaching the unknowns of the stepchild state. The force which dictates what that state will be is seen in each step along the way to the step family. It is intensely satisfying, in the drama of discovery, to identify it bit by bit, to test its validity and to know its direction.

The courage to harvest its knowledge may allow the stepchild to emerge in the twentieth century in vigorous honorable relation to the people in his world, who, after all, have created it.

Chapter Two

CINDERELLA PERCEIVED

"Wisdom is the principal thing; therefore get wisdom: and with all thy getting get understanding." —PROVERBS 4:7.

Cinderella is the stepchild everyone knows. Her story, told around the globe, has survived for centuries. Little children delight in its cruelty, believe in its magic and rejoice in its triumphant ending. They remember it for the rest of their lives.

Stepmothers, it says, are wicked, jealous, cruel, and step-children, their innocent victims, are gentle and kind. In the story's vivid imagery, good and bad are absolutes, never qualified. No fragment of well-meaning lightens the step-mother's black venality, no shadow of self-interest sullies Cinderella's purity. The stepchild is good, the stepmother is bad. This, the story says, is the way it is. Folk tale trappings make it palatable, even beloved, to the parent who reads and the child who listens. As it is harsh, it is healing, blurting out feelings that have to be hidden and silently suffered in life. In disguise it says what no child would dare to say outright about a parent and what no parent could admit to. Un-masked, it is not a lovable story; it would, in fact, be unbear-able bedtime fare.

You don't have to be a stepchild or stepparent to appre-ciate *Cinderella.* The violent tale reaches to the very center of every child's sensitivities and touches the vulnerability of every parent. When there is a step relation in the family, its effect is even more powerful. Children are wary. Stepmothers are defensive. Glance at the magazine articles they write: *The Cruel Stepmother, I'm a Stepparent but not an Ogre, Stepmothers Can Be Nice.* Who said they couldn't be nice? Cinderella said so.

It is part of her message—but not all of it. There is more
in the memorable tale than a description of the step relation.
Its particular eternal wisdom is welcome and satisfying to
the nursery audience just the way it is, it penetrates without
being completely understood; why not leave it that way?
Fairies, witches and ogres stay obediently within the confines
of "Once upon a time . . . and they lived happily ever
after," where the glorious goodness and badness is unchal-
lenged, untrammeled by qualifying reality. Why shouldn't
Cinderella and her stepmother stay there too? Why probe
for the story's meaning?

As Cinderella is everybody's stepchild, she is everybody's
child. What the folk tale has to say about modern marriage,
family relations and step families is too important to ignore.
Uncomprehended, it does damage. Understood, it illuminates.

The story matters to people wherever they are in time and
space. It has to be told, over and over again. There is not just
one Cinderella story; there are 500 versions, perhaps more.
They come from all over Europe, from Africa to India,
Scandinavia to Australia, from Ireland to Iceland, North to
South America. Always they tell the same basic tale of the
widower's daughter who is abused by her stepmother and
stepsisters. Somehow she gets supernatural help—from an
animal, her dead mother, a fairy godmother—meets her
prince, runs away from him, is found, identified, and lives
happily ever after.

Because there are so many versions, it is possible to cull
out the elements of the story that are universal from those
which are cultural window-dressing of the particular place
and era in which the story was told. To make its decoding
even easier, there is an amazing and fascinating catalogue of
some 345 versions of Cinderella, plot by plot, symbol by
symbol, the life work of a nineteenth-century British folk-
lorist, Marian Roalfe Cox. Because of her unique scholarship, guesswork is ruled out of knowledge about Cinderella,
the only folk tale to have such an encyclopedic study of its
own.

The heroine's name, Cox says, is always connected with
ashes; there's the French Cendrillon, Aschenputtel from
Germany, Askepot (meaning "pot of ashes") from West Jut-

land, La Cenorientola from Rome and the Russian Zama-
rashka, which translates as "a dirty person." The much-loved
fairy godmother is seldom the magic savior. More often it is
a helpful beast—a white bear in Sweden, an eel in Jutland,
a toad in the Hungarian version, a mouse in the Annamite.
Shoes are ever-present; at least half are golden but they are
diamond in the Venetian story, galoshes in the Danish, boots
in Jutland, sandals in Turkey. The glass slipper, a marvel
in those pre-plastic days, is unique to the French Cinderella
and believed to have come into being by a mundane, un-
romantic recording error.*

There are endless other adaptations to surroundings and
culture. The version told by the Zuni tribe of North American Indians is a striking example:

> "The abused daughter is a turkey herd. Her turkeys take
> pity on her and furnish magic clothes. She attends the
> tribal dance and attracts the chief's son but she disobeys
> her turkeys and overstays her time. They punish her by
> taking away all her beautiful clothes." (THOMPSON, S.)†

The earliest known Cinderella story is presumed to be a
ninth-century Chinese version; it includes the animal friend
and the lost shoe. "One thing is plain," Andrew Lang, folklore scholar comments, "a naked and shoeless race could not
have invented Cinderella."

Who did?

How does it happen that the same girl springs Phoenix-like
from ashes on every continent to know the same adversity
and achieve the same victory? Why, from many cultures in
many places, the ubiquitous wicked stepmother? Why is The
Stepchild always the father's child—and a girl—although
mother's children are stepchildren too? Why the name from
cinders, the prince, the helpful animals, the happy ending?

---

* Perrault, the French folk tale collector, heard the slipper described by a
storyteller as *"vair,"* the fur of a kind of weasel now extinct. What he wrote
down, the sound-alike *"verre,"* meaning glass, created the image treasured by
generations of bedtime listeners.

† The name in parenthesis here and following is the quoted author; the
title of the work quoted is found under the author's name in the bibliography
at the back of the book.

Cinderella's lineage goes back to the earliest stories people told each other, the myths and legends of centuries before Christ. When these were discredited by knowledge or no longer understood, some of their raw material was used in folk tales, handed down from one generation to another by storytellers and recorded by collectors such as Perrault, Lang and the German brothers Grimm. They were told by simple people for entertainment when work was done, allowed the use of imagination and ways to express the hope that goodness triumphs and happiness is possible. Some social scientists say that folk tales reflect only the specific culture which invents them; others argue that the stories passed over oceans and continents much as a good joke travels from California to New York and Paris. This "driftwood theory" is contested by still others who, tracing the routes of early traders and crusaders, show the necessary connecting links were non-existent. But regardless of how it got there, a story meaningful in China would not have survived in Germany unless it had had equal impact on coolie and woodsman. *Cinderella,* it appears, did.

No one can know if all stepmothers who lived in the centuries of folk tale invention were cruel to stepchildren; one can suspect that the pragmatist who argues that the tales report fact has his own personal reasons for hoping that the story is just a primitive form of journalism. For even if every single stepmother from China to Chile was cruel and every stepchild deprived, there could never have been enough of them to have made the story a universal necessity to tell. The chorusing of hundreds of Cinderella stories may report fact but are only indestructible because they report feeling too.

The neglected child and cruel stepmother make sense in Asia, Africa, Europe and America as symbols of emotions, the same emotions that keep the image alive today and give the prefix "step" its power.

All children know how Cinderella feels because they have felt the same way themselves. The infant's first great need is to be fed, warmed and comforted by mother, its first great disappointment is to feel less than totally cherished by her. Although it is nature's design that mother must deny and regulate, the infant does not understand why this must be; there is fear, then anger, when his desires are not totally met. The essential nature of the family makes mother the parent who denies the earliest infant needs; she is the child's first introduction to the hard lesson of reality, which suggests a reason for the ubiquitous wicked stepmother and the absence of wicked stepfathers.

The most difficult and perhaps most important struggle of a child's life is in learning that a parent cherishes him and continues to cherish him even when there is a denial of his wish to be completely loved. Boys become rivals with their fathers for mother's love and entertain certain murderous thoughts about him. Girls, who have an equal need of mother's protection, turn their desire for cherishing to father; although they yearn to be loved by mother too, their feeling for her is divided. It is not until children come to trust, admire and know the firm affection of both parents that they can resolve this first enormous set of passions.

Every small female would like to have her father to herself; the mother who makes this impossible seems cruel, jealous, wicked and punishing, and small girls wish her out of the way, wish her dead. Triumphant, then, they can be singularly father's child. It becomes evident that Cinderella—and all the company of folk tale stepchildren—must be father's child to make the point of mother's venality. It is this rationale that makes wicked stepmothers happen in every corner of the world. And it is this that accounts for the absence of boy Cinderellas. The difficulties that boys suffer in growing up are evident in literature from Sophocles' *Oedipus Rex* to the most recent explosion of an angry young man. But because boys do not have the early divided passion toward mother that girls have, they do not make as dramatic source material as their sisters for the particular device of the stepmother folk tale.

Grimm's fairy tales—known as *märchen* or household tales —are merciless with the stepmother and her daughters, tender with the stepchild.

In *The Three Little Men in the Wood* "The woman became her stepdaughter's bitterest enemy, and day by day did her best to treat her still worse. She was also envious because her stepdaughter was beautiful and lovable and her own daughter ugly and repulsive."

In *Mother Holle,* the mother was "much fonder of the ugly and idle one because she was her own daughter and the other who was a stepdaughter was obliged to do all the work. . . ."

The proud and haughty queen in *Snow White* was "shocked and turned yellow and green with envy" at the mirror's message. Whenever she looked at Snow White "her heart heaved in her breast she hated the girl so much."

The woman in *Sweetheart Roland* was "a real witch with two daughters, one ugly and wicked and this one she loved because she was her own daughter and one beautiful and good and this one she hated because she was her stepdaughter," hated so much that she decides to chop off her head.

"God pity us," cry the stepchildren in *Brother and Sister,* "if our mother only knew!"

They cry for the good cherishing mother they once knew. She is gone now; thanks to folk tale magic, the good mother is conveniently dead. In her place is the bad rivalrous mother for whom hatred is justified; she does not seem a mother at all but distinctly and disastrously the enemy rival, father's wife. What better symbol could there be for the woman who comes between a girl and her father than the stepmother? She is the perfect bad-mother effigy.

Comprehension deepens with a look at the supremely well-chosen detail in the Cinderella story.

Grimm's *Cinderella* is a hair-raising tale, closer to most versions than Perrault's, which gives us the fairy godmother, coach and enchanting glass slipper. In the early nineteenth century, two young German brothers, Jacob and Wilhelm Grimm, wrote down the folk tales dictated to them by a Frau

Katherina Viehmann who was about fifty-five when they discovered her in a village near Kassel.* The story Frau
Viehmann remembered explains Cinderella, Cendrillon, and
Cenorientola, and a good deal about millions of folk who
let the cinder girl tell the story of their own souls.

Here, in brief, is Grimm's *Cinderella:*

> Cinderella's mother dies and her wealthy father then
> marries a woman with two daughters. They force Cinder-
> ella to work hard and sleep in the hearth cinders. Father
> asks what he should bring the girls from the fair; the sis-
> ters want dresses and jewels, Cinderella "the first branch
> that knocks against your hat on the way home." She
> plants the little hazel twig he brings her on her mother's
> grave, waters it with her tears, and it grows into a tree
> to which comes a little white bird that grants all her
> wishes.

> Stepmother refuses to let Cinderella go to the festival
> at which the prince will choose his bride unless she picks
> lentils out of the ashes. Pigeons and turtledoves help
> Cinderella with her task three times, but the stepmother
> breaks her promise and Cinderella is left behind. She asks
> the tree for clothes and the little bird throws them down
> to her. She goes to the festival, meets the prince, runs
> away and lays her beautiful dress on the grave, and the
> bird removes it. A second time the process is repeated
> and a third, when she gets the most magnificent dress of
> all and golden slippers.

> The prince finds one of her slippers; in his search for
> Cinderella, the sisters try it on but it is too small. Mother
> tells her eldest daughter to cut off her toe so it will fit,
> which she does and rides away with the prince but the
> birds on the hazel tree tell him of the ruse. The second
> daughter is advised to cut off her heel with the same re-
> sults.

> The slipper fits Cinderella; she rides away with the

---

* "She retains fast in mind these old sagas," Wilhelm Grimm noted, "a tal-
ent which, as she says, is not granted to everyone. . . . Never does she alter
any part in repetition and she corrects a mistake herself, immediately as she
notices it. Among people who follow old life ways without change, attachment
to inherited patterns is stronger than we, impatient for variety, can realize."

prince and the two white doves leave the tree to perch on her shoulders. As she enters the church for her wedding, with the sisters on either side, the birds pluck out an eye from each sister and on their return the other eye. "And thus," the tale concludes, "for their wickedness and falsehood they were punished with blindness all their days."

Cinderella's wishes are the theme. Folklore scholars, who disagree on almost everything else, concur that wish-fulfillment is a basic motif of most folk tales. "Like dreams," the Freudian-minded Franz Ricklin states, "the tales are expressions of the general human tendency to create a healing, wish-fulfilling surrogate for reality." The stepmother tales have a special set of wishes which center around sexual wish-fulfillment. Like every girl child, Cinderella wishes to be completely loved and cherished by her father; this, she believes, is her right. She wants what he can give her, the privileges of his wealth, the most beautiful face and clothes, the supreme ability to have him, or a reasonable facsimile thereof, for herself.

In reality, a girl's wish for her father must be compromised; in the story, Cinderella's can be magnificently granted. She thinks only of herself, as many children would like to do most of the time (and do do, as parents can testify, for a not ungenerous proportion of their childhood years). "The egoistic standpoint dominates, the altruistic has not yet appeared," Ricklin says. It begins to be perceivable that Cinderella is not, as she appears offhand, as pure as driven snow. She wants what she wants when she wants it and is extraordinarily skillful in her effort to have her own way. Neatly she kills off the loving mother, and with unerring aim conducts her campaign to advertise the wickedness of the woman who has married her father.

In a dozen villainous ways, stepmother persecutes Cinderella to prevent her from getting the man she wants; each act conclusively demonstrates that mother is her sexual rival. Because of stepmother, the rich man's daughter has to sit in the cinders, the lowliest place in the house. She is named a cinder girl, and cinders are dirty, indicating unhappiness and punishment (as in the biblical combination with sackcloth).

Stepmother makes Cinderella wear an "old grey bedgown" and wooden shoes, unlike the good mother who, from her grave, gives her splendid adornments. Stepmother sets Cinderella impossible tasks, breaks her promises and is even cruel to her own daughters.

Why all this punishing? Cinderella would like to believe herself superior to her rival and so makes it appear that the stepmother is jealous, afraid that the young beauty will vanquish her. In *Snow White,* the same theme is more directly stated; the beautiful queen who becomes the stepmother *does* believe the heroine to be more beautiful even than herself and therefore determines to destroy her. Perhaps Snow White was simply playing a ventriloquist's trick with her long-suffering stepmother's mirror, but by her story she turns self-doubt into its opposite. She insists that her father's wife lives in terror of the daughter's superiority. In some folk tales the mother herself is the persecutor; this, Ricklin comments, "fits splendidly into the theory that the stepmother signifies the true mother as a rival."

Cinderella's stepsisters underline their mother's wicked character. They, too, are rivals "beautiful and fair of face but black and vile of heart." They help express the fear of a small girl that her wish to be completely loved can never be granted and that she herself is not able to compete successfully; it would be less poignant if the rivals—conquered after terrible travail—did not present the total threat of being very beautiful. It's the heart that matters, Cinderella is saying, and over and over she proves that in contrast to their black hearts, hers is solid gold. The sisters also serve a literary value, setting off the heroine in her own generation. Their bullying domination of the unprotected youngest child, subject to sibling rivalry then as now, tells of the injustice she feels about the preferential treatment given to older children. Only a bad mother could prefer the dreadful sisters to the heroine "pious and good," the small childlike innocent who surely arouses the listener's sympathies. There are precedents all through literature for the youngest daughter of three being the fairest and the best; Cinderella is in good company with such as King Lear's Cordelia and Aphrodite in the *Judgment of Paris.*

To get her wish, Cinderella asks her father to give her a hazel twig, a masculine sex symbol. The first green twigs of spring are a sign of fertility; the phallus signifies the same meaning and the twig has become one of its symbols. Symbolic language has a different logic from the one we speak, Erich Fromm says in *The Forgotten Language,* a logic in which "not time and space are the ruling categories but intensity and association. It is the one universal language the human race has developed." For the skeptical, other versions of *Cinderella,* and other folk tales, too, support the symbolic meaning; magic dresses come from an assortment of phallic symbols—nuts, wands, staffs and animals. In *The Little Hazel Branch,* the youngest daughter asks her father to bring her "a beautiful green little branch with golden nuts." It belongs to a bear who becomes a prince when she breaks his spell. In *Oda and the Serpent,* Oda asks for "the first thing that runs under your wagon" which is a serpent who turns into a prince. Animals represent sexual power, Ricklin says, because "the life-preserving principle is considered as the animal in man."*

The bird that helps Cinderella is small and white, a pigeon, a turtledove, as gentle and pure as the heroine herself. The birds help her do the impossible tasks the stepmother demands, they perch on the wish tree and throw down the dresses. They are the good-mother surrogate, all-giving, helpful, understanding and kind. As the story progresses, they seem to represent Cinderella herself as they help her to conquer her rivalrous feelings about mother. Cinderella returns the dresses to the grave and the birds cooperate in her deception by removing the evidence; they inform on the sisters' tricks to make the slipper fit and ultimately it is the birds, in all their purity and goodness, who take revenge on the sisters, plucking out their eyes for punishment. It would be too painful for Cinderella to admit to vengeance on her own part; the birds—or any helpful beast—are her happy if violent solution.

Cinderella wants to grow up and get her man. In folk tale

---

* In a burst of enthusiasm for the subject, he tells of a story in which Zeus changes Amor into serpents, flames, a bull and a swan and adds the note, "What a beautiful collection of masculine sex symbols!"

language, her wish is for the prince, the chieftain's son, the tribal leader or whatever man represents the zenith of the culture she lives in—in other words, her father. Father's gift to his daughter represents father himself. She has to battle great adversity to get the gift. Oda's serpent and the bear in *The Little Hazel Branch* immediately turn into the prince; Cinderella must first plant the phallic symbol on her mother's grave and water it with tears, symbol of her persecution. Only then does it grow into a wish tree which gives her the dresses that ultimately enable her to snare the prince, a more roundabout process but the same basic idea.

The extra effort has a persuasive logic; by her horticultural activity Cinderella has, in a sense, joined her mother and father together again. She has resolved the enormous conflict that made her want to get rid of mother, to have father to herself. Free of the guilt those early wishes engendered, she can cast off the covering of cinder shame and enjoy her mother's and father's joint beneficence by virtue of which her own native quality can then be discovered.

Beautifully constructed, the story builds toward its climax. All Cinderella's wishes lead to the moment when the prince finds the slipper, "small and dainty and all golden," on the staircase and says, "No one shall be my wife but she whose foot this golden slipper fits." The shoe incident is believed to be based on an ancient custom of using a shoe at betrothals; the bridegroom brings it to the bride and, as soon as she puts it on her foot, she is regarded as subject to his authority. It represents elegance, fine breeding and delicacy. Again Cinderella triumphs over the stepmother. Because of the inheritance in the very bones of her feet, Cinderella gets her wish.*

"She seated herself on a stool, drew her foot out of the heavy wooden shoe, and put it into the slipper, which fitted

---

* "Studying the story psychoanalytically," writes Dr. Donald Marcus, "it is apparent that the little Cinderella gets her every wish, including an oedipal victory and unlimited access to a good-giving mother. Moreover she is entirely blameless and, therefore, suffers no punishment because the wishes are denied and projected onto others. To begin with, the good mother of the earlier pregenital period is carefully preserved by being forever dead. The victory is then won over a cruel step-mother, who is the mother seen as the sexual rival of the oedipal period. The victory is total and complete since both mother and siblings are vanquished."

like a glove. And when she rose up and the King's son looked at her face, he recognized the beautiful maiden who had danced with him and cried: 'That is the true bride!' The stepmother and the two sisters were horrified and became pale with rage; he, however, took Cinderella on his horse and rode away with her."

Centuries of feelings about growing up have been poured into the making of the Cinderella tale. Its wonderfully expressive language tells of everyone's passionate longing to be completely cherished and ominous fear that it cannot be, of the difficulty of learning to love and be loved, to give and take, to be parent and child. It says that wishes can come true and that it is safe for little children to grow up in the presence of parents who both cherish and deny, that they will grow up to live happily ever after.

It was a brilliant literary coup to make the child who feels neglected and deserted a stepchild and the denying, rivalrous part of mother a stepmother. By this eminently successful disguise, the attack, so deeply felt and so rarely directly expressed, avoids blaspheming the sanctity of mother and child and heaps its vengeance on the step relation. It creates difficulty for families today because there is something of Cinderella in every stepchild as in every child, something of the wicked stepmother in every stepmother as in every mother.

In this era when people choose remarriage for themselves and the stepchild state for their children, it is essential to separate symbol and reality. The folk tale, understood, is a gain instead of a threat. It provides an implacable backstop for the getting of wisdom combined with understanding.

Chapter Three

THE STEPCHILD'S HERITAGE

"Now began a hard time for the poor step-child."
—GRIMM'S FAIRY TALES.

At a parent's wedding a child becomes a stepchild. The ceremony which makes his mother somebody's new wife, or his father a new husband, makes him a relation he knows nothing about. Newly cherished, newly abandoned, his loneliness quickens amid the rejoicing. He is curious, mystified, afraid. His idea of the freshly-minted family is separate from that of the smiling bridal pair; he does not share their celebration or their hopes. The heritage he brings to this day is what has happened to him in the past. One experience over all others, shared by every stepchild, is overwhelmingly important: somewhere, in his tender years, he has lost a parent from his home.

If there is an aristocracy among step families, it consists of those who have the perception to understand the stepchild's heritage, the compassion to respect it and the humanity to give it decent dignity.

The "hard time for the poor step-child" began once upon a time when he had a mother and father together . . . and then did not. The process of learning to love and be loved was interrupted. Few adults can take death or divorce with composure; no child can. The terror and confusion cuts deep and the scar is slow to heal. The tearing apart of parent and child, at any age and under any circumstance, causes pain.

Queen Elizabeth's mother, Anne Boleyn, laughing hysterically, was beheaded on Tower Green by order of her husband, Henry VIII. Her daughter was not yet three, but old enough to feel the impact of this violent parting. Before she was nine, her kind stepmother, Catherine Howard, was dragged back shrieking as she attempted to beg Henry for mercy, and she too was beheaded, biographers relate, on the same spot where Anne had died before her. It was in that year that Elizabeth was first heard to say, "I will never marry," the resolve of a lifetime for the Virgin Queen who chose the motto *Semper Eadem* ("Be Always One") to live by.

Four centuries later a British war orphan, whose father had been killed in action before she was born, felt the deprivation as intensely, perhaps, as the royal orphan before her. She asked about her Daddy as soon as she could talk, Susan Isaacs, child specialist, reports in her study of war orphans. The baby girl hugged and kissed the photograph of her father. "Why doesn't he speak to me?" she said. "Why doesn't my Daddy come? Doesn't he want to come to see me?"

Whether the baby sees its mother murdered or has never even seen its father, the need for both parents is primeval, the strongest need of its life. If something goes wrong, if one parent isn't there, the primeval force is deflected. Inevitably it grinds the lens through which the child sees its stepparent.

The parting is certain deprivation to the child. To know the character of this deprivation is essential to good step family relations; it determines what the child needs from parent and stepparent. The suffering of an infant at parting from a parent differs from the misery of an adolescent; calendar and emotional age make it different. The sex of the child is another variable; a boy who loses his mother may not have to endure the guilty torture which his sister does if she, Cinderella-like at that precise moment of her life, had been wishing mother was dead. The result of the shock of parting is different again by virtue of its cause. The quick strike of a fatal disease leaves one kind of wound, the bitter, drawn-out divorce wrangle another; visiting father on weekends is not the same as visiting the cemetery. Each circumstance of parting has a special character which can be defined. Each, as it will be seen, contains the heritage of deprivation and the legacy of hope for some variety of paradise regained.

The generally accepted logic of human behavior, developed by generations of philosophers and scientists, is that the first emotional adjustments to mother and father form the basis of every relationship of life. Cinderella's wishes and their magic gratification tell of the first massive conflict and its resolution. Freud named the struggle after the mythical King Oedipus who unwittingly slew his father and married his mother. It was Freud's conviction that the fate of Oedipus is born into Everyman and that character derives from the individual's ability to repress or redirect the energy in those eternal primitive wishes of childhood. There are dissenters, of course; "Freud," *The New York Times* commented on the occasion of a film biography of the father of psychoanalysis, "still is by no means forgiven for unlocking the mysteries of the human mind. . . . Many circles that consider themselves respectable still shudder at the name." And Erich Fromm, philosopher, says, "When we have a society in which the respect for the integrity of every individual, including every child, is realized, the Oedipus complex, like the myth, will belong to the past."

Yet every day a small stepson struggles with an unreasoning hatred of a "new father" who disturbs his plan to have mother to himself, and a survey of 184 college women showed *Cinderella* way out ahead as the childhood story favorite. Its wish-fulfilling theme was named the most appealing, the rags-to-riches aspect was last on the list. (COLLIER, M.) Regardless of nomenclature, school of thought or individual conception, man's nature persists in a discernable pattern of growth. Customary divisions are three: infancy, when the massive compromise between world and self begins; childhood, the productive learning time when sexuality is latent; and explosive adolescence.

Each of us manages the emotional obstacle course with more or less success; at every stage there are difficulties, disappointments and problems which hamper achievement. If they are too disturbing the emotions are unable to move ahead. Even in the best circumstances some remnants of earlier feelings persist along with higher levels of maturity. Dr. Otto Fenichel, psychoanalyst, makes the process vivid with this striking comment:

> "Freud," he remarks, "used the simile of an advancing army in enemy territory leaving occupation troops at all important points. The stronger the occupation troops left behind, the weaker is the army that marches on. If the latter meets a too powerful enemy force, it may retreat to those points where it had previously left the strongest occupation troops."

Two kind, tender parents and the army goes marching on. But what if one departs? A disaster of this dimension calls for a sizeable number of occupation troops whether a parent dies or leaves via Reno. Understanding bereavement makes a base line to which can later be added the variations of parting by divorce.

PARTING BY DEATH

The loss is most serious during the time that the child's emotions about his parents are still precariously balanced. The child has his own ways of expressing the message of the black-banded sleeve; he may be overcheerful and boisterous, rebellious and defiant, or clinging and suddenly spoilt beyond measure, but in one manner or another he is deeply worried:

> A boy whose father had died when he was an infant had moods of unhappiness, tantrums and distress at age four. His mother had to go to work and her young son worried about her poverty and loneliness, Susan Isaacs' war orphan study reports. The boy resented his father for having died, said he was "a bad Daddy"; if he'd been good, he'd be alive and helpful, not only to mother but "to love, help, and guide the little boy too," Isaacs comments. "He came to feel intensely guilty for his father's death because of his own rivalry for mother's love. It was his fault that father died; his hostile wishes had killed him."

It is this same haunting conviction in the lines:

PRINCE HENRY (to his dying father):
"I never thought to hear you speak again."
KING HENRY:
"Thy wish was father, Harry, to that thought."
                                  —*Henry IV, Part 2.*

Or, even more abstruse, in Shaw's *Man and Superman:*

"You may remember," Don Juan says in the Hell Scene, "that on earth—though of course we never confessed it— the death of anyone we knew, even those we liked best, was always mingled with a certain satisfaction at being finally done with them."

If the parent of the same sex dies while the child is still questioning his affection for this rival person, it is difficult for him to complete the all-important process of learning how to love and be loved. The child's natural wish to see his rival dead has come true, a devastating blow indeed. Such angry wishes are too dangerous, now, because there's nobody there to love the child in spite of them; he banishes his hostility— suppressing it mightily—to quiet his unrest.

The terrible guilt of achieving his primeval wish is intensified when the grieving parent turns to the child for comfort; the warmth of the small body in bed, sitting in Daddy or Mother's place at the table, all the sudden new closeness, sparks anxiety. The child may do something "bad" to deserve punishment which relieves his guilt, or have moods and tantrums like the little four-year-old war orphan.* Or, he may cling to the surviving parent to the point of tryanny to make sure he is loved in spite of his imagined mayhem. If the bereaved adult absorbs all the child's love, without the buffer of the same-sex parent for balance, it makes the child overwhelmingly guilty, and may cause inversion.

---

* Oedipus' horror at discovering that he had killed his father, married his mother and had children by her, propelled him to gouge out his eyes (the same punishment meted out to Cinderella's stepsisters) and banish himself from his native land forever.

In any event, the small boy or girl who loses a parent of the same sex during the Oedipus period leaves large occupation troops at that point. Ensuing relationships are haunted by this unfinished business; any successive love remains mixed with hate.

If the opposite-sex parent vanishes, there is bewildered grief. "Why doesn't my Daddy come? Doesn't he want to come and see me?" There's poignant longing and disappointment in the cry of the little London girl. Left without the comfort and protection of the loved parent, the child wonders who will shelter him, whom can he trust? The parent who lives is his rival but the only parent he has. Hostility and aggression are buried; the child is apt to be docile, well-behaved, helpful, hiding as well as he can the mixture of feelings of girl-for-mother, boy-for-father. He tries to conceal his longing for the lost parent, assuming what Isaacs describes as "a hard brightness," a noisy cheerful gaiety which, if it becomes too deep a pattern, may lead him dangerously close to an inability to feel any emotion for anybody.

Underneath it all, a tiny needle-sharp doubt whether mother or father, now dead, really cherished him. Would a loving parent leave his child? Because he cannot comprehend the parting, the child idealizes the lost parent, makes him into an image that can do no wrong. The marvelously kind, all-loving person thus invented can never lose his temper or be busy when you want him. He is both menace and blessing. He is a menace if used as protection against another hurt in the thought that no one else can possibly measure up to the ideal, so no one else is worth loving.* He is a blessing if the ideal of the missing parent acts as a bridge to a replacement; father or mother was good, so everyone like them will be good, is the rationale. Whether idealizing is help or hindrance, many observers find that it happens. It is a documented fact of human behavior.

David Copperfield's thought about his parents' death is

---

* "In all his love relationships," Dr. English and Dr. Pearson, the psychiatrist-pediatrician writing team, comment, " (the child) remains true to the parent who was unfaithful to him, and either cannot love another person, or, if he does, his love is combined with an actually causeless feeling of fear, disappointment, anger and aggression."

as revealing as the most modern textbook example. About his mother: "In her death she winged her way back to her calm untroubled youth and cancelled all the rest," he says. "The mother who lay in the grave was the mother of my infancy." He was able, as will be remembered, to find a substitute in his aunt, the redoubtable Miss Trotwood.

In contrast, his musings about his father, who died before he was born, have the suggestion of ambivalence. He talks of the paternal gravestone: ". . . the indefinable compassion that I used to feel for it, lying out there alone in the dark night when our little parlor was warm and bright and the doors of our house were—almost cruelly it seemed to me sometimes—bolted and locked against it."

Adults, perhaps unwittingly, encourage the idealizing. The child knows genuine grief when he sees it; equally he recognizes the hypocrisy of much of our mourning mores—the hushed voices, serious speeches, cocktail-hour visits to "show respect" to the departed, the unanimous praise. This is the grown-up world he sees, and it is catalytic to his instinct. At eight David Copperfield felt "a dignity attached to me among the rest of the boys and that I was important in my affliction. I felt distinguished . . . the importance was a kind of satisfaction." He is more candid than the pretentious mourner who uses current funeral customs to bolster his own ego.

Older children, Oedipus alumni, can accept a parent's death more easily. If they have emerged from the struggle of the first years with a healthy affection for both parents, they can find father's strength and mother's love in their expanding world. Brothers and sisters, friends, teachers, relatives help by giving and receiving love, hostility, affection and rejection. The isolation of infancy is gone; grief and confusion can be shared with trusted parent-surrogates. The children mourn, of course, but are not crippled by the loss.*

But maturity is not always obedient to the calendar. If the infant emotions were not resolved—if too many energy

* "Usually by eight, ideas of death have become more realistic and understanding," the Gesell Institute tells parents, "and many children have progressed to a more or less intellectual interest in what happens after death."

troops were left along the way—the loss of a parent throws the child of any age, or, for that matter, the adult, back to the place where his emotional growth is impounded. The ten-year-old mama's boy, the overdependent adolescent, the fearful, angry, or lonely children to whom the reassurance of mother or father *there* is still necessary, will be as deprived as the baby. The intensity of their reactions is some measurement of their need . . . and their longing. A doctor describes two degrees: a temporary revival of thumb-sucking after his mother's death gave a nine-year-old a mild and expected bit of "oral reassurance"; his older brother's prolonged bout of compulsive eating, for the same purpose, was a cause of serious concern.

More extreme still, the extraordinarily violent childhood of Elizabeth who was to become Queen of England produced an equally violent emotional turmoil from which, it appears, she never recovered. Her ruthless, compellingly sexual father, Henry VIII, allowed her no permanence of parental nurture; the motherless girl was in and out of his favor at whim and the political requirements of the moment. When he died she suffered "intermittent ill health, migraine and pains in her eyes," a biography reports. She was a magnificent statesman and queen, nevertheless, but she could never bring herself to fully love again. Nor could Thomas Mann's hero Hans Castorp, who traveled almost back to the womb.

> "[He] privately recognized life to be hopeless, helpless and viewless." Hans Castorp's mother and father died between his fifth and seventh year, his grandfather-guardian eighteen months later. His retreat was, of course, to the Magic Mountain, where there was "the hermetic enchantment to which he proved so extraordinarily susceptible that it had become the fundamental adventure of his life."

Mourning has twin goals: to keep an affectionate or at least realistic memory of the dead parent, and to give him up as an object of love, so to be free to love again. The hundreds of separate ties to the departed must be dissolved one by one. The child's capacity to form healthy scar tissue is enormous but it needs time—time, opportunity and adult awareness. If he can and wants to talk, a response like "How *can* you say such things about your father when he's dead!" sweeps agression under the rug and forces idealizing. If the child is silent, a querulous "You don't seem to care" is equally damaging. The child's wish to be closer to the surviving parent may be harmful if accepted too willingly; keeping the adult eye on long-range goals for the child asks for particularly unselfish parental gallantry at this moment.

Parents have their own emotions to deal with, their own ambivalence and loneliness, discussed in the next chapters. It is difficult to make time and opportunity for the child to mourn, and to accept his many-faceted reactions with serenity. The loss can never wholly be made good; the parent knows it, the child knows it. But its gradual comprehension can make it possible for the child some day to find a comfortable place in a new family setting.

PARTING BY DIVORCE

It is popular opinion that the child of divorce must suffer even more than the orphan. For those who self-righteously clasp this belief to their own shaky marital morality, the fact that it is not true will remain uncomprehended. The bias is reflected in law which insists that one of a divorcing couple is "guilty" and in social mores which imply that divorce has to be "bad" for the children.

Everywhere, divorcing parents are stung with guilt-plated barbs. "Have you thought what this will do to your children?" is a not infrequent comment of self-appointed saviours of the young although they know, as do their victims, that the bombardment of advice from newsstand, bookshelf, relative and friend could not allow a member of this child-centered culture to think about anything else.

A survey of modern novels and plays shows that the child of divorce is almost always depicted as "an innocent victim of parental folly." (SMITH, W.)

In New York City, a Magistrate's Court stamps every en-
velope with the threatening slogan "When family life
stops, delinquency starts."

Edmund Bergler, psychiatrist, administers a literary
scolding in *Divorce Won't Help:* "Frequently the gift of
divorce, which parents present to themselves, is comple-
mented by the Trojan Horse of unhappiness presented
to the innocent children."

"Shall we stay together for the sake of the children?" The
old-fashioned prejudice that divorce is always the wrong
answer to this crucial debate veils modern scientific evidence
that it can be the right one. Individual decisions need professional wisdom based on an understanding of the people
involved. There is such wisdom available. Any other advice is
not only worthless but dangerously irresponsible. The opinion of friends is likely to represent their own problems and
surely presents their own bias. In any case, the debate has no
place here; the present interest is in understanding the effect
of divorce on children in order to know what heritage they
bring to the stepchild state.

Today, most students of family life agree that it is
the climate of divorce that is more disturbing than the fact.
Much of the debilitating effect on children noted as the
result of divorce, actually belongs to what J. Louise Despert,
child psychiatrist and author of *Children of Divorce,* calls
"emotional divorce" of parents "emotionally severed from
each other by deep and serious rifts . . . even though legal
divorce may never have been considered." It is in such
families that torn, anxious, grieving youngsters are found.
The proposition has, by now, been tested and confirmed by
many scholars.

Most deviant behaviour in children of divorce "is not
caused by the divorce itself, but by the divided home
and the bitter conflicts that led to the divorce" is the statement of William Goode, Columbia University sociologist.

At the University of California, Judson Landis queried

thousands of youngsters; one result: "... it is the un-happy marriage that is more disturbing to children than the fact of divorce."

It is the attitude, more than the event, that matters, states Kingsley Davis, sociologist, pointing out that Egypt has a higher divorce rate than the U.S.A. but "has stability of institutions, contentment of people," as does India with a lower rate of divorce. "We need social machinery for proper child rearing," Davis says. "Once this is ac-complished, the incidence of divorce is of little conse-quence to the stability of the larger society."

The child can be released from the climate of an unhappy home by the fact of divorce. By the time he becomes a step-child it is likely that he has been. But at this precise moment his past comes flooding back; it takes time for it to recede again. Even the most constructive divorce is a major event in a child's life.

Death comes uninvited and the shakiest youngster knows, somewhere, that his parent didn't really want to die. But divorce is chosen by at least one parent and accepted by both. It seems to confirm the child's worst suspicions that he is being abandoned and, therefore, is not loved. The anger and hostility toward the departing parent which the orphan feels are even stronger in the child of divorce. Since he, like all children, is primarily concerned with himself, he cannot see any other reason for a parent's choosing to leave but the one that causes so much grief; father or mother doesn't love him. If he did, why would he choose to go away? The same reasoning, cruelly magnified by violence, applies to a parent's suicide.

The child wants and needs his parents together. Since both have agreed to the parting, he is angry at both for destroying his two-parent home. These hostile feelings breed guilt. "By steps mysterious to the adult but quite logical to him, the child can arrive at the conclusion that he is responsible for the separation of his parents," Despert says. The circle is spanned; hostility to guilt to fear, suppression of that fear and back to hostility again.

Divorce means that the child has to know what he cannot bear to know. It shatters the safety of believing that mother and father love each other despite his wishes that they wouldn't. It is not easy to take.

A sophisticated and brilliant boy—ranking second in his class at an Ivy League college—plummeted close to flunking out in his last semester, weeks after his parents decided to divorce, a psychotherapist relates. The boy attributed his failure to "the terrible shock at home." Although the legal ending of the marriage surprised almost no one who had observed the "emotional divorce" of many years' standing, the son's-eye-view obscured his parent's obvious mésalliance. "All that quarreling didn't really mean anything," he said. "They really did love each other." (SOURCE WITHHELD BY REQUEST.)

An amazingly parallel orphaned reaction appears in a report on "dropouts" at Harvard in a *New Yorker* article. The counselor of one student related: "Then, one day, in sheer weariness he let himself—and me—know that he was furious, too, with his father, for having died on him, for having deserted him. His rage fell to pieces in what seemed like guilt and grief. He could hardly speak." (WERTENBAKER, W.)

The stronger the wish to believe the parental marriage indestructible (and childish wishes therefore impotent), the harder the fall to the truth of the matter. If all were perfection, there would be a civilization of perfectly attuned psyches smiling at each other as their paths crossed, and every child would be reassured enough by knowing a "good" marriage between his parents to completely resolve the Oedipus situation. If this were the case, there would have been no great Greek tragedies to write, no *Hamlet,* no *Cinderella*—and no divorce.

As it is, divorce, like death, breaks up the desirable family setting. Further, it gets in the way of the convenient solution, open to the orphan, of idealizing the lost parent. The child of divorce may try to pretend that the parent now gone and the marriage now broken were what he wanted them to be, but his attempt must fail.* The parent denies an image of what might have been ... simply by living, and the child of divorce has to see a new side of him. The scarlet passions of divorce make parental behaviour seem strange and frightening.

One way or another, the child becomes a target for the conflict between his parents; their angry grief and shattered egos hardly encourage kind, loving parenthood. Discussions about custody, support, rights of visitation and vacations are loaded with unhappiness for the child. Mother and father snarl, weep, threaten and bribe, dividing the child's loyalties. They use him as a weapon. The youngsters report some of the ways they were used in a questionnaire:

> One tried to get information from me about the other
> asked me to testify against one parent in court
> asked me to back up arguments of the other in family
>   quarrels
> not permitted to talk to one parent
> not permitted to see one parent
> one told untrue things about the other
> one gave messages to me to give to the other
> one or both played on my sympathies
>
> (LANDIS, J. T.)

Even the most civilized divorce exposes parents' personal problems to the child, despite heady warnings from the advice-givers: "Your job, then," says *Parents Without Partners,* handbook of the organization of the same name and obvious purpose, "is to separate your feelings for and about your children from your feelings about your husband or wife." Ten guidelines and a model separation agreement are

---

* Sociologist Landis questioned 295 young people about their parents' divorce. For all, he says, the degree of hurt is related to how the child saw the home before the divorce. Adjustment was harder for those who thought the home was happy before the divorce, easier for those who recognized the open conflict between parents.

The youngsters supplied a poignant list of their efforts to pretend: "Sometimes lied about where one parent was, said one parent was dead, said one parent was on a trip at sea or would be with us later, talked as though parents were not divorced."

provided, as if it were possible to separate feelings as mechanically as milk from cream.

With or without such exhortation, the ugliness can hardly be disguised. The child must experience parental conflict and the pull of divided loyalty. Actually, one can question how devastating it really is to see parents exposed in all their human fallibility; an advantage to the child is that it is wellnigh impossible for him to escape to enchanted ideals when he lives with this reality.

He has to know what his parents are like and how they feel about each other, and it is often extraordinarily painful to be forced to this knowledge. But it has to be, and the necessity makes parting by divorce different from parting by bereavement, more complicated and perhaps more difficult. And it is in exactly this same respect that the child of divorce suffers less. He still has a mother and father; they are viable ordinary human beings, subject to the same weaknesses and frailties as the rest of the race. The child may wish it otherwise, try and try again not to know or see the common truth, but ultimately he must learn to live with it. A parent becomes a person, with all his faults more comforting than an image.

A child can act toward a living parent and get a reaction. He needs the response to judge whether he is gaining or losing in his effort to grow toward maturity. Orphans use the closest thing to a parental replacement, the stepparent, to express the anger that they feel toward the parent who is dead; the hatred David Copperfield felt for the murderous Mr. Murdstone, Cinderella's resentment for her wicked stepmother, Hamlet's necessity to kill his uncle Claudius—all these orphans had to batter the stepparent with the emotions of growing up.

> "There doesn't seem to be anything I can do for her," a worried stepmother of an orphan reported to a psychiatrist, who prefers to remain anonymous. "Nothing I try is of any value for her; I really don't know what to do."
>
> "You don't have to do anything," he replied, "except *keep living.*"

Having two living parents is an advantage to the child of divorce *de facto*. It can be two living, loving parents, letting the child escape from the unhappy small-family concentrate to what Dr. Peter Neubauer, psychiatrist, calls the "fluidity of two homes" and the certain advantages of parents vying with each other—even if it's for the wrong reasons—to be good, kind, even lavish toward the child. Unlike death, divorce selects for marital and parental fitness and may be a welcome relief instead of a pressing sorrow. The energy which it releases can be put to good use instead of sluicing down the waste pipes of conflict and misery.

There is no easy way to grow up. But there is tremendous resiliency to the trials which start at birth, an ability to bend but not break, to suffer but not be disfigured by sorrow. The child who has had to part from a parent—whether by divorce or death—has suffered more than his peers; he has taken an extra step toward maturity because he has had to. If the parent is able to give him a sense of dignity in the sorrow by respecting his feelings, he can survive the painful experience of parting and emerge from it stronger because of the adversity.

What has happened to the marriage into which he was born is the stepchild's heritage. There are memories of mother and father together, memories of the parting. There is a new sophisticated knowledge of what a parent is like when deprived, grieving or angrily ugly, sorrowful or courageous, self-indulgent or quietly gallant. The child brings all this knowledge to his stepchild state. He has had a rough time of it, and a revealing, learning time, with the built-in chance, not given to all children, to know his parents as people. With this heritage, he becomes part of a new family.

Chapter Four

IT'S A NEW WORLD

"The crown of life is the exercise of choice."
—THORNTON WILDER

The Father of Our Country was a stepfather; Abraham
Lincoln was a stepchild. Each came to the relationship because of a death. But a twentieth-century stepchild in the
White House—Jacqueline Kennedy, until the dreadful assas-
sination of her husband our First Lady—is a child of divorce.
The Executive Mansion has sheltered a pervasive change, as
true for Main Street as for Pennsylvania Avenue. Where once
most stepchildren were created by the accident of fate that
made them orphans, now the overwhelming proportion come
into being by choice—the choice of parents to divorce. The
emotions that spark the Cinderella story are unaltered, but
they lose the protective innocence of bereavement. You assume responsibility when you choose to end one marriage and
begin another; it is the onus of choice, the price of the modern idea of marriage.

You can decide when and whom to marry, when to have
children. You can divorce or not, remarry or not. The determined rigidity of Victorian family rule has gone before the
thrust of individualism. The change has come fast; only a
few times in known history has there been such a swift cultural shift.* It has come so fast that the present generation
and the stepchildren it cradles spearhead an emerging pattern.

It requires flexibility and independence of thought to

*There have only been four times of extremely rapid movement in the
Western family system, according to Harvard sociologist Carle Zimmerman,
". . . the forced movement of the French and Russian revolutions, the period
after the Peloponnesian wars in Greece, and now."

pioneer a new morality, and people pay heavily for the privilege. They suffer the doubts of all who leave familiar for uncharted waters. They sail against a current of nostalgia, conformity and gloomy forecasts of decline and decadence.

Ask a dozen people their opinion of the rising divorce rate, and they are unanimous that it is a disaster. If there are children in the divorcing family, it is worse still. A man who chooses to become a stepfather is regarded with suspicion, a home that shelters his children, her children and their children with dismay and curiosity. Reformers beg for a return to values which, like the grandparents who held them, are good because they are old. They warn that marriage is tremblingly close to doom, the family disappearing, children crying for security. It is assumed that we are coming on bad times, as did the Roman Empire, and that the good old days were good.

But people doggedly continue to change their ways. The family pattern at the turn of the century is as obsolete today as everyday life in 1900 when most Americans had no telephones, automobiles or electricity, and air travel, radio and television were still as unknown as the six-week stay in Reno. Family life has changed since Tom Lincoln brought a new wife to the log cabin to care for young, motherless Abe and his sister, and even more since George Washington married the rich widow Custis and became stepfather to her two children.

It has had to. A collection of revolutions—the Industrial Revolution, the emancipation of women, revolutions in medicine, social science, psychiatry, mobility and automation —have meshed in the twentieth century to make fundamental change in marriage and the family.

The stepchild lives with change. Attitudes fashioned in other times hold back the effort of parents and children to establish healthy families in the modern design of the step relationship. Yet facts point directly to new attitudes; new ideas about marriage, family life and children, new reasons for divorce and remarriage. At this precise moment, men are discovering methods to collect, correlate and communicate these facts. New sciences examine and measure personality, motivation, attitude and intelligence. They poll, ques-

tion, test and count Americans under powerful new micro-
scopes. As their observations join company with historical
perspective, the changing climate comes into focus.

How has the making of the modern stepchild come about?
There is no need to speculate; the facts of change speak for
themselves.

CHANGE IN THE FAMILY

The large, three-generation family, presided over by an
elderly patriarch, once was necessary for the support and protection of its members. Today, a senior citizen living alone
in a neat, golden-age apartment project can remember the
teeming houseful of kin he grew up in; uncles, cousins,
babies, grandparents, together made the economic and social
unit he knew. Its men worked outdoors, its women raised
the children and managed the house. Although it divided
responsibility, the family was primary; its children were expected to be dutiful, cooperative and respectful. Progressive-
minded, psychologically-oriented parents hear its romance
with wistful longing.

The modern American family is the immediate family—as
you see it plastered on billboards with car, refrigerator or
case of Cokes—mother, father, son and daughter, called the
"nuclear" or "isolated biological family" by Margaret Mead,
the "small family system" by the late sociologist James Bossard.* It lives alone, has less contact with relatives, fewer economic functions as a family. It buys what it once produced.
"[It] no longer spins, weaves, makes shoes, tailors men's suits,
makes soap, butchers hogs, cures leather or makes furniture,"
a student of the family states. Gradually disappearing are
the fine arts of home baking, canning, washing, ironing, making clothes and sewing; still with us—cooking, cleaning house
and taking care of children. (OGBURN, W.)

Gone, too, are certain social functions; police and insur-

---

* The term, he explained, came into being in 1913 with the publication of
a book by the same name which attempted to "identify families with some
degree of contraceptive sophistication . . ." The relation of birth rate and
population change soon became known as a way of life.

ance companies protect instead of grandfather and his shot-
gun, television replaces a family sing for home entertainment,
schools educate "the whole child" and warn parents not to
help with homework, churches leave few rituals uninstitu-
tionalized. The urban life provides more money for people
to go their own way, less dependence of children on parents,
brothers and sisters to get them there. The individual is
more likely to be known for himself than as a member of
his family group. Women make reputations independent of
their capacity as housekeepers; one symptom—the magazine
that coined the "togetherness" slogan has dropped it in favor
of being "The First Magazine for Women." Poor relations
now get their social security from Uncle Sam instead of
relying on blood relatives.

Mobility heightens the separation from kin and the new
independence of the individual. The family is constantly
moving, sent to new jobs, able to afford new communities
or just ready to change scenery. In 1958, 3 million people
moved from one main geographical area of the U.S.A. to another and 12 million children moved at least from one house
to another.* Adaptability replaces the old stability.

Without the controls of kin or close community ties, without economic and social interdependence, without the guides
of tradition, the isolated biological family emerges. There
are many nostalgic efforts to hold to past values: the gather-
ing of the clan for a holiday feast, the do-it-yourself work-
bench, the family rumpus room, the high-priced regard for
the "hand-woven" or "hand-made" evidence of craftsman-
ship. Yet the small family system inches its way toward becoming the American pattern.

There are other patterns, too; a variety of families co-exist
in this country.† They vary for ethnic, economic, social and

---

* The 1960 White House Conference on Children provided these figures
and further details: 2 million children moved from one state to another
in the same region, 2 million from one county to another in the same state.
The most mobile—people from rural, non-farm areas.

† Examples listed in a study by Ernest Burgess include the Hopi Indian
(primitive maternal family), Pennsylvania Amish (patriarchal), Ozark moun-
taineers (kinship control), Italian immigrant (semipatriarchal), the rooming-
house family (emancipated), the lower middle class family (patricentric), the
apartment house family (equalitarian), the suburban family (matricentric).
Other sociologists add Negro, Puerto Rican and Chinese-American to the
family patterns list.

vocational reasons and by location, occupation and style of life. Travel to India, Italy, even England, and you find a wider range. From corners of the world now within flying distance, anthropologists produce a torrent of books and films on what primitive people mean by family. There is no one measure for the spectrum; a value sought by one culture is discarded by the next, wholeness for one is disruption for another. Each attitude evolves at its own speed and for its own reasons. In California, for example, the divorce rate races ahead to double that of the rest of the country, dissolving one marriage in two. In New York, stepchildren from differing cultures have separate reactions. A public school teacher asks her pupils from low-income Puerto Rican, Negro and white families, "Is your father coming to Parent's Day?" and the not unusual, freely given answer is: "Whichfather?" *(sic)*. Not many blocks away, the stepchild at a prosperous private school reddens and hesitates, too embarrassed to answer.

The concern of this book is to know the educated, middle-class, more or less typical American step family. Mores of most Puerto Ricans, Pennsylvania Amish or Hollywood stars, however intriguing, must be put aside along with primitive cultures further afield. Otherwise, encyclopedic confusion would obscure the stepchild state in the particular culture of present interest.

Many former family functions are now the work of machines, the state and the community, stimulating criers of doom to pronounce that individualism has destroyed family-ism. Commentators looking for a handy whipping boy for modern ills keep the indictment alive. Often, they castigate the system without the perspective of knowing why it is what it is; change is equated with disaster. "Broken homes," "insecurities," "cultural disintegration," and like expressions are household words for opinion-makers, self-appointed guardians of past values.

More careful analysts examine what the family does instead of what it used to do, and finds it more specialized, strengthened, and perhaps more important than ever. Its essential function as a place where man and wife can know love and affection, where children can be born and the opportunity for individual growth sheltered, remains. These basics require new standards, as qualitative improvements insist on a higher form of health, education, personal adjustment and general well-being, raising the sights and achievements of the modern family.

The long view shows the family steadily developing in value. In the public life of the Middle Ages, everything depended on social relations. Phillippe Ariès, the French cultural historian, tells in *Centuries of Childhood*, "The density of society left no room for the family. Not that the family did not exist as a reality; it would be paradoxical to deny that it did. But it did not exist as a concept." The ancient cultures had been forgotten, but gradually, as private life began to substitute for public and there was a revival of interest in education, the family "assumed a moral and spiritual function, it moulded bodies and souls." As he traces it from the fifteenth century to the twentieth, Ariès makes an important point: "The history of modern manners can be reduced in part to this long effort to break away from others, to escape from a society whose pressure had become too unbearable." The modern family "satisfied a desire for privacy and also a craving for identity." His conclusion; "It is not individualism which has triumphed, but the family."

CHANGE IN MARRIAGE

What has happened to marriage—the act that creates the family? "A dispassionate observer of modern marriage," says Paul Goodman, author of *Growing Up Absurd*, "might sensibly propose, forget it; think up some other form of mating and child care." A decline in the marriage rate could endorse his cynicism; instead, the result—surely unexpected by worried observers—is a lusty enthusiasm for the blessed state. The number of married men and women in the U.S.A. has steadily increased in the past century as has the proportion of those who could get married . . . and do. More people are getting married; over a million and a half marriages made 1962 the fourth year in succession to record a rise of almost

2 per cent. More than 90 per cent of those born in 1948 (92.2 per cent of the boys, 94.6 per cent of the girls) will marry.*

More of them will choose to end that marriage by divorce than their ancestors did. There are ten times as many divorces today as there were a hundred years ago and the incidence, now one marriage in four ending in divorce, is rising. As more and more marriages are terminated by divorce, fewer people remain to carry out the injunction "until death do us part"— at least the first time it is given. In these years, the number of marriages ended by death is even further diminished by the sudden increase in longevity. Modern medical advances catapult life expectancy from ages in the late forties to almost seventy, a fact so recent that it creates a lag in the death rate of the married population serenely celebrating silver anniversaries (770,000 in 1960) and golden (130,000).

There is wisdom in statistics when they take a long copious view; abstracting one set of facts or one year of fact has the dangers of partial truth. The full-face portrait of steady, long-range marriage trends over the past century is presented in FIGURE 1. The startling divorce figure looks different in the total marriage perspective—divorce is up, but so is marriage—and public alarm raised by the all-time high in 1946 may be quieted by the return to a more normal speed of change. Figure 1 shows that more people choose to marry today than a hundred years ago, more choose to divorce and fewer marriages end in death. The increase in divorce and decrease in death combine to end four-per-thousand fewer marriages now. It follows that a larger proportion of people are presently living in the married state than there were in 1861.

There are some objective explanations for these facts. Three major wars have set off a chain reaction to raise the marriage rate which, although temporarily depressed during armed conflict, surges upward in every postwar era. Civil war babies caused a turn-of-the-century increase; post-World War I children, marrying at World War II, elevated the rate

---

* This information and all the statistical facts to follow in this and the next chapters (where not otherwise identified) are supplied by Paul H. Jacobson, Ph.D., of the Actuarial Division, Metropolitan Life Insurance Company, both from his *American Marriage and Divorce* and a special statistical study for this book which provides facts nowhere else assembled.

to the highest peak in a hundred years, and their progeny, now flooding the nation's college entrance offices, are expected to continue boosting it. The state of the economy has its effect, too; more people marry when times are good and postpone marriage when they are bad. The 1929 crash set

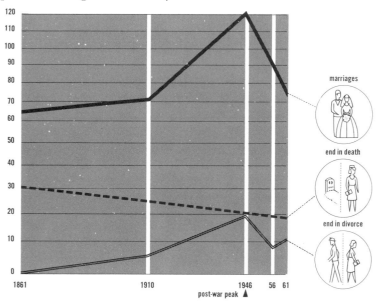

Fig. 1   **A CENTURY OF MARRIAGES**

The rate per thousand of marriage eligibles (single persons age 15 or over and all divorced and widowed persons) who marry each year, and of existing marriages that end in death and in divorce each year.

back the marriage rate, although even this severe depression did not have a lasting influence. It did, however, affect today's stepchildren by its roundabout, unexpected influence on the current adoption practices, described in detail in later pages.

People marry younger; twenty is the median age of brides, twenty-three of grooms, while in 1890 it was twenty-two and twenty-six respectively. The Population Reference Bureau says that more women marry in their eighteenth year than in any other and puts one of every two first-time brides in her teens. Marriage age appears to be returning to the level it was at in the first days of the U.S.A. when legal reflection of what was usual set it at sixteen for women, eighteen for men in

many states (although in New Hampshire thirteen and fourteen was and still is permissible!). The law has remained constant, and in this regard, custom has come full circle to re-
validate it. But for divorcing couples—and for stepchildren—
its lag remains with shocking reverberations.

An unusually high proportion of all stepparents comes from
these young marriages; what is the secret of early-marriage
appeal in the face of doubting parents and the youngsters
themselves.* Investigators agree that a third of the girls in
teen-age marriages are pregnant at the wedding, that favor-
able economic conditions allow parents to pay the young
couple's bills for the first years, and that the Atomic Age—a
catch-all for such pressures as "insecurities," military service,
the live-for-today stance—are perceivable motives.

"It is better to marry than to burn," was St. Paul's measure.
To him, marriage was a last resort. Movies, television, magazines and Madison Avenue copy writers flood America with
quite a different estimate—the key to change in the concept of
marriage. To Be Happy is the goal, marriage the means. Individual fulfillment has replaced the home-centered economy;
instead of making shelves of preserves, the family makes happiness. Americans unanimously want Happiness and are surrounded by the message that it comes in a marriage package.
The rosier the promise, made increasingly so by the cham-
pions of yesterday's values, the harder the fall to reality. Dis-
illusion and disappointment become even more vivid and important in the small family concentrate where every tremor
is a quake. Divorce and remarriage have changed in response.

CHANGE IN DIVORCE

The century from Lincoln to Kennedy made divorce usual.
Margaret Mead measures it as the major change in the Amer-

---

* Many teen-age discussions end up like the recent conclave of 170 youth
representatives of New York State communities which reported "unanimity of
opinion against early marriages. Teenagers are not mature enough. On the
question of hasty marriages, parental influence can be most important. . . .
Steady dating is too confining and feeling may become too tense. This may
lead to bad marriages."

ican marriage pattern, bringing "growing recognition that divorce may come to any marriage, no matter how devoted, how conscientious, how much in love each spouse originally was . . ." What she labels "the terminality of American marriage" was regarded with somewhat less objectivity by another social commentator, Emily Post: "The epidemic of divorce . . . must be rated as a catastrophe along with floods, dust bowls and tornadoes."

One of four marrying Americans will be in her catastrophe category. Despite moral indictment, punishing civil law, and forbidding religious precept, more than 15 million people living today in the U.S.A. have been divorced, and the steady rise indicated in FIGURE 1 augers ever-increasing numbers.

"Thou shalt not plow with an ox and an ass together" *(Deut. 22: 10)* was the biblical quotation Milton used in arguing for divorce. Always, even before these words were given, there has been the possibility of divorce as a solution for marital conflict. It weaves in and out of history, encouraged or frowned on according to the needs of the particular society. To the Greeks in the Homeric Age, divorce was practically unknown; a century later it was an everyday event. Ancient Romans decided it to be in the best interests of the Empire to permit marriage to be entered into or ended by private agreement between a man and a woman. (In a modern version, the U.S.S.R. made divorce as easy as signing your name and as lacking in stigma. Twenty years later, also to advance state purposes, policy, procedure, and attitude were reversed.) When marriage changed from a private or civil contract to a sacrament of the Church, it was ruled indissoluble but right through ensuing centuries of strict ecclesiastic rule, men found loopholes whereby with enough money and influence or both, divorce could be arranged.

Official morality has always been challenged. Current efforts to change our divorce laws have a particularly eloquent antecedent in John Milton's plea. "To prohibit divorce is against nature," he told Parliament in the seventeenth century, asking that "some conscionable and tender pity might be had of those who have unwarily, in a thing they never practiced before, made themselves the bondsmen of a luckless and helpless matrimony." (The blind poet spoke from the heart; his young first wife, Mary Powell, had gone home to mother after one month of marriage and stayed away for two years.) His oratory was not immediately effective; until 1857 it still took a private act of Parliament to get a British divorce and adultery was the only grounds until 1910.

In modern America, divorce is replacing desertion, separation, annulment, or staying in an unhappy marriage as the most usual solution. It is available to Catholic, Protestant and Jew and in every state. This latter consensus came only in 1949, when South Carolina, the last holdout, finally legalized divorce. Where state law is too stringent, citizens go to get a "migratory divorce" where it is not. These migratory divorces account for 3 to 5 per cent of the nation's divorces.* The law throughout the land makes one party to the divorce guilty and the other innocent, forcing most divorcing couples to collusion, fraud, or perjury as their last conjugal act.

Today most stepchildren are children of divorce. In 1900 most were orphans. FIGURE 2 shows the dramatic change. People died at a younger age before the great twentieth-century advances in medicine, ending many more marriages where there were children under eighteen by death than at present (almost half in 1900; today the proportion is reduced to 23 per cent). The numbers of divorces in 1900 were small; in 50 per cent there were children under eighteen, and now with the huge numbers of divorces, we find that that proportion has increased to 58 per cent. Children available to be stepchildren in 1900 were almost 90 per cent orphans; today, 30 per cent are orphans and 70 per cent are children of divorce. The *proportions* have changed and the *numbers* of divorces and children of divorce have skyrocketed; divorce becomes pivotal for most stepchildren and parents.

There were 7,000 divorces in 1860, 422,000 one hundred and one years later! The biggest change has taken place since the turn of the century, ignited by the two world wars and the social revolution. Our current rate of divorce, 10 per 1000 or 1 per cent of all marriages each year, is the highest in

---

* New York had the lowest recorded divorce rate in the country in a recent year, although 10.8 per cent of its white males were divorced during that time, as compared to 8.3 per cent nationally.

the world except for Egypt (where there are also more marriages), but the trend is the same in most Western Hemi-
sphere countries touched by the urban-industrial revolution,
and is everywhere increasing.

This enormous increase has its subtleties. Divorce comes increasingly early in marriage; in 1900 the increase in rate was

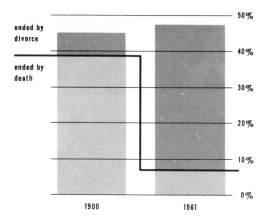

Fig. 2   SOURCES OF STEPCHILDREN

*The per cent of all marriages with children under eighteen which ended
in divorce and in death in 1900 and 1961.*

greatest in four-year-old marriages, by the 1920's at three
years; since 1943 the biggest rise is for marriages of one or two
years. FIGURE 2 shows the increase in divorcing families where
there are children; like their parents, the children know divorce at a younger age.

Most people think of divorce in the limits of their own
experience—how it has happened to them and their friends,
what they read or see in theatre and movies. For the educated
upper classes, divorce is the sleek Noel Coward sophistry
which activates a brace of psychiatrists and a million-dollar
settlement. Such an image is prolonged by the people who live
it and write about it from this particular view. It was once
almost the total divorce picture . . . but it is no longer. Wil-

liam Goode* challenges the stereotype, as damaging as that of
Cinderella and the stepmother. "A revision of certain literary
cliches is due," he says. ". . . the lower-class family as one of
easy warmth, love and stability as contrasted with the neurotic, psychically aggressive, divorce-prone, middle-class family makes for simpler novels, but it is not accurate." It is
only an echo of past fact that divorce was a privilege of the
rich and powerful, or of the sensitive, educated few.

Parents' divorce is part of the stepchild's life, but it is not
a great leveler, nor do stepchildren come off an assembly line
identically mass-produced. Although certain generalizations,
based on universal emotion, hold for all step relationships,
most are qualified by circumstance. The differences become
known when the phenomena of divorce are examined. Social
and economic change in America has altered the image of divorce with broad strokes.

Today, Goode states, there is an inverse correlation between class and divorce. His and other studies show greater
inclination to divorce among unskilled labor and low-income
groups, and greater inclination to divorce among grammar
school than among high school graduates, who in turn are
more prone to divorce than the college-educated. The higher
the income, the lower the rate of divorce.†

In Goode's profile there is more divorce in cities than in
rural areas, more for couples with different backgrounds,
education, and religion, more for Protestants than for

---

* In the welter of studies about divorce, one of the most complete, impec-
cably researched and detailed is William Goode's *After Divorce*. Professor
Goode, Columbia University sociologist, made an intensive field study of 425
divorced women in Detroit; in the process, the major studies were checked
and contrasted to his results where necessary, and precautions taken against
drawing unwarranted conclusions.

† Goode gives a Proneness to Divorce Index. A high index means more
divorce-prone.

Occupation		Income		Education	
Unskilled	179.7	under $1,000	188.6	Grammar school	101.9
Semi-skilled,				High School	
operatives	83.2	$3—4,000	89.2	Graduate	95.0
Professional and					
proprietary	67.7	over $4,000	66.7	College	86.1

An interesting exception comes from a study by Hollingshead; the "arriviste
family," where there is "conspicuous expenditure, insecurity and family instability," shows much higher divorce rate than other in the same economic
and social strata.

Catholics or Jews. The Negro divorce rate is higher than the white. People with shorter acquaintances and engagements before marriage are more prone to divorce. Occupations involving irregular hours, frequent overnight absences from home, and concentrated association with the opposite sex are given as vocational encouragement to divorce. A study of 100 exceptionally successful men in each of six categories showed artists to be the least firmly married; they had 50 per cent more than their share of remarriages. Next to them were doctors, with 25 per cent more than their share; their profession provides all the hazards above. Military men were the most stable (the armed services frown on divorce); business men, college professors and engineers were in between. (NIMKOFF, M.)

Change to the small family system, change in the focus of marriage, and the revolutions on which these hinge suggest valid causes for people to choose the way of divorce. It can no longer be tied to caprice, indulgence, or class, race or creed; in theory it should no longer carry the stigma it earned long ago. With its roots clearly exposed, divorce could mean progress.

CHANGE IN REMARRIAGE

"Since the age of twelve, thanks to God whose life is eternal, I have taken a husband five times from the church porch." Chaucer's woman might be surprised at the attitude of her descendents; the much-married movie queen or wealthy scion who follow her medieval example—now called "sequential polygamy" by sociologists—are freaks. Even a century ago the practice was accepted. Witness two authors writing about the 1850's: Eugene O'Neill has twice-widowed Ephraim Cabot marry a third time at age seventy-five in *Desire Under the Elms* to a widow " 'bout thirty-five an' purty," and Steinbeck's Cyrus Trask—within two weeks—"wooed, wedded, bedded and impregnated" a new wife. "It was quite normal in that day," his *East of Eden* reports, "for a man to use up three or four wives in a normal lifetime."

Today, remarriage has a slightly shady, less than salubrious hue. The change is not mysterious; it is the direct result of the increase in divorce, now the major source of remarrying brides and grooms. What was accepted for the widowed in their unavoidable bereavement is a question of ethics for the divorced who have exercised choice, who account for the huge increase in remarriage in the twentieth century and who give it its present coloration.*

Remarriage has doubled since 1900. (See FIGURE 3.) "At the turn of the century," Jacobson reports, "first marriages accounted for close to nine-tenths of all marriages." Now almost one in four are remarriages. (An even more radical figure, one in 3.5, was reported to the 1960 White House Conference.)† The source of this first important change is that in every 100 grooms, fewer are single than they were two generations ago; half as many are widowers and seven times more are divorcés. In somewhat lesser proportions, the same is true for brides.

There are, a scholar figures, 432 possible varieties of remarriage between the single, widowed and divorced, with and without children, young, middle-aged and old—a provocative potential. Nowhere has change come faster or with matching

* The persistent bias shows up in the community reaction to a large number of remarriages as follows:

	% Favorable	% Indifferent	% Unfavorable
For widowed men	67.0	24.5	7.8
For widowed women	67.9	23.9	8.2
For divorced men	51.7	32.5	not given
For divorced women	56.0	32.1	11.9

This table, by Jessie Bernard, a sociology professor, is from her *Remarriage*, the first book to tackle the subject. It is based on reports of 2009 remarriages from students, colleagues, and friends of the author. The information is valid, the author says, "for native white, predominantly Protestant, middle class, highly educated communities in the northeastern part of the United States." This much-quoted text has a further qualification bestowed by the years since it was published; the material was collected during the postwar time of exaggerated change in every attitude of personal life. It is best used with this in mind.

† There are no reliable figures prior to 1900, perhaps because the totals were so small. The first published national statistics on marriage and divorce were incomplete, due, Jacobson says, to the "wretched condition of marriage records at that time." Massachusetts, longing to prohibit the "social menace" of divorce, collected some statistics ahead of the country. On these Bernard rests a conclusion opposite to the one presented here; she states that "there has been in the past century no consistent long-term increase in the remarriage rate." For the part of the iceberg in clear statistical view, her statement appears inaccurate.

drama. The 1960 portrait is more reliable than it could have been a decade ago before the post-war uproar had settled, at least in family terms, back to steady change. But even this is so unpredictable that a year's facts can alter before the ink is dry. FIGURE 3 proceeds with caution to show the second con-

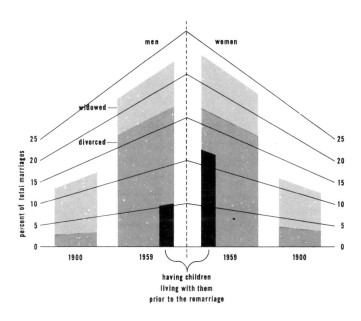

Fig. 3 THE NEW LOOK OF REMARRIAGE

The increase in the per cent of all marriages that are remarriages since 1900, the change in the previous marital status of remarrying brides and grooms, and the per cent of each having children living with them.

crete evidence of long-term change; remarriage now takes its character more from the divorced than from the widowed, a reversal in two generations.

There is a new environment for the stepchild. The age at which he is presented with a stepparent and the character of that person matter in the extreme. Remarriage comes younger to child and parent; although it is still a middle-age phenomenon (median age of remarrying brides is 35.4, grooms 39.7, according to the National Office of Vital Statistics) the increase in remarriage is fastest for young people.

Half the remarrying brides in FIGURE 3 and a quarter of the grooms have children under eighteen because the young divorced parent is likely to want to get married again—and does. In addition to age, a host of personal, practical, and social forces differentiate the divorced from the widowed in remarriage. These differences determine what happens to stepparent and child; they will be scrutinized when the quality of remarrying parents is considered in later pages. The present quantitative look is startling enough; starting in their twenties, divorced people marry more than the widowed at *any given age* and both marry more than the single. At twenty-five, for example, the divorcée's chances to marry are 99 in 100, the widow's 93, the spinster's 88, and for men about the same proportion. By forty-five, divorced or widowed men are more likely to marry than women, especially widows.

The simplest explanation is that there are more divorced people available; two become marriageable at every divorce, one at every bereavement. And remarriage increases the age gap between spouses. The older a woman is, the less chance that she will marry, because the men of her age can happily flatter their egos by choosing her younger sister. The statistics give no quarter to the dream that sends the spinster scurrying to find a rich widower for her security; the widowed are likely to marry widowed or divorced, the divorced to choose other divorced. Whether because of availability, suitability, or compatability, it happens.

The stepfather gains in importance; for almost all children of divorce, he is the living-in stepparent. Orphans live with whichever parent survives, but children of divorce almost always with their mother. The spotlight moves away from stepmother, confining most Cinderellas' difficulties to weekend visits. Stepfathers are older than fathers, and not unusually from a different background from their new wives, who compromise standards in their eagerness to remarry or have changed ideals as they matured.

"All experience is an arch to build on," Henry Adams wrote. Experience in remarriage is just beginning to be an arch for new attitudes. Remarriage follows divorce as a lower- rather than middle- or upper-class phenomenon. However, some say it is ascending the social scale, a fact which is viewed with alarm by Bernard. "Does this mean," she asks, "that the disintegrating forces of modern living, having delivered their blow at the lower status groups, are now in the process of eroding . . . higher status groups as well?" Others see the rise in remarriage as reassuring evidence that divorce is *not* undermining our social structure but encouraging new and often more successful marriages.*

In any case, remarriage has outstripped the conventions of civil and religious law in its sudden burgeoning. Although Catholics and some Protestants still forbid remarriage after divorce until the previous spouse dies, liberal Protestants and Jews are more encouraging; Rabbi David H. Wice says divorce should lead to remarriage because the Talmud says "it is better for four people to be happy than for two people to be miserable." At least one-third of the states impose a waiting period before remarriage on the "guilty" party to divorce, although none have such rules for the widowed except Puerto Rico—300 days. But there is evidence of inevitable, if tortoise-slow, evolution, even in law.†

Being remarried is part of the vast social experiment of the twentieth century. With an almost breathless urgency remarriage as a way of life has become viable for more people than ever in our known history. The quantity has skyrocketed and the quality has changed to meet the requirements of the divorced. In its new form remarriage is of major importance. It almost completes the chain reaction of change in family, marriage and divorce.

Almost. This generation has made its choices to bring

---

* The statement that more remarriages end in divorce than first marriages, made by some sociologists, is invariably qualified with a list of ifs and buts; as they quote and requote each other, the educated guess has become a fact, its qualifications forgotten. It is doubtless too soon to make a meaningful determination; speculation is useless and generalities misleading.

† The 1963 adulterer is prohibited from remarrying the person he committed adultery with in Louisiana, Pennsylvania and New Hampshire. Elsewhere any "guilty party" to a divorce must wait till his first spouse dies or for a period of time which varies from none (rare) to one to five years. For fifty years after the Revolution, Massachusetts, for example, forbade the "guilty" party ever to remarry. Gradually the restrictions have loosened; first an out-of-state marriage for the sinner became valid, then the rule applied only during the lifetime of the former spouse, a pattern much repeated elsewhere. Today the defendent must wait two years. All these restrictions are more important in attitude than effect; neither religious nor civil law appears to stop desired remarriage, which is as migratory as divorce, perhaps more so.

about a social revolution, but it has not made them alone.
Each choice has been affected by children; each affects children. They live different lives from their grandparents or
even their parents, in different settings with different relationships. Born in revolutionary times, they carry the seeds
of change. Their decisions will determine how trends pro-
ceed from here. The change for children, considered in the
next chapter, is the most significant change of all in the world
of the modern stepchild.

Chapter Five

THE CHILD'S WORLD CHANGES

"Childhood shows the man, as morning shows the day."
— MILTON.

The statement—
There Are 7 Million U.S. Stepchildren!
appears here for the first time anywhere. If your child, the child next door or down the street has a stepparent he is one of the seven million. His mother or father has died or, more likely, his parents have been divorced. He has lived through the painful parting, lived with the troubled time afterward, and the terror of uncertainty . . . what next? He has acquired a stepparent, perhaps two, and a new family arrangement wherein each childhood difficulty is multiplied. The changes that create him in such numbers are familiar; the nation's searchlights penetrate bedroom, nursery, and cocktail lounge to bring the population explosion, the rising divorce rate and the remarriage habit into plain view. But their result, the modern stepchild, is still in darkness. The light has not yet reached the 10.6 per cent of the nation's children who live in the stepchild state.

The Bureau of the Census of the U.S. Department of Commerce does not count stepchildren. No other government agency or private organization has been located which has measured their numbers. The search for quantitative information from the U.S. Department of Health, Education, and Welfare, the U.S. Children's Bureau and highly-named societies—Child Welfare League, Child Study Association of America, National Association for Mental Health, Family Service Association, and others—everywhere drew a blank, not only for statistics but for any facts about stepchildren whatsoever. The Census Bureau's explanation suggests that ubiquitous stigma may be a reason.

"The Bureau," one of its officials states, "has never insisted upon the enumerator's making a distinction between children by blood and children by marriage . . . *because it would introduce some embarrassment;* moreover the facts of the situation would not always be known by the respondent." (Italics mine.)

How many stepchildren are there? The elusive figure has been tracked down for presentation in this book by Paul H. Jacobson, demographer. He followed a circuitous statistician's route to find it. He estimates the number of stepchildren under eighteen in the U.S.A. at 7 million for 1961, the latest figure available at this writing, which suggests that published guesses made by sociologists on the basis of small samples are invalid. Until some government agency finds a way to count stepchildren heads, the determination made by this national expert stands as the most reliable figure available.*

The numbers of stepchildren will increase in a year and become a great deal larger within the decade. The trend is established; the 1960's will demonstrate it. It is in this decade that the growing number of children of divorce have crossed the path of the declining number of orphans and superseded them so that now, for the first time ever, there are more children of divorce. Their numbers grow, making more potential

---

* To get the figure, Jacobson calculated the number of children by age who are orphans, illegitimate, and children of divorce; then the number of parents of these who subsequently remarried was estimated, excluding marriages between natural parents that followed illegitimate births. Jacobson gives his sources:

ORPHANS: *Social Security Bulletin* Vol. 24, No. 10, p. 14, Table 1.
ILLEGITIMATE BIRTHS: National Vital Statistics Division in *Vital Statistics of the United States* Vol. 1 (annual issues) with survival from birth to present age, based on 1949-51 United States life table for total persons.
CHILDREN OF DIVORCE: from Jacobson's book *American Marriage and Divorce* p. 130-131, 135, and unpublished data covering the period 1956-1961.
REMARRIAGES: parents were classified according to previous marital status, i.e., divorced, widowed or unmarried, using above sources. The number of children in each category was then grouped into parent units on the basis of statistics by the Bureau of Census in *Current Population Reports* p. 20, No. 67, p. 23, Table 11.

stepchildren. The population explosion also contributes to the certainty of increase, coming so fast that there are twice as many children today as there were in 1900. (See FIGURE 4.) Stepchildren, as it can be seen, have increased at a slower rate and are a smaller proportion of all children today. But

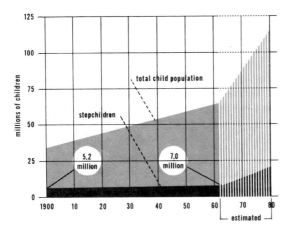

Fig. 4   MORE CHILDREN, MORE STEPCHILDREN

The increase in numbers since 1900 and a projection of the future.

both elements in the trend combine to forecast the growth of the stepchildren number.

This still uncomprehended—even unrecognized—trend forces its way to the light, now, as we choose the stepchild life for more and more children. Already, the figure of 7 million represents more than ten per cent of American youngsters; it will soon be history. The very numbers of stepchildren alone may at last overcome the powerful stigma which has for so long kept eyes averted and minds uninformed, and the child-centered culture of today will be stepchildcentric as well tomorrow.

There have always been stepchildren. The proportion may be no larger now than it was in ancient Rome, medieval England, or colonial America; prestatistical times allow for only speculation about numbers. But although certain emotions are timeless, the impact and expression of emotion in today's 7 million stepchildren is different than it was for their ancestors. Childhood is no more static than the man it creates; both have changed.

The child-centered world is a modern phenomenon. Today's parents have developed it, grandparents inaugurated it. Its antecedents are deep in history. In medieval society achievements of ancient cultures had been forgotten; the idea of childhood did not exist, according to Ariès who traces its emergence in paintings, clothes, games and customs. Jesus said, "Suffer little children to come unto me," and the medieval painter surrounded him with eight little men with the muscles and expressions of adults; only size indicates childhood. The six- or seven-year old, as soon as he was out of swaddling clothes, was dressed like an adult, played the same games, lived the same whirling public life, in effect he *was* an adult. Infants were disregarded; "Nobody thought," Ariès tells us, "that every child already contained a man's personality. Too many of them died."

Tender feelings toward the infant were unexpressed. Little children were believed to be unaware or indifferent to sex; the socially acceptable sexual ribaldry of the times included them quite naturally. If the child was troubled, he found his own solution as best he could. At fourteen, when today's rebellious teenagers send parents quivering for guidance, Louis XIII was "put to bed beside the Queen his wife [age 13] in the presence of the Queen his mother." (Ariès) Across the Channel, Elizabeth saw her father, Henry VIII, marry a third stepmother. It was not until the churchmen and moralists decided that the child was a creature of God to be cherished and educated that childhood was established as an ideal. Schools prolonged the years allowed for childhood; parents took new interest in the child. In the several centuries before modern times, the child became increasingly important in the family circle until he ultimately arrived at his present position in its very center.

In the perspective of centuries this is a new concept. Parents have always mattered to children and children to parents, but the climate has only gradually admitted expression of emotions, and the attempt to understand them is an even more recent phenomenon. Knowledge of the existence of

7 million stepchildren would have been disregarded in a time when even biological ties were quickly cut; it would have been less than sensational when every widowed lady had to remarry to protect her virtue and her larder. It is the combination of social changes that gives the stepchild his present importance.

Change from the large, extended family to the small, biological family is major for the stepchild. In the setting where many relatives were bound together, relations between parent and child were diffused. When Lincoln's mother died, there was the resource of Tom and Betsy Sparrow, relatives, and their adopted son, Dennis Hanks, living in the Lincoln pole shed next door to the log cabin. Lincoln's stepmother and her three children arrived and when the Sparrows died Dennis, too, moved in to the one-room cabin; when John Hanks, another relative, appeared, it held nine souls. Carl Sandburg describes the move to Illinois: fifteen relatives all told and "Abraham Lincoln on and off an ox wagon." Sarah Bush Lincoln was mother-in-general to all as well as mother to her own and stepmother to Abe. Whatever his emotions, he was not isolated in a separate status but shared it with others in Mrs. Lincoln's group of non-biological children.

Lincoln lived in the large family system. Sandburg does not say whether this contributed to his deep affection for his stepmother or whether his lonely moody character sprang from whatever deprivation it inflicted on him. No one studied the family in those days; they had neither the interest, time, nor tools. But the large family's characteristic effect on children has recently been observed; twenty-five families with five or more children were studied by James Bossard in 1948. The results help to understand the past and hint at the stepchild's present circumstance. There is a tendency to take minor crises in stride because they are more frequent and shared by many.

Bossard gives a vivid example: a child spills ink on the tablecloth, and in the small family there is a scene. Father, mother and child work on the mess, and emotion is rife. In the large family, father continues reading his paper, mother sews on busily, and the culprit cleans up with the help, if he can get it, of a brother or sister.

Emphasis is on the group; self-expression is secondary. The large family insists on conformity, defining each member's role and function. Emotions are shared with many, and parent-child intimacy is limited, in Bossard's observation, by the setting. Parents are neither possessive nor demanding and the silver cord is likely to be fragile and short. Children make easy adjustment to change and new relationships.

Add psychological insight and the large family picture is even clearer. It is known now that the baby's relation to mother alone, to mother and father, and then to siblings establishes patterns of response and adjustment for life. The family is the child's first "group." It determines his response to later groups; "It is entirely reasonable to suppose," Bossard says, "that the girl who has grown up happily with six brothers, for example, might be very unhappy in a woman's college, or at work in an office staffed exclusively by women."

The family determines social relations, and equally, personal relations. Mother is the child's first love, father the first expansion of that love. Future loves echo earliest adjustment.*

Youngsters in Lincoln's day lost a parent from their large families without recognized trauma; the very numbers of people suggest that the loss was cushioned by surrounding kin. Arrival of a stepparent was absorbed by group and child together. What was good for the family was good for the child; his individual reaction was secondary. He would not be likely to express resentment and hostility under the ever-present pressure to conform. Concentrated attention to feelings were unusual. Writers with modern insight give stepchildren of past times lines they could probably not have spoken:

* Burgess and Cottrell predict success in marriage by certain personality tests. One finding: children from large families are more likely to make a good marriage because their image of love is not limited to the one-to-one relationship. The youngest child, who has a prolonged and deeper intimacy with parents, resembles the only child; both are reported less likely to succeed in marriage.

Eben cries to his dead mother in the seduction scene with his stepmother in *Desire Under the Elms:*

EBEN: Maw! Maw! What d'ye want? What are ye telling me?

ABBIE (stepmother): She's tellin' ye t' love me.

EBEN: I see it. I sees why. It's her vengeance on him so she kin rest quiet in her grave.

Probably closer to the nineteenth-century stepchild's reality are Lincoln's own words reported by a contemporary:

"Once when Lincoln referred to the fact that he owed much to his mother I asked 'Which mother, Mr. Lincoln, your own or your stepmother?' to which Mr. Lincoln replied, 'Don't ask me that question, for I mean both, as it was my mother all my life, except that desolate period between the time mother died and father brought mother into the home again. Both were as one mother. Hence, I simply say mother.' " (PICKERING, GOV. W.)

The twentieth century catapults the child into the tight embrace of the small family system. Here, where spilt ink can cause turmoil, death or divorce is a monumental disruption. The ballast of the large kinship group is gone; if one parent departs, the child has nowhere to turn ... except to the other parent. If a stepparent appears, the way is blocked; he is a generic threat to the child and the two are soon locked in combat which may never be resolved. Now that marriage is constructed for happiness, and there is a new intensity of relationships, the reconstructed family must evolve a delicate balance to survive.

This is not easy in a system which concentrates on children—and the modern family does just that. It has seized the opportunity of the open-class fluidity of this era and molded itself for ascent. Success—in the social scale, career, education, economic comfort—is the desired end, children the means. With a sideways look at what other families are doing, parents impose their own desire to achieve on their children. They may mask ambition with apparently casual sophistication; the old open delight in children's achievement is too close to the immigrant culture it sprang from for comfort and now becomes the source of jokes. (The proud mother on the beach crying, "My son, the doctor, is drowning!" is still the classic.) But admitted or not, change to the small family system has produced intensive parenthood as a substitute for the secure containment of the great kinship society.

In little boxes of streamlined apartments or split-level houses, rapport and emotion are concentrated. Children share feelings with parents and an occasional baby sitter.* New behavioural sciences, medical advances, time and money are available; intently, parents use every personal and public resource to "do a better job" with children. As the small family system develops, there are wild gyrations from the permissiveness of the '30's to the panic of the '40's to the new concern with discipline of the '50's. Each brings new conclusions and a rash of books advocating change. The earnest parent is affected in direct ratio to his personal convictions; the assault on "momism" sent thousands of vulnerable women to psychiatrists with their guilt, *Fathers Are Parents Too* energized many males to an effort at palsmanship. A recent diatribe, *The Feminine Mystique,* follows Simone de Beauvoir's *The Second Sex* in its attack on an isolated portion of the small family system; it says there is too much motherhood. Harold Taylor, educator, was enthusiastically applauded by two thousand members of Child Study Association for saying there is not enough. As in any time of rapid social change, every conclusion, frail or solid, is heralded out of proportion to its long-range significance.

The new marriage and the new family is a quality system which, for better or worse, concentrates on the child. It produces the spoiled egocentric aggressor and the sensitive, shy, dependent; individualism is encouraged if not manufactured to satisfy authorities who say it is good. In this environment, the child has an exaggerated opinion of his importance in

---

* Margaret Mead, recently a grandmother herself, calls for the return of the grandparental influence. "It is not their experience of the old tried and true ways but instead their experience of the arduous and trying process of continuous adaptation to new ways that is now needed. The retirement of the grandparent generation into a convenient chimney corner or seat at the club . . . is over."

the family group because he is given an exaggerated amount of its attention. Emily Post commented on the beginnings of the child-centered culture: "In the world of yesterday," she said about the 1900's, "the children's right to an unbroken home far outweighed any question of whether Father or Mother might themselves be finding happiness in marriage." This attitude undoubtedly made many miserable people; to-day's parents, conscious of the damage of the concept she de-scribed and intent on their search for happiness, have a differ-ent solution.

If they are not happy, they divorce, regardless of the pres-ence of children. The widely accepted idea that children act as a deterrent comes from early figures now out of date. Dif-ference in the rate of divorce for childless marriages and those with children has steadily narrowed; today the propor-tion is 1.6 (childless) to 1 (with children). There are nine children in every ten divorce decrees, totaling more than a third of a million children each year whose parents divorce. About two-thirds are under ten years of age, considerably younger than orphans, whose parents die at an older age than parents divorce. An educated guess that fewer people are staying in an unhappy marriage "for the sake of the children" is borne out by a subtle change in divorce rates according to the size of the family. Divorce without children decreases, with children it increases and the rise is greater for those with three or four children than for the one- or two-child couple.

Children do not appear to prevent divorce, nor are they the cause of it. The 400 women in Goode's survey, listing the main causes of divorce—spouse's drinking, non-support, per-sonality, values, involvement with another woman—placed "home life"—his lack of interest in home, children and wife —sixth in order of importance.

Now, in the second half of the twentieth century, there are more and earlier marriages, more children in the first years of marriage and more divorcing parents. On the surface, it does not add up to a child-centered world if you believe the popular dogma that divorce must be bad for children. Three sticks of dynamite can blast away this stereotype; they only remain to be bound together and ignited. (1) It is exposure to parents' marital conflict that causes trouble, not the end

of conflict by divorce. Recent studies of delinquent and emotionally disturbed youngsters in whom trouble is grossly apparent increasingly often come to this conclusion. (2) Much
of the misery ascribed to divorce in early investigations is
now seen to belong to economic stress. The confusion came
because social measurements were first taken in the low economic group where divorce is most prevalent. (3) Remarriage of divorced parents recreates a whole home which may,
in fact, give the child his first experience with a happy, reliable environment. Remarriage is growing in significance as
a result of divorce.

Each imperative change is forged against its opposite; it
would be naive and grossly inaccurate to presume that there
are no damaging divorces, no self-motivated parents, no severe
emotional traumas from divorce. But there is a trend which
forces a new perspective; parents who divorce—more aware,
more interested, more concerned with children than ever
before—believe it to be good for their children. Of course,
they are thinking of themselves too, and their judgment may
be mistaken. But it is not lightly made. The effects of the divorce on the children was the primary topic of discussions
between Goode's divorcing couples, far outranking division
of property, support, alimony and remarriage in frequency
of importance. Mothers almost always have custody of the
children—only one-tenth of all U.S. decrees gives it to the
father; 57 per cent of Goode's parents arranged for weekly
or any-time visits from father, 43 per cent for monthly, holi-
days only, or none at all. The almost one thousand parents
studied are widely regarded as representative; 84 per cent of
these mothers and fathers stated their arrangements to be
satisfactory.

Such divorces create a new brand of family, which this book
names the "interim family," whittled down from the all-inclu-
sive, three-generation, patriarchal great household to the
small, biological mother-father-children unit, and now to
the mother-and-children with father-on-alternate-Saturdays
arrangement. It is still classified as sinful; society assumes
that parents' interest in children, no matter how earnestly
pursued, is immediately and forever violated in the establishment of the new family brand.

Most children live in this new family arrangement before they become stepchildren. (Most orphans have the same mother-child experience; 70 per cent under eighteen lose a father, 30 per cent a mother.) It is no longer an oddity to children; they have absorbed the reality faster than their parents. The young are not shocked to have school, camp, or college ask "Parents' Marital Status: living together, widowed, divorced?" (The absence of this question caused many a child of divorce extreme discomfort just a generation ago.) The change in the effect of divorce on children can be seen in the difference between the results of a study made in 1932 and a comparable one of some twenty years later.

The earlier sociologist tells of a marked degree of "disorganization" of children's personality resulting from infrequent contact with one parent, feeling inferior to the two-parent child, lack of adjustment to both sexes and a skeptical view of marriage. (MOWRER, E.)

The later study of children's reactions shows that two-thirds of the youngsters felt that their parents' divorce did *not* affect their self-confidence with friends; they were drawn closer to their mothers and became less close to their fathers. 76.6 per cent said "It has given me more determination to work at making a success of my marriage." 76.9 per cent said "It has made me more aware of the problems of marriage." 1 per cent: "I never want to get married." 2.7 per cent: "I have little confidence in making a success of my marriage." (LANDIS, J. T.)

Nurture in the interim family can strengthen future stepchildsmanship. Because of the contracted size of the immediate family group and the concentrated attention children expect, their needs are more fully met. Most parents attempt an intelligent balance of attention and freedom for their children, assisted by an onslaught of advice from every communications medium. For the many reasons built into the recent social revolutions, children's attitude about being children of divorce are newly sanguine.

In the wake of so much divorce has come a surge of insights, ways to direct and control recrimination, bitterness, competition and other assorted post-divorce ugliness which once went untrammeled. A score of how-to-do-it books challenge mother to refrain from making father's visits difficult, to understand the child's needs for both parents, to maintain a cheerful household liberally infused with security for the children. They insist that father is a parent too, and tell him how to make contacts with his children that are meaningful, if occasional. Throughout the literature runs the major theme—"The child of divorce must be made to feel loved and safe"—and the accompaniment—"There's another marriage for you around the corner."

"Of approximately ten [today it's fifteen] million people in the United States who have been divorced, only about a million and a third are now unmarried." So it was reported to the 1960 White House Conference on Children and Youth. By now, readers can anticipate that even this provocative statement to an assemblage concentrating on children aroused not even a murmur about stepchildren. To adults the suggestive statistic is clouded by prejudicial stigma. Children are able to be more perceptive and to accept the concept of what is to happen to them. It is well-known that children of divorce hope and press for their parents to marry each other again.* If reconciliation efforts fail, they become embarrassingly busy cupids, inviting any visitor to "marry us." Women's magazines are replete with such stories; they report some of the truth. Omitted but omnipresent is the anxiety behind the wish, the two-directional hope that a parent will marry again . . . and won't.

Emotions pull one way, the climate the other. The small family system intensifies closeness and the child's yearnings for exclusive parental affection; what he wants and how he feels is hugely important to the family in contrast to what it was in Lincoln's day. But as the interim family becomes increasingly intelligent and constructive, panic at the idea of losing mother to a new husband and of having to accept a rival to the lost biological parent, and the terror of uncertainty are

---

* Whether for this or other reasons, a good many people do. Jacobson's estimate based on 1948 records: "About one out of every fifteen divorced men who married a divorced woman remarried his former spouse."

somewhat assuaged. At the same time, the pressure of more
and more parents remarrying grows; what other people are
doing matters more now than it used to, replacing the kinship
group as a source of checks and balances. Children know
what they see around them, not from whence it comes. The
pull away from a parent's remarriage is less strong, the pull
toward it stronger.

The presence of children is not a deterrent to remarriage
any more than it is to divorce; in fact, statistics show it to
make remarriage more acceptable. Clearly, parents and children want remarriage; seven out of eight children in the
U.S.A. live with two parents, real, step or adopted. Families
have larger numbers of children. The proportion with two,
three, four or more children has increased in the last decade,
the proportion with only one child has decreased. Remarriage
must account for a sizeable proportion of the much-discussed
rise in the size of families and is significant in interpreting
the meaning of the rise, a favorite occupation of commentators on our social scene. But nowhere is it mentioned.*

There is an inherent prejudice in current statistics; interest
in social phenomena could be forwarded by pressing for details of the new pattern. "All children and stepchildren be-
low specified ages are legal dependents of the parent or stepparent; hence those interested in dependency have never
urged us to subdivide this combined group," a Census Bureau official writes in answer to an inquiry. Because of their
built-in stepchild blinders, present day statistics and their casual interpreters give only part of the picture.

The modern stepchild is the product of the isolated biological family—mobile, adaptable, companionable, paying close
attention to emotional well-being—and of its offshoot, the interim family, wherein a new idea of parenthood incubates.
Here the child learns that parents are divisible, that their
love for him can survive, even improve, on physical separa-

---

* "The number of American women with three or more children doubled
in twenty years," *The Feminine Mystique* announces, "and educated women
after the war, led all others in the race to have more babies." Facts of the
population explosion measured by the Census Bureau are cited as the source
for the statement; it leads on to alarmist concern with what is happening to
women. "The five babies, the movement to suburbia . . . took the place of
those larger needs and purposes with which the most spirited in this nation
were once concerned."

tion from him, that divorce does not have to spell disaster.
And he learns one more thing of major importance to his
future as a stepchild: mother and father are people as well as
parents, people who have not abjured the family system because of divorce or widowhood but are as enthusiastic about
it as others around them. Even in his huge self-centeredness,

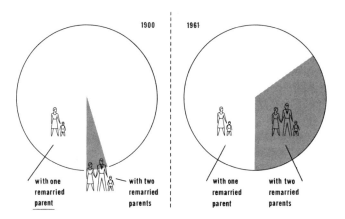

Fig. 5   MANY MORE CHILDREN HAVE TWO STEPPARENTS

*The per cent of all stepchildren under 18 with two remarried parents
in 1900 and today.*

the child wants them to be happy people—a not entirely altruistic wish; parents are easier to live with when they are
happy. He perceives that marriage—first or second—is the way
that most people take to happiness; he, too, believes in it.

All this he brings to his stepchild state. The degree to which
these past experiences have modulated his emotions determines the degree to which he will find the new life agreeable.

At its 1963 graduation exercises, a school was surprised to
find its usual parent section of seats inadequate. The number of students had not increased in a decade . . . but suddenly, they had more parents! FIGURE 5 shows the change
since the turn of the century; the proportion of stepchildren
with one remarried parent has decreased by almost one-third,
the proportion with two remarried parents has increased
more than seven-fold. Father's new wife and mother's new

husband bulge auditoriums across the nation as more and more stepchildren stand up to get their diplomas.

The stepchild of divorce may have four people in the parent category to deal with, a more complicated life than that of the orphaned stepchild who can only have two, but not necessarily a worse one. *What happens is up to parents and the people they marry.* They set the tone, they shape the relationship. They have certain distinct advantages in the modern pattern; on the average, children are younger and therefore more flexible after divorce than after bereavement, their parent's remarriage happens sooner, they are likely to be relieved by the departure of trouble—and one parent—and more welcoming to the new arrival. These possible pros are contrasted to the cons in sociologist Charles Bowerman's unique study of more than two thousand stepchildren, representative although not universal. He places the disadvantages squarely at the parents' door; inadequate parents, unfortunate choice of new spouse, intrusion and disruptive effects of the former spouse, and the failure to learn from the past; "The influence of previous tensions and deep conflicts may carry over directly or covertly into the personality, marital and parental patterns brought to a new marriage."

Change for the child has been extraordinarily fast. The new kind of childhood it makes, the primary concern of this book, has hardly been identified, much less understood. "Childhood," Milton said, "shows the man, as morning shows the day." The kind of men and women stepchildren will be is largely determined by their childhood which, in turn, is largely determined by parents and stepparents. The step relationship depends on adult attitude. Advancing knowledge has brought parents to the very edge of understanding the curious stigma, the pervasive stereotype that dominates thought on the step relationship. The next step is to examine the parents' society, the laws they live by, and the kind of people they are likely to be. Here the dangerous gap between perception and reality that leaves its mark on every stepchild becomes even more vivid.

Chapter Six

THE LAW

"Laws, like houses, lean on one another." —BURKE.

The blood tie that pulsates between parent and child is formalized by law. The state, along with parents, watches over tomorrow's citizens on the theory, old as man, that it must perpetuate itself and that good citizenship is essential to that end. By its laws it protects the child from the moment he is born until maturity; it says that natural children and children legally adopted are to be cared for, supported and educated by their parents. In this way the law reflects the abiding instinct of loving, responsible parenthood.

The law for the stepchild mirrors quite another image. Legally, stepparent and stepchild are as strangers; the mere fact of their relationship confers no rights and imposes no duties. This is the dictum of law.

To the parent happily anticipating remarriage, to the well-intentioned stepparent, and to the securely established stepchild, this blunt position may be a shock. The law's harsh statement is remote from their experience; responsibility and compassion, dictated by their own humanity and the society of family, friends and community, make the rules they live by. Theirs is a social, more than a legal, relationship. Mostly they govern themselves, well within the law, and thus it stays distant, even unknown to them. But should their responsibility waver, or cease to govern—which it can with even the best intentions—the law decides.

You may regard the stepchild as one of your own children; the law does not. It has formulated only the lowest common denominator of the step relationship, giving the stepchild practically none of the protection of a natural child. If it matches your personal concept, it will serve you well. If not, there are ways you can take the law into your own hands to make it fit your particular purpose. You can change your will. You can consider adoption. An able lawyer can tell you how to translate your ephemeral social behaviour into properly sturdy legal form. (He will probably delay suggesting solutions; the situation is so newly important that each of the three expert attorneys and a professor of law interviewed on the subject said he needed time "to look into it," never having given the subject much thought.)

This chapter does not presume to substitute for individual legal advice. It looks at the legal status—or nonstatus—of the stepchild, and how it came to be what it is, because the concise rules of law reveal exactly what society thinks, what each child whose parent remarries must accept. Some of its provisions make sense, some don't; the law has not caught up to this stepchild era any faster than the people who make it, in fact it is slower to reflect habit, pausing always for a generation or two as if to be sure that change is valid. Gingerly, cautiously, it has begun to explore the no-man's-land of the step relationship; it has made changes which, even though they seem tiny, are significant in pointing the direction of larger change. Whether it suits you or not, the law has the fascination for stepparent and stepchild that the mirror had for Narcissus; it reflects you.

"There is no legal pigeonhole for the stepchild," Professor Monrad G. Paulsen, family law expert at Columbia University Law School, comments. "It is an irregular state." Although the step relationship is established by law rather than by blood—or, as lawyers are apt to say, by affinity not consanguinity—there is no statute to make it less than "irregular." It comes into being through the back door of the marriage law; because you marry a parent, his children become your stepchildren and you their stepparent.

Under our legal system, family matters are the exclusive domain of the individual states; each makes its own laws about marriage, divorce and parenthood, but their legislation has practically ignored the stepchild. His legal status has been evolved by court decisions known as common law. Case by case, the law has been molded, deriving its logic from the past. Its beginnings are not only compelling human documents but the only way to understand present practice. First, then, a look at what has gone before.

The town of Dennysville, Maine, once sued neighboring Trescott for the funeral expenses of one Elias Bilbarb. When his mother remarried, Elias, age seven, had become his own master, binding himself to various persons and visiting his mother occasionally. The court decided that although his mother and stepfather lived in Trescott it had not been Elias's legal residence and did not have to reimburse the plaintiff town for the funeral. This was in 1849. The records give no hint of why the small boy left home. At the final reckoning, the law simply says that his mother's home was not his; Dennysville, however grudgingly, had to bury Elias Bilbarb.*

If Elias's stepfather threw him out, he was within his rights. The relationship of strangers was firmly established. As if to emphasize its unfamilial view of the stepchild, the court called him "child-in-law" and the stepparent "parent-in-law." In 1833, a Massachusetts judge made the doctrine brutally clear: "The father-in-law is under no legal obligation to support his son-in-law. The son-in-law has no place in the house of his father-in-law. He may turn the son-in-law out when he pleases." To make the stepchild's lot even harder, there was nothing his mother could do; it was common law then that when a woman married, her husband controlled her property and had an "absolute right" to her earnings. Elias's mother had no means, except her second husband's good nature, to support her child; if his father was dead or had vanished from the scene, Elias had no legal right to support from anyone.

"It is revolting," Justice Holmes stated, "to have no better reason for a rule of law than that so it was laid down in the time of Henry IV." Common law for the stepchild is based on judgments made in England in the reign of Queen Anne. After some indecision, a 1703 case became the precedent; the judge decreed that only a parent "of sufficient ability" had

---

* This case, all others cited in this chapter, and the legal interpretations were collected by Ruth Charles, a law school student, in a special study for this book.

to maintain the children and when a mother, such as the one appearing before him, "has parted with that ability by her second marriage, she is no longer liable. Her husband takes only her debts and this is no debt of hers." Apparently, it was no debt of his, either; in 1790, a Mr. Harrison separated from his wife and stepson, promising to give her fifty pounds a year and pay all her debts for which he was liable. He was sued by an innkeeper who was providing the two with food and lodging. "We are of the opinion," the judge said, "that the husband is not liable for the expenses of maintaining his wife's child by a former marriage."

Across the ocean, the very first relevant U.S. case established some small equity for the stepchild. James Freto's father died and in 1805 his mother married Robert Pierce, who took James into his home and supported him. At fifteen James shipped as a hand on a fishing schooner; boy and stepfather both tried to collect his wages. James won. "The father-in-law is not obligated to maintain the plaintiff (James) and is consequently not entitled to claim his earnings . . . against the minor's consent. If he could, the earnings might greatly exceed the amount of maintenance; the while of which the father-in-law would receive and the next moment might turn him out-of-doors."

The stepchild had a right to work—evidently such as Elias and James became independent at a young age—and to keep his wages, but not much more.* Then, in mid-nineteenth century, two changes significantly improved the stepchild's position.

Married women got the right to control property. The first Married Women's Property Act was passed by Mississippi in 1839; by 1920, all the states had laws which, like New York's, decree that a woman's real or personal property be her own "as if she were unmarried, and shall not be subject to her husband's control or disposal. . . . ." A widow could now support her child with his father's estate if she remarried, regard-

---

* A strange echo survives in Alaska. In *American Family* Laws, C. G. Vernier tells of its "curious statute which provides that 'The power of a mother to bind her children . . . shall cease in case of her subsequent marriage and shall not be exercised during the continuance of such marriage either by herself or her husband.' No case construing this statute has been found and the context furnishes no clue to its meaning."

less of what her second husband chose to do, and a divorcée, marrying again, could keep control of whatever funds were hers.*

At the same time men who acted like fathers were recognized by law; the rule of strangers was modified by their way of life known, logically enough, as *in loco parentis* (in the place of a parent). The stepfather who voluntarily took the responsibilities of a natural father was henceforth treated as a parent in almost all legal matters. A parent has a right to the services and earnings of his child, to collect for his injury, and to correct and punish him, all of which rights, C. G. Vernier says, "can be supported as based on the general right of parental control without resorting to the fiction of mutuality of obligation." These rights and responsibilities end, legally at least, when the child is twenty-one or "emancipated" by marriage or military service.

A New York judge in 1850 was one of the first to explain the reasoning of this important change when he heard the case of Charles and Dan Williams, who worked on their stepfather Hutchinson's farm and were suing him for their wages. They said that what he had spent on their maintenance was less than the value of their labor. They did not collect. "We should not, by our decision, deter the husband from taking the children into his family," the judge said. If he supports and educates his wife's children "as a parent and good citizen, the law should be liberal . . . to encourage an extension of the influence of the domestic fireside. . . . [It] must add vastly to the happiness of the mother and to the children its advantages can scarcely be construed."

But it was the question of money and property, more than happiness at the domestic hearth, that insisted on a definition of *in loco parentis*.

Who pays? Who gets paid? Since money is the crux of most litigation, it is no surprise to find that it was the support of

---

* Two other effects of this change are noteworthy. "A large amount of U.S. wealth is held by women as a result," Harriet Pilpel comments in *Your Marriage and the Law*, "which is changing the economic relationship between man and wife."

Professor Paulsen finds it "startling" that the legal emancipation of woman and her increasingly important economic role have not changed the primary duty of a husband to support his wife; he believes the law is "giving a kind of reality to cherished myth."

the stepchild and the right to his services and earnings that were most often brought to court. The intention of the stepparent became the criterion of modifying the rule that he is as a stranger to the child. Does he *intend* to act as a natural parent? This is the legal measure of *in loco parentis* which does not exist if the intention appears otherwise:

> . . . if parent and stepparent are separated or divorced,
> . . . if the child is not living in the stepparent's home for any other reason,
> . . . if the stepparent has an agreement with the child's natural parent, or anyone else, to be reimbursed for his support of the child,
> . . . if the stepparent intends the relationship to be temporary.

An unsettled question is what happens when the natural parent dies. In 1957 two New York courts arrived at opposite positions. One said the stepfather was liable to support his wife's child even after her death, the other decided that that event ended his legal obligation.

Against this background the present-day law about the stepchild can be understood. The outlines of the corpus are clear; its skeleton is the doctrine that stepparent and child are as strangers, its flesh the relationship of *in loco parentis*.

Who is responsible for the stepchild?

Support is a major responsibility. In a healthy second family, bills get paid, allowances dispensed, and extra change handed out as naturally as affection and care, which have no price tag. It is when there is a breakdown—economic, physical, or emotional—that law rules. It puts the obligation for support of the child on his father. If the father dies, the mother is responsible but if he is divorced from the mother, his obligation to support his child continues.* When he remarries, his natural children still come first; a divorced father defaulted on payments of $200 per month for support of his child because he felt "morally obligated" to take care of his

---

* Either or both parents can be required to contribute, depending on their economic status. Arrangements for children's support are, authorities say, the most difficult of all pre-divorce agreements.

second wife and four stepchildren. The court did not accept his excuse. Some states—Indiana is an example—require a man entering a second marriage, who has minor children dependent on him, to prove that he will be capable of supporting them despite his remarriage.

When a mother remarries, the natural father is still responsible for supporting his child. If the stepfather decides to take on this function, he becomes responsible, having chosen to act *in loco parentis*. (Reports of the father-stepfather-child triangle invariably comment that fathers, particularly if they themselves have remarried, wish stepfathers would support their stepchildren.) Paulsen describes this as "role-playing and the response to role-playing": the stepfather who represents himself to the world as the responsible party for the child is expected by the world, and the law, to follow through and pay the bills. He is required to support the child at the normal economic level of the family, in a manner "appropriate to one's station."*

He can retreat from his position, which was voluntary in the first place. To change his role, he has to undo the image he has established and inform the world of his intention. Lawyers recommend something akin to the solemn "I am no longer responsible for the bed and board of. . . ." advertisements in the newspaper, letters to schools and doctors and other appropriate notice. But at the rock-bottom welfare level, the stepparent *in loco parentis* must support the child who would otherwise be destitute. Social welfare law looks first to the father; if he is dead, has left the country, or is destitute, then the mother, other relatives, the child's own resources and finally, the stepparent—if "of sufficient ability"—is liable before the taxpayers will give public assistance.

New York and California do not give the stepparent any choice; whether or not *in loco parentis* exists, he is liable for support—in this 15 per cent of our population—if it is "shown to the satisfaction of the court that the stepparent

---

* "Necessaries," in addition to "necessities," have to be supplied. Professor Paulsen cites the case of a New York department store, Bloomingdale Bros., which won a judgment against a customer named Benjamin for certain fancy groceries—necessaries, the judge decreed, because "in the gilded world wherein the Benjamins moved, whale meat and caviar may very well have been regarded as plain but honorable fare."

had knowledge of the child's existence at the time of said parent's marriage."* "As between the public purse and the stepparent," a New York social welfare official reports "responsibility for maintenance of the child should fall upon the stepparent." To get it, a public welfare official must sue; the child cannot.

Custody is a second responsibility. Natural parents have the paramount right to custody; if one parent dies, the child lives with the other. If parents are divorced, the court gives one or the other custody, or it may be divided between them. Most children from a broken home live with their mothers.† If the mother's second husband chooses to act as a father, here again he has a father's rights and responsibilities.

An extraordinarily violent example illustrates not only the rights but an unhappy possibility of *in loco parentis*. In Texas, Mrs. Gorman's second husband took full control of her children, supporting them and treating them as his own. One day he ordered his stepson to pen a horse; when the boy failed to do it as directed, the stepfather beat him with a cowhide whip. Mrs. Gorman intervened and he beat her too. The court held that because Mr. Gorman stood *in loco parentis* he could exercise a father's right to chastise his child. Otherwise, he would have been criminally liable for assault and battery and sentenced to a prison term and civilly liable to his wife and stepson for money damages.

If the parent who has custody dies, the other natural parent has a right to custody, not the stepparent, no matter how close he and the child may be. But there is an important "if": the surviving parent may be unfit. Then the court can give the stepparent custody because it is in the child's best interest. Or the parent with custody may be unfit; Harriet Pilpel tells of a child who made the judgment. The youngster "hated"

* In a curious anachronism, New York is one of the many states where there is no place on the marriage license application to record dependent children, although previous marriages must be identified. It offers marriage-minded parents a wide-open chance to ignore their own children's existence, Jacobson points out. "Many remarriages fail," he says, "because the spouse was 'not aware' of the dependent children until after the marriage."

† There are more widows than widowers, Jacobson reports. "Of total orphans in 1955, almost 68 per cent had lost their father only, about 30 per cent had lost their mother only. . . ." In divorce, the mother gets custody in close to 80 per cent of all cases.

the man his mother married and continually ran away from their home to his father's; the mother could not enforce her legal custody. Although her pride kept her from revising the agreement in court, the child is now settled with his father where he believes his welfare is best served.

Can you marry your stepchild? Here the law reverses itself and considers the stepchild as a natural child; more than half the states forbid the marriage of stepparent and stepchild (only one-fifth take the same position regarding in-laws). Presumably genetic proof of the dangers of inbreeding causes all states to forbid incestuous marriage with a parent, brother or sister, uncle or aunt, and some add first or even second cousins to the list. But the prohibition against a step relative, a non-blood relationship, must have a different base.

"And the man that lieth with his father's wife hath uncovered his father's nakedness; both of them shall surely be put to death" is the Bible's straight statement to stepson and stepmother. "And if a man lie with his daughter-in-law [which some theologians interpret as also meaning stepdaughter], both of them shall surely be put to death: they have wrought confusion; their blood shall be upon them." *(Lev. 11:12)*. These biblical injunctions are less concerned with what happens to genes and chromosomes in intermarriage than with the "confusion" that results from intrafamily seduction of relatives by law. Or perhaps the ancient taboos were a result of both social and biological experience; in any event, the words of the Old Testament have had their effect on our laws.*

Whatever relationship the stepparent has established with his stepchild, all the complex structuring of support, custody, rights and responsibilities, ends when he dies. As far as the law is concerned, the intent of his life is irrelevant for inheritance. If you make a will, you make your own law; if you don't, the state makes it for you and says that the stepchild

---

* In Rhode Island, it is spelled out. Jacobson describes a statute that allows "persons professing the Jewish religion [to] contract valid marriages though related, provided that the marriage is within the degree of relationship allowed by their respective rights and ceremonies. Thus a Jewish man may marry his niece since in Leviticus there is an injunction against a nephew marrying his aunt but none against a niece marrying an uncle."

will almost surely inherit nothing. The philosophy of *in loco parentis* is contradicted at the end of life; the basic doctrine of strangers reappears to have the final say.

Most people with property do make a will. Two eminent lawyers say that their clients, almost without exception, insist on a last testament that leaves their estate to their spouse and their "issue," the children of their loins and their children's children. "People's financial roots stay with their natural family," one comments. "If they mention the step-child at all, it's to say that his own parent or family will take care of him. They might make a token gesture to an existing stepchild or stepgrandchild but it never equals the natural children's share." The usual "boiler-plate" provisions lawyers suggest—"to my daughter Jane," "to my natural children and their issue"—make no mention of a stepchild, present or future. "It's the blood line that matters most," a lawyer says.

The state mirrors this instinct. If there is no will, the children get two-thirds, the spouse one-third of the estate in most states. If there are no natural children, the spouse gets one-half, the deceased's relatives the other half; each state lists them—grandchildren, parents, aunts, uncles, cousins. Nowhere is a stepchild mentioned as next of kin. There is one wildly improbable chance for the stepchild to inherit; if there is *no* next of kin, the estate goes to the stepchild rather then pass to the state.* In a few states (Ohio, Oklahoma and California) property that came from an "earlier deceased spouse" is shared equally by the relatives of both; this gives the stepchild another chance to inherit. But most states have rejected such a law, echoing a New York judge's dictum that it "acts as a dislocation of the frame of the English-speaking people. God only, not man, can make an heir-at-law." Just why a cousin's outstretched hand is more God-like than a stepchild's is not explained.

Making a will is one way to alter the nonstatus that the state gives the stepchild, if that is your wish. Another circumvention, more important because it affects the happenings during life as well as after death, is to adopt the stepchild.

---

* This small crumb does not pass by representation; children or other relatives of an intestate's deceased stepchild cannot participate.

The effect of a legal adoption is to give him a status identical with that of a natural child.*

Adoption is a commitment. The stepfather who adopts his wife's child wipes out all the ifs, ands and buts of *in loco parentis;* he makes it permanent and certain that he is, to all intents and purposes, the child's father, giving him his name and everlasting paternal protection. Except for the name, the same applies to an adopting stepmother. The state's attitude is that the welfare of the child is best served by maintaining the natural parental relationship, so that if there is another living parent, as in divorce, he must give his written consent. He may well hesitate; adoption will end his right of visitation, severing all but his biological tie with his child. It also ends his legal responsibility for support, which may soften the emotional blow.

The child must appear at adoption proceedings; if over fourteen, he must give his consent. Some are resentful, particularly if they have or have had a close relationship with the absent parent. On the other hand, the child may want the security of legally belonging in the new family. Mrs. Pilpel recalls a case where a woman married a wealthy second husband, a Hollywood producer. Her daughter, an impressionable sixteen, was dazzled and delighted, anxious to be part of the second family. She asked her stepfather to adopt her; he was uninterested, explaining that he already had four children who lived with his first wife and did not intend to further divide his estate. Furthermore, he had no interest in this girl. The youngster's drive to belong was so powerful that she pretended, using her stepfather's name, "throwing her weight around" at school, buying expensive clothes and generally behaving as though she was his own child. It has had no effect except to divide an otherwise happy couple and may well break up the marriage.

This is an extreme. Of the hundred thousand or more adoptions in the United States annually, about a third are by relatives or stepparents; "I am impressed" a lawyer says, "by

* Although an adopted child inherits as a natural child, there is a conflict of authority as to what happens when *he* dies. Some courts say the estate goes to the natural kin, perhaps influenced by the unpleasantly calculating adoptions wherein a badly-off family adopts a wealthy invalid . . . with an eye to inheritance.

the increase in the number of stepparent adoptions."* Stepparents have no need for the adoption agency procedure the purpose of which is to find the right adopting parent for the right child; the stepfather or mother is ready-made. The formalities, which otherwise take six months to a year, can be completed in two months from the filing date.

The law for the stepchild has changed since Queen Anne's judges identified the notion that child and stepparent were as strangers. The direction of change is certainly not away from including the stepchild in the family; it is toward it. The recognition of man's desire to act and be as father came with the enunciation of *in loco parentis;* then, the stepparent was presented with parental responsibility when the spectre of another destitute child threatened the taxpayer's purse. Now, the stepchild can, albeit with difficulty, qualify under the Social Security Act for stepparent's old-age benefits, workman's compensation and unemployment insurance. He does stand to get crumbs of inheritance. Knowing the law, a stepparent can legalize close family ties by providing for the child in his will or taking the ultimate step of adoption.

The law insists that parents recognize responsibility for their natural children, whether their marriage survives or not. It allows divorce to parents, and remarriage; by its silence, it implies that neither divorce or remarriage must consider the child's rights because neither action in any way alters the responsibility of his own parents to care for him until he has reached maturity.

This is the bedrock of what men have so far been able to agree is just and right. The direction of change is toward the recognition of the step relationship. Since the way people live eventually becomes the way the law says they must live, it is reasonably certain that whichever way it goes, the conduct of the modern step family will some day be reflected in the law.

---

* In New York's Westchester County in 1961, there were 149 adoptions "by private placement" (no agency); better than two-thirds (105) of these were by a stepparent. A decade ago, the number was not even recorded. The implications of the rise in adoption are examined in Chapter 14.

Chapter Seven

REMARRYING PARENTS

"Second marriages represent the triumph of hope over experience." —DR. SAMUEL JOHNSON.

There is a special lilt to the joy of remarrying parents. The new marriage is particularly precious to them because of the adversity which preceded it. The wedding ceremonial, their message to the world, trumpets forth the "triumph of hope" and the triumph of a society which insists on two-by-two conformity, cherishes the whole family, encourages the search for individual happiness, but by custom mutes the celebration of its achievement by the widowed and divorced.

Custom, as powerful as the law it fathers, dictates what is right and wrong. Its unwritten code is persuasive; even the most rebellious non-conformist follows custom at the great moments of his life—when a child is born, a parent dies, when he marries. It insures communication of the vital happening. There is comfort and safety in the pattern constructed by generations; the proud-father cigar, black-suited pallbearer, and white-gowned bride have the assurance of tradition. The nimbus of custom is rarely penetrated to find its whys and wherefores, although each act has a reason and each reveals the judgment of society as succinctly as juridical tomes.

Customs which surround the second wedding reflect conflict newly born, making it arrestingly apparent that society has not yet made up its mind exactly what to think about remarrying parents.

With their acute hearing, children at the second wedding—about to be stepchildren—are aware that custom writes its music in a minor key. No long white dress, no orange blossoms, no wedding veil, society dictates to the second-time

bride. (It is her previous marital status that sets the tone of
the wedding; the fact that the groom has been married before
has, an etiquette book says, "no bearing on the wedding
preparations made by his maiden bride.") A wedding cake
is out of place; guests do not expect to dance at a second
wedding or throw rice. It should be a quiet, simple, small
affair. One attendant is permissible "but not a string of glow-
ing, girlish bridesmaids" and one or two ushers or none.
Engraved invitations and announcements do not make the
good-taste grade, although some etiquette books allow them
to the widow, not to the divorcée. The most remarkable suggestion is that children of the first marriage might better not
come to the wedding at all, certainly not to attend their divorced mother, although the widow "may have her own children attend her if she wishes."*

Most brides and grooms submit meekly enough, propelled
by their wish once again to be enfolded by society. Every
pressure—friends, family, children, and the way of the world—
has pushed them toward this remarriage; now every pressure
infuses it with the sensation of restraint.† Keep it solemn,
quietly arranged; this, they are told, is what is "right." These
dictates cannot be dismissed as arrant foolishness; both cause
and effect of custom are important clues in solving the
society's acute case of second marriage schizophrenia.

"WILL ROCKY WED MRS. MURPHY?" was *The New
York Post's* headline to a classically schizoid story. "If
divorce is considered a classic handicap for a Presidential
candidate, divorce and remarriage *might double the
handicap,* some observers said today. Political experts
feel it is hardly likely to improve his chances. . . . On

---

* Eleanor Roosevelt's *Book of Common Sense Etiquette* is the first to
attack this convention. "This seems to me to be the height of discourtesy; also
cruel and an invitation to disaster in the second marriage," she wrote. "What
a terrible beginning for a new family venture . . . to have one or more members of the family excluded from the ceremony that launches it!"

† Wedding behavior of 900 couples was analyzed according to previous
marital status of bride and groom by A. B. Hollingshead. Each item shows
marked reduction in ceremonials for the remarrying; 69.7 per cent of first-
time brides had a formal wedding, 6.2 per cent if both had been married
before. 87.7 per cent of first marriages had a wedding reception; 44.6 per cent
for remarriages. Remarrying couples had fewer engagement rings, bridesmaids
and ushers, wedding guests. One item which sheds some light; only 3.1 per
cent of the brides' families paid the bills for a second wedding!

the other hand . . . Rockefeller's happy alliance with a handsome and lively woman *might even be an asset."* (Italics mine.)

"The Presidency is a model standing at the pinnacle of the nation's life," James Reston, *The New York Times* commentator, wrote on the same subject. ". . . what he does in his private life lends itself to imitation throughout the land." For this reason Reston believes "Governor Rockefeller is now in trouble." Reston suggests that moral leadership and remarriage appear incompatible to most American voters.

Bridal customs have primitive roots. Before engraved announcements and society pages were invented, wedding rites had the function of publicizing the union. Most of the ceremonial indicated the fundamental purpose of marriage . . . continuity of the race. To make the union fruitful, to obviate dangers associated with sexual intercourse, and to keep evil spirits away from the couple, come a mass of biological symbols, their origins forgotten. Sprinkling grain or fruit over the bride and groom or on the nuptial bed was symbolic of fertility; today we throw rice. And the beribboned little flower girl who hands it around was another symbol of hope that the bride would be fertile. The wedding cake was once broken over the bride's head as a symbol of fruitfulness and to appease the evil spirits, "an inducement," William Fielding says, "to the soul of the bridegroom to remain with the bride." Orange blossoms, from a tree that blooms and bears its fruit concurrently, and in all seasons, have "an obvious analogy to fruitfulness."

Take away orange blossoms, rice, wedding cake and the child attendant, and you take away the fervent primitive wish for fertility. Disallow the engraved announcement and you make furtive the ceremony that was intended to advertise the new union. The couple must hide their burgeoning pride and hope; their children wonder if there is something wrong about the marriage, some vague anomalous reason why it should be hidden from public view.

Primitive man captured his bride. It was a powerful disruption of the old family and the start of the new; sham fighting between bride's and groom's families evidenced the importance of the occasion. Bridal attendants and the division of wedding guests are today's symbols of marriage-by-capture long ago. Bridesmaids once protected the bride against the marauder, who was assisted by friends doubtless attired in more warlike dress than striped trousers. The wedding veil was originally worn by the betrothed as well as the married woman as a symbol of submission to her husband (much as the nun's veil represents submission to the authority of the religious order.) A more practical purpose was to prevent her from attracting other men. The white dress, of course, symbolizes purity, but also joy; the early Romans wore white on joyous feast days; ancient Patagonians painted their bodies white on all occasions of rejoicing. For second weddings, the joy component is over-looked. *The Bride's Book of Etiquette* describes white as a festival color on page 21; on page 62 it warns that for the second marriage "white is never in good taste."

Forbid the wedding veil and you imply that the second-time bride should be less submissive than the first, or at least is not equally entitled to the badge of modesty. Remove the panoply of bridesmaids and ushers and you assert that the basic family change has less importance when it happens for a second time. Take away the long white dress and you state the obvious truth that the remarrying mother is not a virgin, but you also prolong a sadly frayed pretense. Only the most ostrich-minded believe that all modern brides are virgins at their first marriage, and the candid realist knows that many snowy satin folds shelter a pregnancy. If the long white dress is to be a sign of virginity, it should be worn only by the few brides who have postponed sexual relations until their wedding night. If not, it belongs to all brides at any wedding. Distinguishing between first and second weddings on the basis of virginity is strictly wishful thinking.

The second wedding celebration is overcast by sobriety; to conform, remarrying parents must perform the ancient rite shorn of its symbolism. And to be quite proper, they should outlaw their children from the whole proceeding.

Knowing the origin of wedding symbols, it is clearly non-sensical to deny them to a remarrying bride. Nobody consciously wishes her new union to be less than fruitful and contented. But emotion is stronger than reason, and complicated emotions have brought about these customs. A world that believes in marriage cannot endorse the happy ending to a broken marriage without fear; fear engenders cruelty and punishment. Uneasy jealousy gnaws at the long-married who may secretly wish that they, too, had had another chance but are unable to take the plunge, reinforcing the punitive attitude. To encourage the start of the new family in the traditional manner, down to the last detail of Tiffany's shaded roman lettering, implies the wish for happiness and for babies—the concrete evidence that the second union is as complete and firm as any. In righteous if unconscious indignation, society denies the possibility and attempts to shelter the young from the sight that punctures adult illusion.

Barring children from their parents' weddings reinforces the children's fear of dire results; it not only makes it possible for them to absorb society's prejudice, but makes doubly sure that they do. Unless there is something wrong, why aren't they there at the family function? Uneasiness seeps through to them in a thousand ways; no innocense remains unsullied in the face of it. Stepchild life starts off with a slightly improper sensation, the sum of society's custom and individual desire to conform. But the candor of parents who have more faith in how they feel than in what people say communicates itself too. A remarrying mother and her teen-agers spent evenings addressing invitations (engraved) to her wedding, hours shopping for the girls' bridesmaid dresses along with the bride's; a gay wedding day was climaxed for the family when the bride turned back her veil and tossed her orange blossoms to her eldest bridesmaid daughter. Bad taste . . . or affectionate good sense?

Which woman will flaunt custom and which yield to it? What manner of person is chosen to be a stepparent? Does an ex-husband and an ex-wife—alive or dead—dominate or free the couple and their children for the new life? Has bereavement or divorce made them cynical or grateful, shaken or assured, able or unable to love again? The answers determine what the stepchild world they create will be. Second wedding customs only hint at testimony invisible guests at the wedding can give, guests who can be called Experience. Each parent marries again in company with his experience in society outside himself and his experience of emotion within.

WHY PARENTS REMARRY

People who have once been married and now are not could be labeled "de-married," a manufactured word as unemotional as saying someone is or is not married. But current language tells *why* they are de-married; "divorcée" and "widow," and their male counterparts, have become what copy writers call mood words, adding character to past fact.

A magazine picture story about a divorcée is headed with a championship collection of mood words (italicized here for identification). "The *scars* of her *broken* marriage remain, yet JoAnn Morton, 29, must *fend for herself* and her son in the *hurly-burly* of New York City. Here, in pictures, is her *lonely fight* to rebuild her life." (KAPLAN, R.)

"Divorced" summons a flamboyant, slightly disreputable, surely unhappy image; "widowed" immediately appeals to the protective impulse. The words carry a strong charge of emotion toward the de-married; its voltage is determined by what happened to the first marriage.

There is urgent pressure to remarry. Putting internal strivings aside for a moment, the push of society toward the second wedding of both widowed and divorced is evident. "None of us want pity," a single parent writes in the *Parents Without Partners Journal,* "but all of us would like to avoid the feeling of being somehow different." This feeling, later described as being "a social misfit," is well-founded. There is a pattern for the jet-set bachelor, the career girl and, of course, for the married couple. But none for the de-married.* Neither the widowed nor the divorced can conform because there is nothing for them to conform to . . . except to get married again. They *are* "different" and "misfits." Missing from present-day morality are requirements for relatives and friends to support the de-married, economically and emotionally. Single parents cannot easily return to the family they came from; not many men or women will cheerfully go home to mother, nor is mother ordinarily equipped or even willing once again to expand her now contracted household to receive them. There is no prescription for making a new family, no definition of how to act and what emotional attitude to take to deserve social approval.

The absence of a pattern is not a vacuum; there is disapproval in the air. It is stronger toward the divorced than the widowed although it exists toward both. Most people feel secretly almost pleased when misfortune comes to someone else; sympathy is just slightly tinged with malice. "Isn't it a *shame* that he divorced her" often contains a kernel of subtle cruelty. Deprecating the sufferer whose personal and emotional problems are in full view is, for some, a source of strength. The divorced man or woman has "failed"; the marriage of the widowed is ended; many testify that the friendship temperature changes from warm to chilly.

The de-married not only give the married a chance to feel self-satisfied, they also give them considerable unease. The divorced, particularly, are ideological threats, demonstrating the possibility that any existing marriage can end. They are also an actual threat; when the Gay Divorcée or the Merry Widow comes to dinner, wives are challenged and suddenly possessive of their husbands.

The disapproval quotient is heightened when there are children. Friends, families, educators, the clergy and behavioural scientists are convinced, each for his own reasons,

* The divorced woman is not even sure what she should call herself. Custom is indecisive. According to Mrs. Roosevelt's etiquette book, Helen Randall who marries Edwin Howe and is subsequently divorced becomes Mrs. Randall Howe. "The usage 'Mrs. Helen Howe' which was current in former generations is now considered in bad taste."

that "children need both parents." All deplore the lack of the mother-father-children family and encourage its reconstruction. A psychiatrist, keynote speaker to a Parents Without Partners Annual Conference summed up her major theme; "I would like to offer you one attitude in which I believe you as parents without partners and the community will heartily agree. The community wants to see you all remarried as soon as possible and to have you absorbed as a full family in the social life of the group." This was the message to a group whose stated purpose is to manage de-marriage effectively.

Money is another external pressure toward remarriage. "Cyrus wanted a woman to take care of Adam," Steinbeck writes in *East of Eden,* "he needed someone to keep house and cook, and a servant cost money. He was a vigorous man and needed the body of a woman, and that, too, cost money— unless you were married to it." The widower's finances are apt to be in better shape than those of the divorcé who has parted with alimony and must continue to support his children.* In addition to the bald requirements of Cyrus Trask, the lone father must entertain his children on visits and his women on dates. Besides out-of-pocket expenses, his job status suffers; industrial surveys show the divorcé often passed over for promotion for the vague management reaction, "unstable family life."

A woman alone with her children can have pressing money problems. If she doesn't work, she must manage with income limited by her husband's estate or his contributions arranged at divorce. Her living standard is decreased; there is less money for the children's education.

An irate speaker told a social workers' conference recently that the financial plight of "America's half-orphans" affected their motivation to get educated. He

---

* The degree of acrimony and argument that payments engender suggests that they have emotional as well as economic features. The derivation of the word "alimony" endorses this hypothesis; it comes from the Latin *alimentum* meaning nourishment. Together with child support payments, it has gained the proportion of big business; for Detroit's Wayne County alone, the receipts exceed 10 million dollars a year as reported by Jacobson.

called for a "crusade" to point out this result of divorce. He reports a college admissions director's estimate that half the incoming freshmen in 1960 who had serious financial difficulties had such problems because of their father's remarriage and children by the second wife. (DRINNAN, R.)

Her needs increase; to go out as a single woman means more money for clothes. To entertain, particularly new friends and more particularly prospective husbands, requires other than family-style meals, liquor, and decor. She may want psychiatric help for herself, the children, or both, in the difficult time of readjustment; even the most modest fifty-minute hour puts additional strain on the pocketbook. If she goes to work for financial or emotional reasons, she is limited in being a "good mother" by time and available energy. With parenthood no longer shared, "doorkey" children depend entirely on mother who crowds after-office hours with housewife plus maternal activity. Even income taxes deprive her of more money as a lone parent "head of the household" than when she was married. Financially, remarriage seems to make sense to all but the most economically secure woman. She has no thought now that money matters can also be a liability in remarriage; such complications emerge in a later chapter.

Strong as societal and money pressures may be, even stronger are the demands of emotion. A small percentage of the de-married do not want to remarry; psychologists identify them as "lacking in marital aptitude."* Most people will not throw the baby out with the bath water and give up the institution of marriage. Rather, motives spring from the past to propel men and women toward another union. Internal pressures to remarry—loneliness, longing, desire to love and be

---

* "The pessimistic, cynical, and recessive type of person, as well as the overly cautious and the extremely independent, may prefer not to remarry," Bernard remarks. Other reasons are fear of fortune hunters, of sharing children, of sexual relations. "The sexually unresponsive or cold would tend to be selected out of the remarried population," she says. An exception—the frigid woman or "wolf" who must constantly search for release from basic inability to love.

loved, to "be happy"—are common denominators for the de-
married. But here past experience separates the divorced from
the widowed adults as the children of divorce from orphans.

THE WIDOWED

Death is an unavoidable crisis. A parent dies and the child
feels deserted, resentful, even angry at the departed for leaving him. But the child has a surviving parent to turn to; his
parent-child world is only half destroyed. The adult's man-
wife existence is totally finished, against his will, or at least
against that part of his will that wanted the marriage to
continue. Every married habit has to be given up, every wish
opposes that necessity. Sex life, support for the ego, shared
routine of every day and night, solidarity that had come
from weathering the storms together and working toward
common goals, are gone. The immediate reaction is colossal
frustration at every level. The widowed try to escape difficult
reality by taking tranquilizers (chemical or social), repressing
feelings, deliberate forgetting. Some race into an immediate
remarriage for comfort. The impulse, exaggerated to be sure,
is expressed in the story told of an inconsolable widower at his
wife's funeral. A friend tried to comfort him: "In a year you'll
have found another wonderful wife." "I know, I know," the
bereaved sobbed, "but what will I do tonight?"
    Mourning is not a planned process. It happens. Bit by bit,
old habits are relinquished and new ones take their place.
Bereavement can end in complete readjustment if there
is time for reconstruction. Otherwise the sense of loss, and
anger at that loss, persist to affect every subsequent relationship—as a parent and lover and in a new marriage. Tradition
has always honored mourning time; the original widow's
quarantine lasted forty days and came from fear of contam-
ination of the stock. The patriarchal family encouraged
mourning as a sign of respect although it did not always
follow the rule. Periods of necessity—like that of early colonists—or extremes of emancipation—like that of the war

generation—have discouraged adequate mourning.* The results, where observed, have been less than sanguine.

The bereaved parent, bewildered by the annihilating sense
of loss, becomes newly egocentric, leaning heavily on children
and friends for support. The outpouring of sorrow can increase family solidarity if the children can accept the proffered closeness, or cause conflict and rebellion if they cannot.
In either case a parent feels guilt at making such demands,
even though compelled by massive needs, and, in anxiety,
tries to compensate to the children.

> George Washington was taken aback to find that Martha
> had ordered elaborate toys from England for her chil-
> dren just after their father died. For Jack Custis, age 8,
> "a tiny coach-and-six with a little stable that sheltered
> six additional horses. A toy whip was included for the
> boy, and for Patsy [age 6] a corner cupboard and walnut
> bureau." The new stepfather Washington, hardly a
> spendthrift, was presented with a later bill, too, for a
> Persian quilted coat, "one fashion-dressed doll to cost a
> guinea, a prayerbook bound in Turkey, a silver-laced
> hat and silver shoe and breeches buckles for Jack."
> (FREEMAN, D.)

Every marriage contains some hostility. This, too, the
widowed must face.

> A psychiatrist tells of a man whose wife died in child-
> birth; he disappeared for some days thereafter, returning
> only when relatives had made plans for the children. In
> the process of understanding what had happened, he
> realized that he had had hostile wishes about his wife;
> these made him so guilty at having played a part in her
> death (by impregnating her) that it was impossible for
> him to face the fact that it had happened.

---

* "The colonists," an historian tells us, "married early and they married
often. Widowers and Widows hastened to join their fortunes and sorrows. The
father and mother of Governor Winslow had been widow and widower seven
and twelve weeks respectively, when they joined their families and themselves
in mutual benefit, if not in mutual love. At a later day, the Governor of New
Hampshire married a lady but ten days widowed." (EARLE, A.)

Other parents blame their children for the death instead of drawing closer to them because of it. This particular part of grief appears to alter character; if the anger is turned outward, children and social relations suffer. If it is turned against himself, the widowed person becomes anywhere from melancholy to wildly promiscuous in his masochism.

Remarriage can make trouble for the widowed if it happens too soon. Love for the departed spouse will eventually be absorbed, but along the way the survivor struggles; give it up or hold it forever? Customs which play down the second wedding play into his hand. "This isn't a *real* wedding," says society, "the first one was." Emotions are not dependable until the intense longing for the dead dissapates itself, making room for a new love. The widower who remarries fast finds the sight of his children uncomfortable; there is a sense of being unfaithful to them, the representatives of his still-treasured wife. Repercussions in the woman he makes a stepmother can cause misery for the family. The same applies to widows; a psychologist writes of the dangers under the title *A Little Widow Is A Dangerous Thing;* Paul Popenoe, a marriage counselor, heads a chapter *Beware of Widows, Divorcées.* Both concern themselves with the effects of incomplete mourning; the new husband will be a second choice, a "sentimental halo" for the first; widows have already formed a sexual pattern and will always compare the new with the idealized old.

But unless society presses too hard, the widow or widower can stand at his second wedding with mourning complete and the potential for success as spouse, parent and stepparent.

THE DIVORCED

The divorced mourn too, but with the huge difference that their marriage was *de facto* unhappy, the break by choice, and the ex-spouse alive to be reckoned with. For parents, particularly, this multiplies guilt ("What have I done to my children?"), insecurity ("I failed"), and hostility toward the symbol of that failure, the former husband or wife. Because society believes marriage is best for children, it gives little support to parents who defy the rule. Disorganization of home and family, self-doubt, sexual longing and ubiquitous loneliness must be managed, once the crisis of separation and decree have passed, pretty much alone.

No matter how acceptable the cause of divorce, it engenders torment. The Shah of Iran divorced his wife because of the pressing political necessity for a male heir; his tragic mien appeared in every newspaper photograph. When Napoleon divorced Josephine for the same reason, he committed what one biographer, Emil Ludwig, describes as "temporary suicide."

> "Napoleon went alone to Trianon which was at this time unoccupied. There he held a death watch . . . he remained there for three days, absolutely inactive. . . . He received no one, he never dictated a word, read nothing, noted down nothing; for three days the mighty wheel stood still. . . . Soon afterward he visited his divorced lady at Malmaison."

Reasons for divorce are rarely as well-defined as the need to beget a son; modern investigators no longer accept the indictment of psychiatrists such as Edmund Bergler, who believes it undeniable evidence of neuroticism (to the degree that he entitled his book *Divorce Won't Help*) or Kinsey, who argues that its roots are inevitably in sexual incompatability. Neither is it always a sign of emotional immaturity, incomplete courtship nor general malaise and restlessness. It may be for one or many of these reasons; all are sheltered under the copious umbrella of the present marriage-for-happiness ideal which can and generally does spring disillusioning leaks.

Depression and sudden euphoria, listlessness and energy, self-degradation and self-justification seesaw the divorced person. Although he blames everything from ex-spouse to bad luck for the event, he has had a part in it himself. If he recognizes this basic fact—it could be as simple as having made an unwise choice of whom to marry or as complicated as a revival of an unsolved Oedipus complex—he accuses himself of failure or redoubles his efforts to blame and villainize the wife or husband from whom he has parted.

Children are the continuance of the legally untied knot. Their joint creation is not and cannot be undone by divorce. Although no longer man and wife, parents are still mother and father and on this battleground warfare rages. With the same motives as the widowed, the divorced parent tries to make up for his "sins," courting his children's affection, asking for their understanding (although this is almost impossible for a young child to give) and holding to the letter of his legal rights until it becomes too inconvenient. New difficulties between parent and child, born of divorce, are taken as a signal to redouble efforts, reinforcing the conviction that troubles are due to abominable behaviour in the enemy camp.

Anger, jealousy, hostile aggression and bitterness between spouses result in some degree from any divorce. They overlay one's honest assessment of the other's character. Yet in a dozen magazines each year, in lectures and psychiatrists' offices, in books such as *Children of Divorce* and *Parents Without Partners,* the divorced parent is told that both emotion and reason must be hidden from the child, that he must not derogate, criticize or downgrade the other parent to the young. Intellectually the parent gets the message: his emotion must be swallowed in colossal repression, and along with it his very real—and crucial—opinion; better the parental stomach be ulcerated than the psyche of the child. Whether all parents can follow these instructions is a question mark to the pragmatist; whether they should is a moral enquiry rarely raised. The protective injunction is so firmly established in divorce mores that to challenge it is almost heresy.

Yet we are forced to speculate whether lip service—and it can be no more than that if divorce was necessary—to the sterling character of the absent parent, the practice of ersatz friendship with the person one could not bear to live with, the parroting of aphorisms from the how-to-do-it books, are not more a vice than a virtue. Can pretense build more confidence than candor? Even if concentration is solely on the child, the lie told in his interest is a questionable asset;

children are rarely fooled. If interest extends to parental well-being, the search for truth should be encouraged. But because society looks askance at divorce, it clouds reality with prejudice and cannot allow parents the splendid freedom to be honest with their children, or foresee that what is healthy for parent will be healthy for child.

There are limits, of course. The child's image of the other parent can clearly be damaged if he is exposed to antagonisms born of personal hurt; this is strictly private business between man and wife. But opinion, soberly thought out to its logical end of firm conviction, can be shared with children; in fact, muzzling parents often does what it is supposed to prevent. If the child cannot know the truth as his parent sees it, he cannot understand the divorce. He must assume that it had no solid base, in which case there was no respect for his childish needs. His view of parents and self is thus diminished; he is suspicious of any future marriage.

The old marriage is over, but the tie continues with the monthly check and the weekly visit. One parent has more responsibility for the children, one has less. Both suffer. Fathers find full-time support and part-time relationship hard to swallow. Some simply forget about the children. Others make heroic efforts, and (although they need only conform to the child-centered ethic on weekends) complain that the arrangement is untenable. *I Was An Uncle To My Sons* and *The Torment Of The Divorced Man* explain that weekend visits force an entertainment schedule of avuncular proportions, while father would like "just to be home with . . . [the children], have pancakes for breakfast, and read the funnies together." Mothers may assume the self-sacrificing stance and "devote themselves to the children" as though this unasked for and unhealthy concentration could ease the discomfort of self-doubt. Others allow the sins of the father to be visited upon his representatives, the children; his character becomes theirs and mothers escape into various pockets of behaviour, from reckless sexuality and bohemianism to religious zeal or sudden creative ferment. Despite all this, Goode's divorced mothers were almost unanimous that things were better after divorce. Only 7 per cent regretted that it had happened.

The divorce can help or hinder the next marriage. Those

whose ego will feed forever on the lush pastures of injustice done will as easily repeat mistakes as make them the first time. The clear view of self is harder to come by than the luxury of feeling wronged. A more dependable route to successful remarriage is charted by the bare truth about the past. It leads away from self-pity and revenge—and a new mate chosen for his ability to indulge it—away from a sense of failure and incompetence, toward understanding and achievement. It requires effort; it hurts. And there is no guarantee of worth built into the truth. But most investigators find reality to be a firmer base for human relations than fantasy.

What the divorced can achieve for themselves and their children, after the first euphoria of freedom has faded and sexual adventure no longer appeals, is what one of them has called "the marriage of limited expectations." Writing about a modern divorcée in *Harper's,* Midge Decter says, "marriage need not be any of the things her contemporaries, particularly the American ones, pretend. Its proper justification is the one that her own future marriage will have; namely, it is the most sensible economic and physical arrangement available for most people's lives." This realistic if not particularly romantic definition omits the all-important catalyst of self-knowledge and the ability it releases to love as well as to be loved. Add this element and remarriage for the divorced can accomplish what a first try, permeated with indulgence, could not.

WHO REMARRIES WHOM

Remarrying parents are a select group. They have been married once, they want to be married again, and someone wants to marry them. The new mate agrees to become a step-parent. He may be innocent of what is in store for him, since neither law nor custom asks for recognition of the new responsibility—there isn't a stepparent-preparation course or counseling service in the land. Nevertheless he chooses to marry a person who endows him with the state that has no definition other than prejudice, no honor except the most personal, and undoubted complications.

"At thirty," writes the author of *I Was An Instant Mother,* "I was a confirmed career girl who had had no experience with children. My marriage to a widower with three children was considered the height of folly by my friends. And as I walked to the altar I couldn't help but agree with them."

"A woman wants her man for her own," another testifies, "and wants her children to be his first. If they are his third or fourth, will she be strong enough?" She married a divorcé and suggests that if strength is lacking, a second wife "remain barren" rather than chance trouble.

Comments such as these are symptoms, like the second wedding customs, of pervasive prejudice against divorce that has spread to remarriage and stepparents. Professionals who look at the rising divorce rate with "anguish" and want to stop the tide, lump all the divorced together and condemn them as marriage prospects along with the widowed.

"Divorcées," says Paul Popenoe in his marriage guide, "are biologically inferior." He states them to be three or four times as likely to become insane, commit suicide and be sent to prison as married persons their own age; that their life expectancy is half as good and that they have a high degree of sterility. These attributes also apply to the lower economic strata where there is most divorce; by quoting them out of context, a cruel (and inaccurate) comparison of apples and oranges forwards prejudice. Ignored is the fact that the remarrying parent has particular assets or he would not be getting married again. Despite the uneasiness, the de-married remarry.

Previous marital status is not as important in choosing a second mate as needs and expectations. Each pressure has something to say in their formation; outside pressures of social existence, children, finances and status, and inside pressures of feelings. To the degree that the old marriage survives in the emotions, it influences choice; if it was satisfying, the hope is to reproduce it, if unhappy, to improve on it.

Age makes a difference. In their twenties, people are likely to repeat the first marriage choice; their needs and expectations have not had time to change. Some older men and women are not ready to change, and they, too, repeat the early choice. A man who looks back to the first years of a first marriage as happy days remembers his wife as the enchanting girl of his youth and marries a young bride to replace her, an effort to turn back the clock. A woman who holds an obsolete image of her husband as a young man tries to replace this ideal and although she has, as a gentle investigator puts it, "declined in her bargaining power," would want a younger man as a second husband. (Failing this, she overrelies on a growing son, young minister, or doctor; the extreme is recourse to the gigolo.) The young stepparents thus created, near in age to their stepchildren, have a strange role, discussed in future chapters.

Men and women who find satisfaction in their middle age have altered goals since the first marriage. A middle-aged parent, accustomed to the comfort of companionship, chooses a new spouse who can enjoy a relaxed family life. The older stepparent has status and respectability that work for the new family, exaggerated reactions to children that work against it. The children seem more troublesome to the older stepparent and he less understanding to the children. Firmness comes too close to rigidity for comfort, solicitude too close to pathological concern. A mother who remarries an older man for security may find it lacking; although he represents a fatherly person to her, to her children he looks like a grandfather.

Parents in a hurry to remarry compromise ideals and settle for what's easily available. An interclass second marriage is not uncommon;* Reno is filled with marriages between the cowhand and the lady from the city who went there to get her divorce and got a new husband into the bargain. A man finds that some women he would like to marry are afraid of the stepmother stereotype; the woman to whom he represents increased status will overlook the fear and marry him.

* Social class is used here as a descriptive rather than a snobbish term. Bossard says it describes "the realization that the normal population lives and thinks at a number of different levels." His observations on interclass marriages, although not specific to remarriage, are the basis of conclusions summarized here.

The result of interclass marriages is a lack of inner harmony, open disagreement, different methods and objectives in child-rearing. The child is ashamed of the lower-class parent or stepparent and accepts the standards of the upper. If the mother is of the higher class than her new husband, it's harder for her, easier for the child. If the father is superior, difficulties are more serious, especially for girls, and further complicate the stepmother's role; unflatteringly compared to the natural mother, she feels herself defeated and a handicap.

Unfinished business in the personality—be it lack of insight about the first marriage or childhood-bred conflict still unresolved—contributes to choosing another spouse. Everyone has some neurotic trends; they can be as minor as a twitch of the eyebrow or as major as compulsive self-destruction. Psychiatrist Bergler makes a provocative comment: "Since the neurotic is unconsciously always on the lookout for his complementary neurotic type, the chances of finding conscious happiness in the next marriage are exactly zero. These," he says, "are the clinical facts." This and similar statements of "fact" have the danger of generating misleading conclusions. It is risky, today, to generalize about remarrying parents and stepparents since they are created in such an infinite variety.

An accurate generalization, and one worth considering, is that parents who remarry are, after all, just people, people who are special because of their experience. The ending of the past marriage put them in the equivocal position of outcasts in the world of parents, which of necessity continues to be their world. To satisfy the long list of pressures from without and within, they marry again. Arbitrary second-wedding customs forecast a prejudicial attitude toward the second marriage. But parent, stepparent and child are not likely to recognize that the halo will be less bright for the second than for the first marriage. They step into its dimmed light from the darker time between marriages.

Chapter Eight

BETWEEN MARRIAGES

"He that observeth the wind shall not sow; and he that re-
gardeth the clouds shall not reap." —ECCLESIASTES 11:4.

Making a stepchild is a three-act drama; Act One, the
marriage into which the child was born; Act Two, the ending
of that marriage and the readjustment parent and child must
make as a result. When the curtain rises on Act Three, the
parent is ready to marry again and the child knows it. His
sensitized antennae report an almost imperceptible shift in
parental attitude. Act Three climaxes what has gone before
in scenes sober and hilarious, and so complex that as each
individual plays out his part it appears impossible that the
drama will resolve to the final curtain—another marriage.

These are crucial months, a period when parenthood and
adulthood are antipathetic. Parents search for ways to in-
corporate both.

A mother looking for another husband has less time for
her children; there are days when she wishes they were some-
place else. She may not marry a man who turns pale
at the sight of a female under thirteen or shudders at the
impact of a boisterous boy child; still she prefers to introduce
the glories of family life in small doses. The children are
not likely to be cooperative. Although they encourage the
casual friend to join the family, the telegraphed report from
the antennae that mother or father is actually considering
marriage galvanizes fears once comfortably remote. A prospective stepparent is subjected to a pack of encircling youngsters who sniff, snarl, and scuffle like half-grown wild dogs
at the introduction of a threatening stranger. They seem to
have forgotten their hard-taught manners; mother's whispered

suggestion ("Please . . . go and shake hands with him!") finds
them suddenly hard of hearing. Her careful plans for a
pleasant family outing are sabotaged by the savage young
who can turn a picnic into an unmitigated disaster; no suitor
enjoys the scorn engendered by the way he peels a hard-
boiled egg or wades a brook.

Ostensibly, children are in favor of their parents' remarriage. Not many rejoice if their mother or father is popular
and out every evening; it's better to have a parent safely at
home when needed. If he is at home, a lone parent is a responsibility; the child worries about leaving him alone,
taking care of him when he's sick, being "a trouble," and
would be glad to place the onus in adult hands. He would
like to have his parent settle down and be like other parents.
He is pleased at the idea of restoring the family balance;
at best, the interim family is a compromise.

Still, the message that marriage is imminent is a red flag
to children past the baby years, and since most parents marry
anywhere from two to five years after their first marriage has
ended, their children are old enough to react. Suddenly, what
is seems infinitely preferable to what will be—the unknown
of another marriage. No matter what the child has imagined
about his mother and Mr. X, Y, or Z, or about his father's
private life as a de-married man, no matter how blatant the
love affairs or how exposed the affection and desire, the news
that they intend to marry is different—frightening, upsetting,
bad news. It forces the child to face what he ignored in his
natural family and instinctively shied away from knowing in
the interim family. The mother or father who wants to
marry unalterably presents the alarming, unsettling fact of
parent sexuality.

> "I have a very nice youngster as a patient," Dr. Milton
> Levine, pediatrician, remarks. "He likes me. If I was
> going to marry his mother he wouldn't like me. I would
> be a very real threat."

> "I was jealous," says David Copperfield of Mr. Murd-
> stone, "that his hand should touch my mother's in touch-
> ing me—which it did. I put it away as well as I could."

In *Desire Under The Elms,* Eben is less polite about his father's approaching marriage, "Her—here—sleepin' with him—stealin' my maw's farm! I'd as soon pet a skunk 'r kiss a snake!"

The shock is powerfully disturbing.* The reaction depends on the child's general equilibrium and age; if he is already troubled, symptoms of distress can be as severe as running away from home or attempted suicide. A mother found her young son unconscious beside a gas fireplace when she returned from dinner with the man she intended to marry. "There's no use in living," the boy said when revived, "nobody loves me." His one wish was that mother would marry father again. More stable children have less violent reactions. But almost all children, although they want and need the marriage, will do what they can to stop impending disaster.

They can do plenty. A houseful of wary youngsters is at best not an ideal setting for courtship. Many a second thought has crossed a lover's mind as he is cross-examined by a potential stepchild, dressed for the occasion at his untidy worst, or when evenings at home with a beloved include a procession of hostile children in and out of the living room. Any woman who experiences the disdainful shrugged shoulder or monosyllabic reply from his children hesitates; she is feeling desirable and romantic, yet she must maintain a motherly stance; her thoughts are for her man yet her attention, tact, and a reasonable facsimile of warm affection must be for his children, and her own. The older the children, the more difficult the situation. A baby can be cuddled into security, a small child entertained without violent emotion; but as adolescence approaches, with the need to achieve personal identity, evidence of a stepparent-rival is unsettling.

A teen-ager answers her mother's phone: "Mom," she shouts, "it's Mr. Wrong!" She refuses his candy and presents (if he is foolish enough to try to please her), finds fault with his looks, clothes and conversation, or even worse, may

* The onset of symptoms in forty-one disturbed stepchildren brought to the Institute for Juvenile Research in Chicago was studied; in half the group, trouble started at the parent's remarriage, in less than 10 per cent it came at loss of a parent, during the interim period, or after remarriage. (WHITE, A.)

appear to be completely accepting and not mean a word of it. Visiting his father's bachelor apartment, a prep school boy discovered a lacy negligee among the suits; the father was sheepishly pleased at the boy's long, low whistle, dismayed to find that his son refused to say a word to the lady when she appeared for dinner. The boy's sister dismissed the whole incident as "disgusting."

"*En garde!*" cry the children.

"I'm in love," the parent murmurs.

Even the most romantically entwined parent cannot prepare to marry as a childless man or woman can. (A possible exception is the divorced parent without custody who is willing and able to cut himself off from his children completely.) The marriage has to work for the children, too, or it won't work. If each of the couple have children of their own, complexity is multiplied. Parents are tempted to sweep the children under any convenient rug while contemplating, searching for, or achieving another marriage. But for all but the most calloused, the fact of the child, source of pride, trouble, or extraneous nuisance, is ever-present. The existence of one's own flesh and blood is not easily ignored. A very small child makes it poignantly clear:

> "After taking the adults' orders the waiter turned to four-year-old Allen. 'And what will you have, sir?' he asked. Astonished, the youngster paused for a moment and then, turning to his parents, said with wonder in his voice, 'He thinks I'm real!' " (OSBORNE, E.)

The child is "real" and has real needs between marriages. Dr. Graham Blaine, Jr., psychiatrist, defines the essential needs as "the presence of an adult man and woman in the home" although not necessarily the actual parents or the same two adults for the entire time of childhood and adolescence, and "a place which can be felt as home." Some parents, particularly divorced mothers, worry about these needs; one reported to a psychiatrist that she tried to visit the homes of happily married friends with her daughter "so that the girl could see that marriage could be good." Many parents contemplating another marriage ignore their children's emotional needs, mothers because of the difficulty in combining roles, and fathers because of the necessity for substitute care.

While romance takes root and grows toward marriage, parents often share the responsibility of caring for their children with others.

> "WIDOWER, with well brought-up school-age daughters, 5-12-15, needs housekeeper-governess young in spirit, run house, supervise children. Own air-conditioned room and bath. Good salary. Other help employed. Should be cultured, able handle household for television VP. References required." (SATURDAY REVIEW)

The substitute mother who answers this not unusual advertisement has certain advantages for the children; she is not emotionally involved, doesn't compete for father's attentions and can be objective. She may be able to give the children a great deal of affection to answer her own needs. David Copperfield's Peggotty was such a woman; long years after she responded to the message that "Barkis is willing," David continued to be deeply attached to her: "She did not replace my mother; no one could do that; but she came into a vacancy in my heart, which closed upon her, and I felt toward her something I have never felt for any other human being." It is intriguing to speculate whether Dickens intended to contrast David's mother, who remarried against the boy's wish, with Peggotty, who would not marry "if my Davey was anyways against it."

On the other hand, a housekeeper is likely to be a person thwarted in her own life, who uses her job for inappropriate satisfactions; she can be ambitious, with an eye on the widower so accessible to her air-conditioned room. Or she may be over-indulgent; Jane Austen's motherless Emma had "an excellent woman as governess who had fallen little short of a mother in affection . . . the mildness of her temper had hardly allowed her to impose any restraint;" the results, for Emma, were "the power of having rather too much her own way, and a disposition to think a little too well of herself."

Grandparents are a resource. It is said that they are indulgent, pampering and overprotective as they relive the parental role a generation after their own children have grown up. If they had trouble letting go of their own, they get a second chance to hold tight as they again take a parent's place. They are trouble-makers to a stepparent; hostility directed at the daughter-in-law or son-in-law who left is easily transferable to the replacement. "Do not live within walking distance of grandparents!" a stepmother warns. If the children have lived with their grandparents between marriages, another testifies, stepmothers will have to cope with "extreme egotism, tantrums, impudence, crass selfishness and disorderly personal habits."

Despite weaknesses as parent-substitutes, grandparents have advantages;* Bossard's study of 100 students (61 girls and 39 boys) chosen at random in a large university shows reactions to grandparents; a sense of continuity of the family, identifying self with kin and their function as custodians of the family reputation. The single parent usually turns to his own rather than to his former spouse's parents for help (half of Goode's working mothers called on their own parents, 9 per cent on husband's relatives). The statement repeated most often in one form or another by the hundred students clarifies: "Mother dislikes all of father's people and father hates all of mother's people."

The boarding school-camp circuit is a solution. Top boarding schools average 40 per cent more pupils from broken homes than the comparable day school; second- and third-rate boarding schools expect and get the child of divorce, orphan, or stepchild in such profusion that the child of still-married-to-each-other parents is an anomaly. "Boarding school often seems to be the easiest and most appropriate solution," Dr. Blaine comments "but for children under twelve it rarely turns out to be successful. More individual adult attention

* A seven-year-old girl's relationship with her grandmother was a continuation of her brief, satisfying relationship with her mother, a clinical study tells us. "It gave her a positive experience to which to cling psychologically in an otherwise negative environment." When her father remarried, loss of grandmother's protection furthered the youngster's feelings of deprivation and rejection. (ESTRIN, A.)

is needed at this age than can be provided by the average boarding school. Teachers may seem to be excellent parent surrogates, but the siblings in such a school are too numerous and too needful themselves to allow any one student the degree and depth of relationship he needs."

Sometimes children are shifted around so much during the time between marriages that any stability, even the most horrendous stepparent, is welcome. There will be pain at leaving the grandparental cookie jar, at the departure of a bossable housekeeper, or at returning from the family-free school or camp; "The accumulated effect of successive shocks, disturbances, and by-play of antithetical forces in the background," says Bossard, "may make the child difficult to manage, at least for a time." A parent will adjudge this a magnificent understatement. He does not expect the consequences in the children caused by his intent to remarry. Although he has managed the interim family as well as he could, the de-married parent ready to marry again now has something else on his mind.

The search for a new spouse is on. It occupies fathers; even more, it occupies mothers. There are more women available than men, and de-married women hardly continue the pretty fancy that men pursue while women wait. Even the purest of women's magazines puts the seal of approval on this new race of Dianas; articles such as *How To Choose A Second Husband, An Encyclopedic Approach To Finding A Second Husband* appear with regularity. Where to look, when to look ("Wait six months to a year after mislaying your first husband," one remarks, "to take off the five to fifteen pounds gained during the marriage."), how to look ("Suggestions for stalking"), and what to look for are standard items in the literature.

A widow with a fifteen-year-old son fastened her eye on a bachelor newly arrived in town. She sent her son to ask a favor of him which he was forced to grant; he was second in command to a man who had a close relationship to the widow. She quite properly invited the bachelor to tea to thank him; again, his job required that he accept. Within a fortnight, the widow wrote him:

"You no longer come to call on a friend who loves you; you have left her quite alone and you are wrong indeed, for she is tenderly attached to you. Come to lunch with me tomorrow, I must see you and I want to speak to you about your affairs. Goodnight my friend. I embrace you."

The stalking was efficient—she married the man—but it did not come from the slick pages of a current magazine. The letter, written some centuries ago, was signed "The Widow Beauharnais"; the man, of course, was Napoleon, who thus found his Josephine.

Modern women are advised to be as calculating as the charming Creole; suggested methods range from the relatively innocent change in coiffure and home decor, the move to Texas or Alaska, where, it is said, there are more available men, to blatant immorality such as that related by Morris Ernst, lawyer and author. A respectable literary monthly published his account of a remarried client's visit to his office for advice. This was her tale as Ernst reported it:

> " 'It isn't easy for a middle-aged widow to find a marrying type man,' she said. 'I started writing to men whose wives' names showed up in the obituary column. I never lied to them. I didn't say I had known their wives; I just offered my condolences. If they jumped to conclusions was that my fault? Nearly every man acknowledged the letter. Eleven invited me to lunch or tea. The last of them was Clifford. He answered my sixty-third note!' "

Her question was whether to tell Clifford, now her husband, what she had done: " 'Shouldn't marriage be based on complete frankness and mutual understanding?' " she asked. Ernst writes, "The notion, I told her, was utter nonsense. A sound marriage is not based on complete frankness; it is based on sensible reticence. Moreover, all mating-rituals involve a certain amount of trickery. . . . My considered advice was for her to stop fretting, keep her mouth shut and live happily ever after. Apparently she did."

The telling and publishing of this incident is hardly a

symptom of respect for remarriage. Few de-married women will sacrifice their internal gentility to follow its lead; nor are they likely to accept the vulgarity of a guide served up in racing form style: *"—bachelor:* too little experience; apt to falter in the stretch—*widower:* excellent bet; proven to be able to go the distance—*divorcé:* another favorite, much depends on the handling—*miserably married man:* long shot, can be a big-money winner." Nor will they obediently cross off advice-giving author Marjorie Roulston's bad bets: the older man, the man who is always late, the fortune hunter, the alcoholic, the man whose sole interest is business, or one who is tight with his money. The absurd lists of qualifications ("He should be charming, kind, have a variety of interests, and now and then talk about *you.*"), warnings ("A man is like cement. You can mold him up to a point. But once he's set, you have to take him as he is or not at all."), and directives to travel or stay home, to have an affair or not to have an affair, vary according to the author's measure of human relationships, his sensitivity . . . and the degree to which he is infected with second-marriage prejudice.

Most women will marry out of personal and private conviction but the onslaught of advice is virulent. It attacks the susceptible de-married where they are most vulnerable. They are tempted, like Lot's wife, and although a single look at the obituary pages will not turn the husband-hunting lady to salt, it might endanger the resultant marriage. Calculated trickery, however successful, ignores a primary qualification for a mother's new husband.

A man who marries a mother marries a package—mother and children. More than half of today's remarrying women have children under eighteen. *But not one single article examined, mentioned sensitivity toward children in a prospective second husband.* Neither the printed word nor the law asks a mother to consider her children in choosing a second husband, the man with whom most stepchildren will live, nor is there any such enjoinder to a father. On the one hand, morality insists that the de-married mother be a better mother; on the other, it propels her toward remarriage with no thought of her children. These simultaneous strictures are mutually incompatible; to manage both, the remarrying mother must

have the tensile strength to follow no other counsel than her
own.*

For fathers, too, the child-centered ethic takes a vacation
when it comes to remarriage. Men choose stepmothers for a
variety of reasons, mostly unrelated to parenthood. It is understandable that divorced men without custody ignore children's needs but, even here, an unsuitable stepmother can
cause considerable havoc as will be seen in the next chapters.
Ibsen's widower chose Ellida, the lady from the sea, who
questions her own qualifications as a stepmother:

> ELLIDA: The real truth of the matter is that you came
> out there and bought me. You couldn't stand the
> emptiness of your house any longer. You looked
> around for a new wife . . .
> WANGEL: And a new mother for my children, Ellida.
> ELLIDA: You didn't know if I was at all suited for that.
> You'd only spoken to me two or three times. Then
> you—wanted me, and—
> WANGEL: Call it what you like.

Although men do not stop being fathers when they start to
look for another wife, they tend to put their own needs before the children's and are sure that once they are married
everything will be all right.

Not many romances are broken by children's disapproval.
When the parent has doubts of his own, the protests of the
young are reinforcements, but if his conviction is firm, it
withstands offsprings' most demoniacal offensive. Parents rationalize: "The children don't know how wonderful it will
be." "Wait till they get to know him (or her) better." Or, in
a kind of reverse rebellion, they determine to make a purely
selfish decision, just this once, "whether the children like it
or not. . . ." The biblical injunction "He that observeth the
wind shall not sow; and he that regardeth the clouds shall

---

* Whether mothers are thinking of the children or of themselves—or some
happy combination—those with more children remarry faster than do those
with one or two, Goode reports. The younger women in his study had more
dates, fewer children; the older women seemed to "waste less time with men
who were not serious" and married sooner. Furthermore, they interested men
who found a good mother and homemaker attractive.

not reap" warns men and women in love that if they pay too much attention to threatening remarriage weather, they may never get around to harvesting happiness. The words at the start of this chapter seem to urge them to overlook the wind and the clouds created by their children, be it the jaundiced eye or the impenetrable silence, and to marry in spite of apparently inclement conditions.

However risky the gamble, the foundations of the new family can be more secure if the children are allowed to get used to the idea before it happens. When the process is abrupt —one embarrassed father broke the news to his daughter at boarding school by sending her an engraved announcement of his marriage—resentment overwhelms the chance of a positive relationship for many months and perhaps forever. Before behavioral sciences could peer into reasons for action and reaction and recommend a valid course for parents to consider, most introductions were sudden and disregarded the child's emotions.

> " 'Here's your new Mammy,' his father told Abe as the boy looked at the strong, large-boned rosy woman with a kindly face. . . . As one of her big hands held his head against her skirt he felt," Sandburg says, "like a cold chick warming against the soft feathers of a big wing. She took the corn husks Abe had been sleeping on, piled them in the yard and said they would be good for a pigpen later on; and Abe sank his head and bones that night in a feather pillow and a feather mattress."

The physical comfort Sarah Bush Lincoln provided may have diminished whatever troublesome feelings there were. In contrast is David Copperfield's reaction:

> " 'What do you think,' " says Peggotty. " 'You have got a Pa!' " David "trembled and turned white." Later he reminisces. "I might have been made another creature perhaps for life, by a kind word at that season. A word of encouragement and explanation . . . might have made me dutiful to him in my heart—made me respect instead of hate him."

Modern prospective stepparents cannot rely on feather pillows to ease them into the child's affections. Proffered bribes are likely to be regarded with suspicion. It is now understood that subterranean emotion prevents speedy rearrangement of feelings. "An overpowering advance by a strange man brings mixed emotions," Despert remarks in *Children of Divorce.* "It is rather like the occupation of a small helpless country by a too-powerful ally." There is no reason to expect love-at-first-sight from the child, and every reason to know that at any age past infancy, memories will prevent it. If the stepparent-to-be needs the reassurance of immediate acceptance, he will be frustrated; he might better be prepared to be insulted, rejected and criticized, and summon the strength to respond, not as adult to adult, but as adult to child, continuing a slow, gentle courtship, which may some day become mutual affection. If he considers the child, he will be neither overzealous and aggressive, nor unaware of the child's existence, but somewhere in between; warm, accepting and easygoing, he courts his future spouse's children with a delicate touch.

The discipline demanded before the wedding requires extraordinary maturity from the person about to marry a parent. Not only must the children be considered per se, but they affect the conduct of the adults. "Ardent embraces in the child's presence are *out,*" advisors rule. Dr. Levine tells of a child who became violent at the sight of his mother being embraced by her future husband: "I hate you," the child screamed, "why don't you leave us alone!" To manage, the future stepparent must like children; unless tactful behavior comes from the heart, the remarriage supports he establishes will be shaky.

Most important is the way that the child's own parent—the picnicking mother, the father with a negligee in his closet—presents the idea of another marriage. The misbehaving child is a foreign body in the eye of romance; a parent concerned that the child may irritate the future spouse enough to frighten him away is hardly in the mood to comfort and reassure that child. On the other hand, the remarrying divorced parent is worried lest the child's loyalty be diminished by the marriage, turning the child toward his other parent. Outward bravado ("I have a right to live, too.") and inner remnants of insecurity ("At all costs, I must protect my child.") interlock in painful confusion.

"The child takes his moral views from his own parent," Dr. Dora Hartmann, psychoanalyst, told a visitor, "therefore the attitude of this parent concerning his coming marriage is of vast importance, much more important than the unrelated, unknown stepparent-to-be." She suggests that the parent explain to the child that mother or father, as the case may be, needs, wants and loves the new partner, that this is his beloved, that he wants the child to respect and try to love the future stepparent, too. "There is no sense," she says "in saying this is 'a friend.' The child knows this is the man who will sleep with his mother."

Interaction between parent, intended spouse and child writes a tortuous drama. It is built on what has happened to each in the past and builds toward what will happen to them together in the future. As the curtain falls on the second wedding, the child starts his stepchild life, the new spouse becomes a stepparent and the parent leaves de-marriage for marriage again. Hopefully, in the face of insidious prejudice, misapprehension, a degree of cruel disfavor in the world around them, and a measure of doubts within, but still, hopefully, they start a new family.

Part Two

BEING A STEPCHILD

Chapter Nine

CALL ME STEPCHILD

"What is this new stepparent to me?" The child asks the central question. No one can answer.

Parent and stepparent, suffused with pleasure in the second chance at a happy marriage, are brought up short when the question comes. Insistently it hammers at the adult pair. "What is she to me?" is unspoken in the first awkward stepchild kiss, the first act of rebellion. "What is he to me?" is in the ferocious independence, the truncated conversation, the first tentative request for help. Louder and louder the question thunders, *"What is this person to me?"*

The step relation is a maverick. Without the base of a blood tie, a legal action, or voluntary self-propulsion, it defies simple definition. Child and adult have not sought each other out but are lightly bound together by the slender thread of remarriage. There are no rules, no precast mold. It takes time to evolve, weeks of cautious circling, months of testing and retesting, years to put down roots of personal involvement. Yet one small practical matter must be instantaneously decided, and because it indicates relationship, it has importance. The child must call the stepparent by a name and this name cuts straight to the heart of his question,

"What is this person to me?"

Most parents answer with a wish, a wish to be a family again in the world of families . . . mother, father, children. They look back to the natural family for nomenclature: "This is your new mother" and "This is your new father" assumes that names will magically translate into relationships to reincarnate the family as they knew it. It is a wish to expunge the former mate by replacing him, not only as a spouse but as

a parent, to avenge the former marriage, to offer the stepparent the dearest possession—the children. Stepparents endorse the wish: "I will love the children as my own and they
will love me as their own" is a standard warm-hearted intention. This way the new marriage is complete, the old forgotten. The name is a symbol of intent, the intent to be as a
natural parent. Accounts of stepparenthood make much of the
wish to be called mother or father, and its difficulties.

> An extreme but by no means atypical example, except
> for the method, which is cruder than most, is a step-
> mother with a child of her own who was so eager to be
> called mother by her stepchildren that she gave each of
> them fifty pennies; the children were to forfeit a penny
> to her own child each time they failed to call her mother.
> "The children's own mother was deeply hurt when she
> heard about this," the stepmother relates. "I made a
> bad mistake." (HOFFMAN, B.)

The inclination to be a family again is logical enough in
this era which pronounces marriage and family to be the way
to happiness. But although a second marriage is a marriage
as the first one was, the second family it creates is different.
Husband and wife are not equivalent parents to each other's
children. The modern family—so new and varied that it has
as yet no definition—tries to fit step relationships to the old
family form, symbolized by its names. The wish is destined
for frustration.

The child sees what adults don't want to see, that a man
can have a new wife, a woman a new husband, but that he,
the child, cannot have a new parent. There is no such thing as
an ex-mother or ex-father. He has a parent, alive or dead, in
his mind, and this new person is an impostor who wants to
seize the only exclusive non-transferrable word in the language . . . and the relationship that goes with it. The child
does not easily confer the parental title. Some may want to
call stepparent mother or father right off; when they discover
the hazards, the word may become a travesty and be withdrawn. The child's loyalty to his natural parent is challenged; if forced to say mother or father, he is forced to

a lie. The biological truth of parentage persists in every cell in his body, in the color of his eyes, the shape of his fingers, face and figure, where his parents' genes have fused to create him. They remain intermingled in him for life whether parents divorce, remarry or die. Even in legal adoptions, parents and children usually face physiological facts sooner or later. In remarriage they face them sooner, in fact immediately, in the choice of a name

Parents recognize lineage at least with their intellect. Children know it too. Fathers who come to visit the children of divorce embody it; the portrait of mother who died hangs in the child's room as evidence. Over and over children make it clear that they remember: "I don't have to do what you say, you're not my *real* mother!" or "You're much nicer than my *own* father." Still, the stepparent hungers to be called by the parental name.

But the child, wondering what this new person actually is in relation to him, generally prefers to avoid investing his emotions in saying mother or father until he has had a chance to find out.

> "I was five years old when my mother died," a stepchild relates. "After two years my father married again. I remember yet how one day a beautiful young woman came to us and how they said to me that I must call her 'mother.' I thought 'Shall I say "mother" to the beautiful young woman; she is no mother.' My stepmother, who was then twenty-two years old, stood opposite me and waited to see if I would say 'mother.' And I stood and waited to see whether she would be lovely to me and if she would perhaps say anything because of which I could more easily say 'mother.' But she stood and waited and I waited. And there it has always remained." (SMITH, W.)

The stepparent is in a position unlike any other the child knows; not parent, not teacher, not housekeeper or grandmother, not uncle, doctor, or family friend, but with something of all these functions, he is uniquely related to the child by its parent's marriage. He may function as a parent;

the degree to which he does depends on need and circumstance. Stepmother is almost completely mother to the orphaned infant, not mother at all to the college freshman who lives with his own divorced mother. A stepfather who volunteers to stand *in loco parentis* acts the father role, another, uninterested and detached, assumes no parental function and asks for no filial response. The stepparent, however parental his responsibilities, is set apart from the natural parent; his relation with the stepchild is anomalous and the biological truth ever-present.

A fresh face can be welcome at the dinner table, unbalanced in the interim family; a small girl explores stepmother's wardrobe, tries on her shoes, watches her take a bath in quick acceptance, just as a boy may immediately join forces with the new man of the family, tagging along after him in silent or noisy delight. The stepparent is often an improvement on the real parent, the child ready and able to luxuriate in a pleasing new companionship. Such children have managed the parting from the natural parent well; conflict in mother-versus-father loyalty and step-versus-real parent loyalty is at a minimum, and there is freedom to enjoy the relationship that they do not know how to name. But even to these children and stepparents, the title is a quandary.

The assumption that there is something wrong about being a stepchild or stepparent—pinpointed in the Cinderella emotions and in the climate of divorce—makes private and public candor difficult. The most sophisticated parent stumbles over the introduction, "This is my son and this is my stepson." Adjust the inequality with "These are my sons," and the villainy is compounded; real and stepson feel put upon with equal parts hostility and vengeance. Children mumble a suggestive "This is my father and this is his . . ." allowing silence and a wave of the hand to finish the sentence. The difference between a stepparent and a natural parent is there to be reckoned with biologically, functionally and in two final inexorable truths: the stepparent has had no shared history with the child, and he has a predecessor who has.

Child and stepparent had lives apart until the marriage brought them together; habits were formed under separate circumstances. Small things—the way to pitch a ball, make a bed, the hatred of tomatoes—and larger dimensions of character formed over the years are all a mystery to be discovered in fractions. A stepfather's habit of concentration on the newspaper appears as indifference, a stepmother's insistence on table manners or orderly closets, well-known to her own children, seems harsh and unfeeling. Stepparent and child alike are deprived of the years of intimate knowledge. They can never know each other as natural parents and children do, lean on the staunch support of a shared life, or reach for the reassurance of known assets to ease difficulties. "When I remember carrying my child, giving birth and nursing her, and the good traits I have seen in her over the years . . . she doesn't seem like such a monster at thirteen," a mother says. The young lady in question, finding her mother equally unbearable and wishing for her early demise, is candid enough to note, "She used to be a wonderful mother, so I guess I'd miss her."

Stepparents start out as strangers to the children; how then can they expect to be instant parents?

The orphan remembers the parent who died and is likely to hold fast to an idealized image of him; this, in fact, is one of his sharper tools for the stepparent vendetta, "Remember what *fun* we used to have when mother was alive?" is a barb constructed with more than innocence to reach stepmother across the most crowded room. The child of divorce not only remembers his other parent, he sees him, visits with him, and in most instances has a continuing relation with him. Although parent and child no longer live together, this natural parent and his new spouse, if he has one, is part of the child's life, a private, personal part not shared with the other parent and stepparent, who inhabit the dark side of this particular moon. Only the child knows what awaits him on Saturdays or in the allotted vacation times he spends in his other parent's home. There are hints, a few tenuous guidelines; a sensitive stepparent will skirt areas staked out by the child's own parent if he listens with the hearing aid of conscious respect for the other relationship. To him, "Dad says he will teach me to sail" is not a signal for stepfather to dash to the closest shipyard, but a directive to stay in dry dock.

The child's usual preference is to call the stepparent by

his first name—a noncommittal solution. From this impersonal position, the relationship is free to grow in any direction. Most professional advisors agree that this is best for all concerned.

> "I feel," says Dr. Spock, "that the parents should generally speaking follow the child's preference as long as they do not deny the actual fact (of the real parent) or encourage the child to forget it." He reassures the stepparent: "My hunch is that almost every stepchild, even though he develops an excellent relationship with the stepparent, will want to continue to think of this as different from his relationships with his own mother and father. He may not want to call a stepfather 'father.' This should not be felt as a sign of reproach by the stepparent or as a sign of his failure even to a slight degree. . . . The wise stepparent should show that he understands this distinction and respects it."

First names have their own hazards. The child calls his friends by their first names and may be unaccustomed to such informality with adults. (It is even hard for young married people, with childhood behind them, to get used to calling parents-in-law, a not dissimilar relation, by first names.) Stepparents who need a title to back up their shaky authority find it lacking in "Hey, Joe!" But the most committed first-name-only child can almost always be heard substituting "my mother" or "my father" when talking about the stepparent to friends. He, too, would like to avoid the "step" label.

When each adult has his own child, and then they produce one together, mixed terminology has a touch of the Mack Sennett comedy; the baby, a natural mimic, hears his mother's stepchild calling her by her first name while calling father "father"; at the same time his father's stepchild calls father by his first name and mother "mother." The baby finds it something of a problem to sort out who is what to whom and what to call them.

Because of the infinite variations of relationship, it is premature for the stepparent to insist on the parental name that categorizes what he will be to the stepchild. The relation cannot be defined in advance and will not flourish if forced in the hothouse of adult anxiety.

A small boy's comment is witness that the relationship cannot be made to match what you call it. Carefully instructed by a progressively-minded mother that her new husband would be his friend, he was asked by a visitor some months after the marriage, "How do you like your new father?" "He's not my father," the youngster replied, "he's my friend . . . and I hate him."

It seems simple enough for a stepparent to realize that everyone is born of his own parents and gives birth to his own children, and that a healthy regard for the difference between step and natural gives decent dignity to what has gone before. But the half-world of being a stepparent, fogged in with emotion, begs for definition. The incentive to avoid the dread title of stepmother or stepfather, infused as it is with prejudice, to wipe out the past, to be as a parent, impels stepparents to the word and the stance of parenthood. It doesn't work. Stepparents can be many things to the child, but the one thing they can never be is his own mother or father.

What they can be builds slowly. It may become a deeply felt bond, a reliable friendship, peaceful coexistence or an armed truce. There is no pattern, but there are countless mutations which stepchildren find comfortable. If their individual integrity is guarded rather than invaded and the fact of their parentage allowed, they can find the relationship to thrive within . . . and a word for it.

Chapter Ten

CHILD AND STEPMOTHER

"Those who educate children well are more to be honored
than those who produce them." —ARISTOTLE.

This may be the era that unmasks the stepmother stereotype. The old established equation—stepmother = wicked—which has been a convenient depository for the misery all mothers cause their children, cannot hold up much longer against the assault of new insights. The compact child-centered family forces knowledge of the conflict built into motherhood itself. Mothers can, they do, they must deny some primitive wishes of children; it is nature's plan to provide for this denial so as to insure a healthy growing up. Its pain is real to every child, bearable for most and greatly eased by the allowable attack on the stepmother, the perfect bad-mother effigy. She is such a convenient target—this woman who, though not mother, commits mother's most horrendous sins—that no one has stopped to separate out what part of the fabled character actually belongs to stepmothers. Mothers are not eager to share the poisoned heritage and would, if they could, prolong the wicked stepmother image forever. Is it for literary values alone that continuing generations read *Cinderella* and *Snow White* to their children?

Today's parents and children, immensely more important to each other than ever before, find disruption of the mother-father-child triangle serious, and trouble again magnified by the addition of a stepmother. But stepmother earns only her own opprobrium. Mother is not conveniently dead in most modern step families but very much to be reckoned with and able to assume her own burdens. Mother and stepmother exist simultaneously; each has her own place in the child's life and her own kind of family.

In the intimacy of the small family, stepmother can be an asset; children who have known only parental conflict can with her presence begin to steady in the assurance of parental joy. Good will, tenderness and objective understanding are qualities that work for positive stepmotherhood; they are not always inborn, they can develop. As adult and child adjust to each other, their relationship can become an improvement over the past, but its evolution is a slow, arduous process. It does not come completed in the remarriage package.

Instead, remarriage ignites each tinder-dry potential of intrafamily trouble, and if the fire is allowed to spread, it endangers the gains that can come to every member of the second family. There are those who say the conflagration is inevitable because of the nature of primitive emotion it arouses. Others demonstrate that the stepmother can put out the fire, or at least keep it to manageable proporions, that the modern concept of marriage promotes her best efforts because she wants to be happy and quickly comes to see that she has only Hobson's choice; she must make a relationship with her husband's children that is comfortable for him, for them, and for herself in order to achieve a happy marriage.

"I thought," a stepmother says of her stepchildren, "that all I had to do was to bake them batches of cookies and give them lots of love and they'd fall into my arms in gratitude." (HOFFMAN, B.) She found that neither commodity could eradicate difficulties. In spite of good intentions, she had wicked stepmother tendencies, shared with many millions of women who marry men with children.

It is not an army of sadistic women who march into the remarriage arena; in fact they were not necessarily such women before, any more than every mother is necessarily good or every child loving.* But it is more than haphazard coincidence that almost all stepmothers seem to share the legendary traits; they come to resemble the stepmother stereo-

---

*Some centuries ago, Mme. de Sévigné noted an unhappy daughter-mother relation. "Her behaviour was inhuman, a public scandal, and she stood up talking and cleaning her teeth at the very moment her mother gave up the ghost."

type because they become stepmothers. Behavioral science now allows us to understand that the situation has little to do with the character of the woman or, for that matter, the child. It is the relation between them that sparks the fire.

There is a kernel of truth in the stepmother fiction, but it is the result of interaction, a generic not a personal truth. To some degree, a stepmother *is* jealous, hostile, competitive and at times even cruel toward her husband's children; they are all this and more toward her. She *does* intrude on their relationship with their father; equally they intrude on her marriage to him. She married a man, not his children, only to find that they are indivisible. The children insist on being included in the marriage and here appear to be obstacles to achievement of the happiness goal. In the atmosphere of this give and take, the stepmother's venality is born.

The kind of a woman the stepmother is and the arrangement of her step family affects the form and intensity of her wickedness toward her husband's children—and the ultimate result. But it does not touch the root of the matter. That lies deep in the simple fact of being a stepmother.

The classic step family, in which children live with their father and his new wife, is on the wane. Only a fraction of all stepmothers with children under eighteen in this country are in the traditional stepmother position. The great preponderance are of a new variety . . . stepmother by remote control; their husbands' children live with their own mothers. Four times as many stepmothers live apart from stepchildren as live with them, according to Paul Jacobson's statistics for 1961. This typical twentieth-century stepmother has a life, problems, and a chapter of her own, "Remote Control Stepmothers." When she brings children of her own to the new family, the basic problems here described multiply. Mother and stepmother meet in one woman, father and stepfather in one man in the chapter "The Combination Family."

Problems are more intense and can be more clearly seen when stepmother is the hub of the family wheel. Here, she and the child *have* to have at least a working relationship for the everyday routines of living, whether they want to or not. "Creating another family doesn't solve problems," Dr. Peter

Neubauer, psychiatrist, comments, "but it does provide a setting in which they have a chance to be worked out."

Every stepmother will recognize the problems contained in the step family setting; to a greater or lesser degree, they are part of each day she lives. Colliding with them are stepchild emotions, determined by the age and sex of the child and, equally important, by the noncalendar vital statistic of his development forces—how many emotional energy troops he has had to leave behind in parting from a parent, living in an interim family, accepting father's remarriage. What happens between the child and the woman his father has married is most vivid in the classic step family.

The name child calls stepmother attempts to define their relationship. Each homely action also asks its central question. The luxury of treating stepchildren as she would treat her own is denied a stepmother who does not have the understanding of a lifetime for these "new" children. Toward them she tempers her natural way of motherhood. Simple matters— how to dress, household chores, routines and rules of the family—all need to be settled; does a stepmother impose her own rules, disregarding the child's habits, or accept what has been established before she entered the family? Where does she compromise, where insist on her way of doing things? More important values, too, ask the question: does she endorse beliefs antagonistic to her own, in religion, in the morals learned from television (and, not unimportant in the electronic era, how much TV-watching should there be?), in self-sacrifice or self-indulgence, in attitudes toward learning? How does she discipline the child that is not her own? The simple command she can easily give her own child she questions for the stepchild, yet the gingerly-offered request, polite reprimand and raised eyebrow does not, she knows, replace the healthy smack on the bottom and "Go and do it!" spoken freely with maternal authority. How much should she ask her husband's help in these quandries, how much should she protect him from decisions ordinarily in a woman's sphere?

Stepmother problems and the childhood emotions affect and answer the questions of relationship.

STEPMOTHER PROBLEMS

The way a woman loves her husband creates the first problem. The reasons why she marries have been documented; do they match what she finds? Her chief interest is in her marriage . . . but there is the obliquely situated child who interferes with her dream. If she is a tender, motherly wife she can most easily be a tender stepparent, Dr. Helene Deutsch explains in *Psychology of Women.* But women love in many ways to meet their own needs; Dr. Deutsch spells out the results: the narcissistic woman, "erotically desiring and wanting to be desired . . . will either reject the child's demand for love as troublesome or will make the father himself jealous of her tenderness toward the child." Another woman may want to be loved and admired by child as well as father to insure her security. The troublesome feeling of interfering in a private relationship can thus be banished; this woman "wants to be considered the saviour of the orphan and not an intruder," Dr. Deutsch tells us. Substituting the satisfactions of rescue for those of labor pains generally doesn't work; to be loved by the children, she must woo them and they sense in this wooing something alien to motherhood.

Whatever the character of her marriage, it includes a fear that she will lose her husband's love if she and his child are at loggerheads; "Roy began taking extended business trips out of the state." "I don't know how to tell my husband about Mary's constant hostility; it will make him think less of me." Women tell of the fear that marriage success depends on stepmother success: "If it were not for the children, everything would be all right." The evidence refutes the sugarcoated formula in *Stepmothers Can Be Nice,* which says that if there is contentment and confidence between man and wife "the atmosphere will be relaxed and the child's intrusions and misbehavior coped with." It is an open question whether the chicken of a contented marriage can come before the egg of stepchild intrusion and disruption, or if it is not the egg that predetermines what the character of that chicken will be. Many stepmothers reiterate, time and time again,

"If it were not for the children. . . ." Perhaps fortunately for the survival of optimism, they can never find out whether ". . . everything would be all right." The children, unavoidably, are part of the marriage.

The child's presence makes a stepmother feel guilty in her marriage . . . problem number two. An ever-present reminder of the first wife, the child is evidence that another woman was loved by the father. If the mother has died, the second wife feels guilty at taking her place in her husband's bed and the children's nursery.

> Daphne DuMaurier's Rebecca haunted her successor even though there were no children. When the denouement comes, the second wife's guilt and fears are finally banished: "He did not love Rebecca. He had never loved her," she triumphs. "I . . . was no longer afraid of Rebecca. I did not hate her anymore—now that I knew her to be evil and vicious. I was free now to be with Maxim, to touch him and hold him and love him."

> Lord Roseberry, Napoleon biographer, tells how Marie Louise felt about Josephine: "When the Emperor tried to take his second wife to see his first, the former burst into tears and she endeavored every possible ruse and device to prevent his going there."

If the mother is divorced and has relinquished custody of the children or has been judged unfit to keep them, her successor must prove herself to be a better wife and mother to assuage her guilt and conquer jealousy. If perchance wife number two has been the cause of the divorce—"the other woman," "the home-breaker"—she has indeed transgressed society's rules; victorious she is—and even more guilty

Guilt and jealousy, twin demons, drive stepmother to outlandish desperate action to make the children accept her marriage to their father. It is as if the small persons had the power to grant sanction or, even more troublesome, to withhold it, and could, by their acceptance, confer absolution on the stepmother, as if once the children say she is mother, they have exorcised the devils that disturb the marriage bed.

A girl of ten, eldest of three stepchildren, had been the woman of the house between her father's marriages. She was not pleased at the arrival of a stepmother. Returning one day from school, she threw her coat on the floor, the stepmother relates, and refused to pick it up. In response to her stepmother's insistence the child said, "I don't have to do what you say. You're not my real mother."

"Stung by hurt and anger," relates the stepmother, "I swung her over my knee and spanked her. Thus," she concludes, with strange logic, "does one become a mother." (FANCHER, B.)

Other stepmothers, even more direct, agree to marriage only on condition that the children are never to be told that the stepmother is not the real mother. Still others insist on a boycott of any mention of the mother, or contact with her if she is alive, or with her relatives. Sylvia Bauman, psychotherapist, tells of a woman's words to a marriage-minded widower: "I can do it if they're *my* children," and explains that her wish to start fresh came from the fear of taking over another woman's children and so becoming "wicked." Over and over again, children, and sometimes even stepmothers themselves, in unconscious candor, tell how mother becomes forbidden.

"We never dared speak of our first mother. All pictures of her were removed and on the anniversary of her death we dared not go to the cemetery. I have never seen a photograph of my mother, but I shall resemble her very much. . . . (SMITH, W.)

Such fantastic efforts to destroy the mother is evidence of the high voltage that guilt carries and hints at the strength of child loyalty.

Guilt in combination with the oppressive conviction of the community that she is a wicked stepmother, can have an

exactly opposite effect too. The stepmother may do everything she can to preserve the mother's image. The home becomes a shrine that cherishes each memory of the departed.
In this way, Dr. Deutsch explains, the stepmother is "unconsciously taking her revenge upon [the children] for the
fact that they have had another mother." This stepmother
comforts herself with the image of being "a good, self-sacrificing mother to the other woman's children." Oversolicitude,
self-effacement, and saintly patience toward the young eases
guilt and temporarily douses flickers of wicked stepmother
feelings which she has in spite of herself.

A brief little scene in Ibsen's *Lady from the Sea* concerns two adolescent daughters' efforts to honor their
dead mother's birthday in a "secret family celebration"
which excludes their stepmother. She appears with flowers. "Come, children," she says. "Let's put my flowers in
water with the others." She cuts short her husband's
thanks: "You wouldn't want me to be the only one not
celebrating—Mother's birthday, would you?"

A few moments later, her husband tells her of the impact of memories with the same logic as Deutsch's scientific statement: "To you," he says, "it's almost as if the
children's mother were still alive. . . . You think my love
is divided between you and her. . . . You feel as though
there were something indecent in our relationship.
That's why you can't—why you don't want to live with
me as my wife any longer."

The guilt trap is triggered by jealousy of a love that is over
(or is it, wife number two wonders, when her husband absent-
mindedly calls her by the name of wife number one or otherwise shows that he has not completely detached himself from
his former spouse) and by jealousy of a love that survives—
his love for his child. She is not a part of it any more than
she was of the marriage from which it sprang. To accept the
time and interest her husband gives his child is difficult; unlike the natural family, this is not a joint venture with a
common aspiration where wives urge husbands to "spend

more time with the children" and where even a fading mother enjoys her husband's pleasure in their blooming daughter.

Jealousy is disallowed in the current worship of possessing an "integrated personality." The modern stepmother cannot admit to the urge which drove Snow White's stepmother to the mirror with the crucial question. In the fairy tale, punishment was murderous: "Iron slippers had already been put on the fire, and they were brought in with tongs, and set before her. Then she was forced to put on the red-hot shoes, and dance till she dropped down dead." (GRIMM'S FAIRY TALES) Her present-day descendant fears another retribution; she may lose her husband's love, her hope for happiness, and the potential of being a "good" stepmother. She is expected to love the stepchild; she can hardly admit to acid jealousy.

> "In this house I have nothing to keep me," the lady from the sea says. "I have no roots here. The children are not mine. They don't love me. They have never loved me. . . . I haven't even a key to give up, or any instructions to leave behind. I have been outside—outside everything. From the first day I came here."

In this poetic expression, Ibsen recognizes what sociologists now call "cleavage systems in the families of remarriage." Despite her fears, the stepmother, unlike the lady from the sea, usually has "the protection of a coalition with the biological father," Jessie Bernard says of the two thousand remarriages she surveyed. When it is parents versus children "the new mother has won the child's father to her side, or has neutralized him, so that the child is unprotected, except by his siblings."* One would wonder whether this victory, too, might not be inexorably clasped to guilt, whether someday some mirror will reflect the questionable triumph of the unequal contest, woman against child.

Problem number three is hostility. A woman who has es-

---

* This pattern, which Bernard formalizes in a diagram imposingly entitled "Cleavage Model 2 b," is her explanation for the folk tale stepchildren being almost always the father's children. Additionally, she says, the mother is the parent who most often comes into conflict with the child in the daily routine of living; ergo, evil stepmother.

caped from the prejudice focused on her because she was de-
married finds she has simply exchanged it for another equally
devastating attitude. She is now challenged to show the
world that she is not a cruel stepmother. She must live out
her intention to love the stepchild as her own . . . and she
finds it impossible.

> Dr. Robert Seely, internist, tells of typical situations in
> his practice: "Three stepmothers have said almost the
> same words to me during the past months. What they
> *say* is 'The child doesn't behave, doesn't listen to me.'
> What they *mean* is 'The child doesn't love me.' They
> think they have failed—and that is hard to face."

> "I can hardly stand the sight of her . . ." a stepmother
> writes Dr. Spock about her stepdaughter. "Yet it makes
> me feel very sad, because, goodness, if a woman can't
> feel affection for her husband's child, what good is she
> then?"

> A woman of fifty asks Dr. Rose Franzblau about her
> eighteen-year-old stepdaughter's dirty wash: "I do wash
> certain things for her, but am I expected to wash her
> personal things such as panties and the like? All my
> pleading has no effect on her."

> *"Don't Be Afraid of Your Stepchild,"* is another's bra-
> vado title.

Because most women discover that the task set them is impossible and because they do not know it is the relationship
itself which makes it so, they blame themselves and feel defeated; from defeat to resentment is a short distance. Shorter
still is the step from resentment to hostility.

The child who presents stepmother with the necessity to
fail, who makes her feel there is something wrong with her,
makes her guilty, fearful, jealous and full of self-doubt—asking Dr. Spock "what good am I?" or Dr. Franzblau what to
do about laundry—is the object of her hostility. Two separate
studies of cases brought to clinics for help, one in Hartford,

Connecticut, one in New York City, demonstrate the problem at its most extreme.*

"He's not my child. It would be different if he was my own," was the refrain of all the Hartford stepmothers. Anxiety was characteristic, appearing in some degree in all but four of the twenty-seven women. (The four exceptions either considered the stepchild as their own child or "frankly accepted him as a stepchild.") A third of the stepmothers resented having to cope with the results of previous poor rearing and having the child come between stepmother and husband,˙ another third partially rejected the stepchild or adamantly refused to take future responsibility for him. Fear of failure to be an adequate mother showed up in six stepmothers.

Stepmother sentiment was a close parallel in the New York study. A third of the stepmothers were openly hostile, expressing dislike for the child, refusing to assume responsibility for him; one "could not stand" the stepchild, another believed her stepdaughter "touched in the head," others inaugurated rigid discipline or requested placement for the child. Another third had "some understanding of the stepchild problem" but no satisfying love for the child. Stepmothers with acutely disturbed and hostile children were helpless, "didn't know what to do." Only two had a strong tie of affection and, in an unsatisfying marriage, were trying "to soften father's attitude toward his child." Echoing our number one problem, half the stepmothers had a poor relationship with their husbands and said that the child was an important element of the conflict between man and wife; the father blamed stepmother for the child's difficulties or was himself too lenient, these women said.

Forty-nine stepmothers, *in extremis*, give terrible clarity to what in less violent relationships is often hidden by a patina

---

* Both are social work masters' theses; one of a representative sample of middle-class population in the Hartley-Salmon Clinic, Hartford, Conn. is of 27 stepchildren living with stepmother and own father. *(Pfleger, J.)* ˙Ages range from 6 to 16, stepmother's age from 22 to 45. The clinic treats both. The second study is of 22 stepchildren in the Treatment Clinic of Manhattan's Children's Court *(Estrin, A.)*; 10 adolescent boys and 12 adolescent girls with I.Q.s from 75 to 111 and a wide range of behavior problems: truancy running away from home, sex delinquents, ungovernable behavior. Referred by the judge after a court hearing, children and stepparents were both being treated.

of acceptable behaviour. No matter how adept a woman may be at acting civilized, she is possessed of the three problems: fear for her marriage, guilt and jealousy, and hostility toward her husband's children. This is the foundation on which she builds.

But the foundation has more than problems, or all stepmothers would surely be destined for a padded cell. Its cement is the magnificently expandable humanity of a womanly woman, a motherly person. Selected from the population at large to be a stepmother, she can be said to have the aptitude to be understanding, even kind, patient, even absorbed in the interest of her adventure. For her own and her husband's sake, she respects the stepchild's person and with determination begins solving their mutual dilemma.

STEPCHILD FEELINGS

A stepmother who has sharpened up her sensitivity can draft THE STEPCHILD PRIMER on which a stepchild of any age and either sex bases his behavior.

1. THE CHILD WANTS HIS MOTHER. But mother has gone— she is dead or divorced—and has thus betrayed him. Whom can he trust?

2. THE CHILD TURNS TO HIS FATHER. Together, the child thinks, they will accept mother's departure. Father will cherish and protect him.

3. FATHER DESERTS THE CHILD. He marries another woman and loves *her*. Can he, will he continue to love the child too? What is a stepmother?

4. STEPMOTHER IS THE ENEMY. She comes between child and father, child and mother's memory. If she is gentle and wooing, the child thinks he's right in feeling wronged. If she is hostile, he is convinced of it.

5. STEPMOTHER IS LOVABLE. The child who no longer contains primitive hatred toward his own mother can accept a place in the restored family.

Each of these primary facts are qualified by calendar and emotional age because they determine what the child needs and how powerful his needs are at the precise moment the stepmother appears.

If the child is a tiny infant who needs physical care and the comfort of feeling loved, it is of no concern to him whether mother or stepmother or any other maternal pair of hands and capacious lap provides for him, since he can't tell the difference. "If a stepmother takes over before a child is old enough to have formed a union between himself and his own mother . . ." Dr. Deutsch states, "the prospects that her stepmotherhood will develop into genuine motherhood are most auspicious."*

Before a year has passed, the baby comes to know mother and father as people; before he is six or seven, the child has to some degree taken the first huge emotional step of sorting out his desires toward mother and father so that he can begin to enjoy new relationships out in the world of school, friends and relatives. At adolescence, he battles for independence from parents while maintaining their affection and encouragement. In each stage, as has been seen when he parted from his natural parent, his reaction depends on his emotional needs, which may or may not coincide with the number of candles on his birthday cake.

At ten, Lincoln seemed to need the physical comfort and emotional acceptance a motherly person could provide; he had a tender memory of his mother, which helped him accept a "new mother." According to Sandburg's interpretation:

> "The blowing weather awoke some sort of lights in him and he went to the door and looked out into a night of fierce tumbling wind and black horizons. And he came back saying, 'I can't bear to think of her out there

---

* It is wildly improbable for this to happen very often. Either mother must have died in childbirth with father having another wife ready in the wings to instantaneously take her place; or a divorce has been consummated from the natal bed, and mother has renounced the infant to its father, who has immediately remarried. The statement above has less of a practical application than a theoretical one; it does serve to set off the ensuing problems of the child who most combine a conception of mother with stepmother reality.

alone.' And he clenched his hands, mumbling, 'The rain and the storm shan't beat on her grave.' "

"Sally Bush, the stepmother, was all of a good mother to Abe. If he broke out laughing when others saw nothing to laugh at, she let it pass as a sign of his thoughts working their own way. So far as she was concerned, he had a right to do unaccountable things . . . so she justified him."

A sharp contrast is Steinbeck's Adam Trask, whose memory of his own mother twisted his thought of himself and stepmother:

". . . he knew that he had once had a mother and that she had done some shameful thing. . . . And as a result of her fault she was not here. Adam thought sometimes that if he could find out what sin it was she had committed why, he would sin too—and not be here.

"Toward Alice Trask [his stepmother] Adam concealed a feeling that was akin to warm shame . . . And he ached toward her with a longing that was passionate and hot. He did not know what it was about. . . ."

A long-shot conjecture might bring Queen Elizabeth to mind in this connection; she too, knew her mother had somehow sinned; she reached out toward each stepmother in yearning. At middle age, her emotions were still confused, as expressed in her own eloquent lines:

> "I am and am not, freeze and yet I burn
> Since from myself, my other self I turn."

GIRLS

Girls face different conflicts than boys in their earliest emotions and continue a different relationship with mother for the rest of their lives. Every young child loves his mother and needs her protection . . . and wants her out of the way at the same time. In a girl, the negative feelings are stronger; mother is her rival for her father. "I want *Daddy* to put me to bed" is an expected bias from daughters at which most mothers smile benignly; their acceptance makes it easier for the child to love both parents.

When stepmother hears the same words and views the clinging annexation of huband by the small (or any size) female, she is not likely to accept it happily; her own desires are stronger than her intellect. Girl and stepmother are embattled rivals for father at this moment; will he put his daughter to bed or make a martini for his wife?

Stepmother writes the ending of this cliff-hanger: it is some kind of a compromise between her marriage hopes and family realities. She may have to prove that she can win, or her inner structure may allow the child-father pair to be separate from herself. Whatever she does, she can justify; almost always, her stepdaughter feels hostile toward her and shows it in a hundred invidious ways. Without the safety catch of filial devotion, the girl can freely release pent-up hatred toward her stepmother-rival, just as Cinderella could.* She needs no magic fairy godmothers; with fantastically accurate aim, the stepdaughter's provocative behaviour goes straight to the Achilles' heel of father's wife and almost forces even the best-intentioned woman to become the punishing character of the legend.

The thought that "Daddy was available and free but he picked another woman," as one psychotherapist expresses it, has to be revenged.† Anger at the very person of a

---

* "Absence of the real bond of parenthood and its accompanying incentives to tender feeling cause hostile tendencies to meet with less resistance," J. C. Flugel relates in his book on family relations. Such feelings are inhibited or "at least repressed by considerations of general or traditional morality in the case of the girl's true mother."

† Examples of extreme reactions are found in clinic histories. "Girl L., who showed great ambivalence over her feelings toward her father, accusing him of raping her and killing her mother. Thus she revealed her own desire to take mother's place and her guilt over mother's death."

Another, seventeen-year-old Virginia, had been placed in foster homes since she was three; her mother had been unable to love the child "because of her ungratified desire to be mothered herself," had separated from her husband and died when Virginia was sixteen. "Virginia is particularly dependent on adult approval. She identified with her mother very strongly, idolized her. After mother died, she showed great devotion to her father and is frightened by the thought that he might remarry and have a baby, in which case she would no longer be 'his little girl.' "

stepmother takes all kinds of forms; in a study of troubled stepdaughters, one accuses her stepmother of having an affair, another says stepmother makes her do all the housework but pays no attention to her; a third claims stepmother is jealous of her. Via the stepmother route, the girl humiliates and debases herself too, thinking that she is not worthy of her father's love.

A girl of eighteen whose mother had died felt her stepmother to be a rival for father, psychiatrist Heilpern tells us. She felt abandoned as she imagined her mother was. She met a man who shortly abandoned her and quickly she replaced him with another. She thought, "If my mother could have been abandoned so easily perhaps her value was not so great, nor is mine." She needed to go back to being a child again, loved and cared for. Her father died and the girl became "desolate and hopeless."

In a milder way, the girl who wanted stepmother to do her laundry was revengeful, making stepmother her servant, and as Dr. Franzblau suggests going back to "childish habits and behavior that may have been given up long ago." A stepdaughter might choose to disobey stepmother's every rule, to lie, steal money, be restless, nervous, unable to concentrate, or make any adjustment anywhere. Or in severe trouble she might follow Dr. Deutsch's conjecture about a patient: "Her next step would not have been Snow White's glass coffin but a dirty room in a disreputable hotel and the lost love of her father would have been given back to her not by a marvelous prince but by one of many sailors."

"A father cruel, and a step-dame false," cries the stepdaughter in Shakespeare's *Cymbeline* . . . echoed by an endless chain of stepdaughters if in less elegant prose. But modern insight shows unwritten longing accompanying the revengeful accusation; in each hostile act is the little girl who wants her mother to love her (Point 1 in THE STEPCHILD PRIMER) and her father to love her (Point 2). This is her need, not easy for stepmother to discern in the smoke of battle with hostile stepdaughter guns pointed at her. While being attacked or asked for love, or both, by the stepdaughter,

stepmother is, as we know, having her own troubles and is
not likely to react with quiet, calm assurance based on intellectual understanding. She thinks about herself, too.

"Haven't you noticed what Hilde has been yearning
for day after day?" a stepdaughter asks Ellida about the
second stepdaughter. "Ever since you entered this house?
One single loving word from you."
Stepmother's reply shows not unusual stepmother
blinders. "Ah," says Ellida, "could there be a place for
me in this house?" (IBSEN, H.)

Years later, Hilde becomes the woman in *The Master
Builder,* who in her ultimate act of revenge, sends the
man she had seduced to his death. But first, he asks her
an important question:
SOLNESS: Have you never been—really fond of anyone,
Hilde?
HILDE: (in a hard voice) What?
SOLNESS: Did you have a happy home with your father,
Hilde?
HILDE: I had only a cage.

Some stepmothers can make the step family cage a home.
"I don't have to do what you say, you're not my *real* mother"
and "I want *Daddy* to put me to bed" lose the sting of barbed
attack when they are recognized for what they are . . . the
passionate plea for reassurance, for a safe harbor after what
can be recognized as a stormy voyage for a small girl to
weather.

BOYS

There are few male Cinderellas in folklore. Boys are not
disposed to their sisters' intense mother-stepmother rivalry.
In the young male emotions of THE STEPCHILD PRIMER,

stepmother is more likely to appear lovable (Point 5) than as the enemy (Point 4) to her stepson. As he loved his mother, so he can love stepmother. If he managed to resolve his early passions, he can enjoy father's affection too, and start to emulate the man who is his progenitor. But if his longing for mother-love was never satisfied, the coming of a stepmother reawakens early boyhood jealousy of the father who interfered. There is plenty of drama in this plot to match the Cinderella story; it was recognized by Schiller when he wrote the powerful tale of *Don Carlos,* the Infante of Spain who loved his father's wife.*

"A monstrous secret is burning in my bosom," Schiller's Don Carlos says. "Listen, freeze, but do not make reply. I love my mother." (He was referring to his father's new wife, his stepmother.) "A son who loves his mother;—world-wide usage, nature's order and the laws of Rome condemn that passion. Also my claim comes in fearful conflict with my father's rights. I sense this yet I go on loving."

A small boy can happily love his mother but in a man, small-boy longings and grown-boy abilities make for danger. Stepmother, no blood relation, increases the risk as incest taboos are less firm. If father has married a woman much younger than himself, a not infrequent result of current marriage mores, stepmother seems even more fascinating to the stepson near her own age. It is not in spite of the fact that she happens to be married to father but because of it, authorities say. In this way the boy tries to settle his score with his father.

Heilpern tells of a boy of seventeen whose mother died; his father married a girl of twenty. The boy became much attached to his young stepmother and feeling helpless in being denied mother and stepmother by father,

---

* Actually, the Spanish prince, born in 1545, was in no way romantically involved with any of King Philip's wives or mistresses. There was a strong father-son antipathy, which ended in Philip sending his son to prison, where he died some months later. The Don Carlos legend as we know it has taken many forms; the drama constructed by Schiller has a pertinence here beyond its value as an aesthetic creation.

made an attempt to replace father, calling him "an old fogey," trying somehow to defeat his father, Heilpern states.

If father marries the children's nurse or housekeeper, she may become a wicked stepmother to the boy; her first relationship was to take care of him, but now, attached to father, she must deny even his dreams. Dr. Deutsch points out the alternative disaster; a stepmother may be "seduced by the erotic suffering of her tenderly loved stepson." She excuses her transgression of the taboo by the fact that the boy is not her own son, and that she is "compelled to assuage [his] passion."

The incestual urge has not changed since Saturn was emasculated by his son Jupiter. But when it appears in the boy-stepmother relation, it is confused by the absence of a blood tie; if the pretend-mother responds to the flattery and ego-building of a stepson's desire, she can wreak havoc where most mothers fear to tread. "A good stepmaw's a curse," a stepson mumbles in *Desire Under the Elms,* predicting the disaster to come with the seduction perpetrated by his father's new young wife. "Bright and clear I feel what was meant to remain forever dark to me," Don Carlos says to stepmother in his great cry of despair before he relinquishes the semi-forbidden love. "Oh, in this I feel my hell. Another hell lies in his possessing you. Alas, I cannot grasp it."

Some stepmothers know that the surface signs of a loving youngster may mean trouble underneath. A nine-year-old boy daily presented his new young stepmother with carefully-wrapped presents, a stick of gum, a pencil, a flower or two, each neatly labeled "From Your Sweetheart." Gently she told him the truth ". . . but I'm your Daddy's sweetheart," and the presents stopped.

If the campaign to win stepmother away from father fails, as it does more often than not, another problem emerges. The boy believes father is more interested in his new marriage than in his son, and in all probability he is right. Feeling neglected, unable to capture stepmother or father's attention, he tries to accomplish this aim by asocial acts: stealing money (a symbol, some say, of love), being "bad," and sometimes

showing signs of delinquent behavior. Five of the ten troubled adolescent stepsons in the New York clinic study mentioned above developed delinquency symptoms at the time of
father's remarriage that were not there before; truancy, running away from home and stealing were frequent; one forged
a check in his father's name "to get even with him for marrying again.'* The stepmother seems to have caused diminished
paternal affection because father who has cared for his
sons in the interim family now is able to relinquish the job
to his wife, and enjoys understandable relief when he can
say "They're all yours." If he or she believes it to be a happy
ending they will be disappointed; it is just a beginning.

Every baby wants his mother to himself; tender parents
make it possible for boys and their sisters to grow from
this starting point to an expanded affection span that includes mother *and* father and then many others. Some children can immediately include stepmothers in their affection;
girls might want to be like the woman that their father
has chosen to marry, particularly if they see her as a gra-
cious welcoming figure on occasional weekends. For boys,
the guilty triumph of actually having a divorced, unre-
married mother to themselves can be eased by an attachment
to stepmother who lives with his father at a comfortable distance; "Remote Control Stepmothers" looks at these relationships in detail. The stepmother discussed here lives with
her husband's children. For her to become a nurturing help
to a boy's maturing is admittedly a harder job than it is for
the absentee stepmother or natural mother.

But it is not impossible. She can, if able to look, see what
the boy really wants from her; such insight was recorded
more than a century ago by Jane Austen when she wrote in
Emma of a young man and his stepmother, "nothing could

---

* This is not intended to imply a relation of delinquency with the stepchild state but merely to show that remarriage can cause onset of symptoms
in youngsters so inclined. Smith's statement in *The Stepchild* is that stepchildren furnish one-and-half times their quota of delinquents, and that more
of them are girls than boys. In *Remarriage,* Bernard comments that Smith
drew conclusions without allowing for class differences: "It may be that step-
relationships are damaging when they occur in some contexts but not necessarily in others." Her middle and upper-class study did not show any connection between being a stepchild and being a delinquent child.
The facts are more thoroughly examined in later pages.

be more pleasing than his whole manner to her—nothing could more agreeably denote his wish of *considering her as a friend,* and *securing her affection.*" (italics mine)

THE RELATIONSHIP

"Those who educate children well," Aristotle said, "are more to be honored than those who produce them." He may not have been thinking of stepmothers when he conferred the ultimate honor, but his words have meaning for them. Stepmothers are educators; their subject—Modern Marriage. They can teach children that the new human relation can be distinguished in its own right. They qualify for the highest teaching post in their subject by dedication to what is fact and passionate rejection of what is outworn prejudice. The most learned among them would believe with Aristotle that theirs is an honorable task, but would part company from him in comparing themselves with the mother that produced the children. Knowing their function to be separate from hers, they no longer compete with her for honor. They are too busy living their own lives.

They both teach and learn. The first lesson is that their marriage comes first. They are of immediate value to children if they establish this belief. The sureness of the woman of the house that the new marriage will be what she and her husband hoped for is what can make it that way. Her primary contribution to the stepchildren is demonstrating the give-and-take of a sound marriage.

Every day she is challenged by the children; every day they test and try to find out where they fit into the new family. "I don't have to, you're not my *real* mother," "I want *Daddy* to put me to bed," and "From Your Sweetheart" impel her to take a discerning look at the ghosts in her reactions. Her fear for her marriage, guilt, jealousy—her whole apologia for being a second wife and stepmother—becomes less important in the bright light of perception.

Stripping away inappropriate emotions, she begins to see that she is spearheading a new kind of marriage and pristine brand of adult-child relationship. She is not the stepmother of the old-style family and knows it; she can cheerfully accept the efforts of unknowing friends to type-cast her in the wicked stepmother role by enlarging her student body to include them. With the second lesson, she makes a start at unmasking the stereotype for herself, her husband and his progeny and the society in which they live. With deadly serious intent, she can mix a bit of humor, even gaiety, into her learn-by-doing classroom. She can say "This is my stepchild" and smile; she does not want to be called mother because the deception would add another obstacle to the new concept she is developing . . . the idea of a constructive step family.

As her curriculum progresses, she sees that she alone can make the step family work or allow it to be broken. Her husband cannot handle the daily, even hourly, decisions she has to make; the stepchildren are not able to think for the family but must act in their own interest as their emotions dictate. The stepmother commits herself because of her marriage; she relies on her intellect because she has no backlog of intuitively *feeling* like a stepmother. She starts depending on her head; eventually she may chart a way to her heart.

Stepchildren find it somewhat disarming to realize that stepmother is aware of the facts of their lives, simplified in THE STEPCHILD PRIMER, and that she is not overwhelmed to discover that they miss their mother, want father to themselves, think she is the enemy to be conquered or seduced. It does not overly concern her; she is intent on achieving a workable compromise between what they need and what she is able to give them within the frame of her marriage to their father. Discipline, which troubles most stepmothers, challenges her because of her own problems; the stepchild's hostile behaviour is only his way of pointing out what he needs. When he finds stepmother oversolicitous or self-effacing, too strict, too punishing or too anxious to be a "good" stepmother, or too sensitive to the devotion to real mother, he is confused, feels lost and tries again in ever-more demoniacal demonstration.

". . . patiently ignoring misbehaviour or submitting to abuse" is not the solution, Dr. Spock says. "This doesn't work any better than becoming openly antagonistic or harsh with [the stepchild]. When a child gets away with murder, it's apt to have two unfortunate effects. He feels guilty underneath and responds to this by worse behaviour, hoping unconsciously to provoke the firmness of discipline he knows he needs. He senses also that the parent who permits such abuse is guilty about something, so he feels tempted to be more mean. (It's impossible for any of us not to take advantage of a submissive person.)"

"No, I am not your real mother," one woman said to a rebellious youngster, "but I am The Mother in this house." (FINCH, M.) The stepmother cannot rely on mother love for the child since she does not and cannot feel like his mother and in fact is not. She substitutes knowledge for feelings, acknowledges that she has different values than mother had, no better or worse but different. She can compromise when it is unimportant to her equanimity and ask for change when old habits and behaviour are disrupting her marriage. She can take a degree of hostility because she knows its source, but equally can insist on cooperation when it is essential to the forwarding of the step family.

With this measure, she herself knows how important or negligible TV-watching, household chores, manners and morals are to her. A stepchild's tall tales about his fate—his almost invariable conversation piece—may appear as sinful lies to a threatened stepmother, to another, less fearful, they seem a convenient way for a child to let off the steam of angry feelings, better aired than bottled for later explosion. Bad manners are unimportant to one stepmother, untenable to another. A stepmother fighting the past hesitates to enlist her husband's help, but she turns to him free of fear if she is intent on forging their future.

Time works for the child-stepmother relation. A year or two or three of living together builds mutuality where there was strangeness, the beginnings of understanding where there was none. No child or adult makes a friend without the pain of living through some bad times together. The modern stepmother's unique meld of friendship and responsibility has no formula in its twentieth-century setting. It can only grow . . . in time. The excitement of exploring Modern Marriage catches up child and stepmother in its adventure; like all scholars they keep learning so as to be always better teachers.

Chapter Eleven

CHILD AND STEPFATHER

"Oh my prophetic soul! Mine Uncle!"
—HAMLET. Act 1: Scene 5.

A man who is a stepfather in our modern matriarchy is more important to his stepchild than he thinks he is. To make this discovery, he must penetrate quite another prejudice than the stepmother does, a prejudice as shattering to the ego, as devastating to dignity, and equally as challenging as the wicked stepmother stereotype. It is so newly important that it has never even been identified, although it signals from between the lines of locker room conversation and the rare stepfather confessional in popular literature. The prejudice is that he doesn't count very much at all, that his role is to have no role.

Today's stepfather has lost the easy prerogative of his forebear who married the pretty widow for her looks, money, or availability, and either became father to her children in all but the ultimate siring . . . or assumed his legal right to ignore their existence. He combines qualities of a Mr. Murdstone (David Copperfield's bad stepfather), a George Washington (good stepfather), and a Claudius, King of Denmark, who aroused the immortalized struggle within his nephew's prophetic soul. But he is no one of these, nor is he the conventional husband and father of this era. Who is he then?

He has the pain and the privilege of creating a new *genus* family man.

Men make the twentieth-century definition of husband and father in response to what has happened to their women. When wives tore loose from the submissive housebound tradition to become liberated careerists, every cartooning satirist reflected the Battle of the Sexes. When the child-centered ethic sent mothers scurrying back to the nursery, fathers resigned themselves to cocktail-hour lessons in Spock and Gesell. With equal parts awe and impatience, they observed the intense intellectual precision their wives applied to becoming modern mothers and, in their desire for a happy life, cooperated. When gradually unmesmerized, men started once again to balance the state of things familial; today they chisel new proportions for the head of the house. They ask for, and more often than not they get, a companionable wife's respect for their desire to be rule-maker, pacesetter, guide, and resource. Increased leisure time allows them to be more active parents; they enjoy the pleasures of fatherhood and extend its responsibilities beyond the economic to staunch emotional support.

It is not to be easily thus for any stepfather, although each one's situation is different. Men who have never been married before have the advantage of a completely new experience and equally its disadvantages. For widowers and divorcés, the carry-over of a previous marriage and fatherhood makes stepfatherhood more complicated, laced as it must be with the idealized memories of the widower, the resentment and bitterness of the man who has been divorced. Processing a dozen step family biographies of the 1960's reveals that the divorced, remarrying father's conundrum is typical.

Stepfather is head of the house . . . but his wife has a responsibility independent of him that she shares with another man. He lives a family life . . . but in its conduct are reflections of a family that predates him. He knows too much to try to be father to the children whose own father appears on weekends, pays their bills, and supplies the father-image to their psyches. He has a special pocket of understanding for this father because he, too, has become a part-time father to the children of *his* first marriage, visiting and entertaining them, providing paternal comforts within the framework of a divorced parent, seeing his children's closeness to him slip away, and slipping himself into a casual parenthood, as interest in the new family frays bonds with the old.

He is involved, intrigued and in love with his new wife

(more than his grandfather could have been with his grand-mother, surrounded as they were in the large-family system), yet because of her children, he is less than a complete husband. He is less than a complete father to the stepchildren who live in his house and to his own children who live with their mother. He is disabled from giving complete support of mind, heart, and bank account in any direction; he finds this troubling. He also finds that he is freed to achieve a new form of family relations.

Some say it is easier for him than for stepmother, as it is for any husband vis-a-vis any wife, because male home needs are less intensely concentrated. Some say it is harder:

> "In most of the parent-child and age-sex combinations the stepfather appears to fare better in comparison with the real fathers than do stepmothers in contrast with mothers in normal homes," Bowerman's and Irish's study of more than 2000 stepchildren shows.

> ". . . the stepfather was more likely than the stepmother to be reported as having an affectionate relationship with the children," was Bernard's research finding. Her explanation: "The mother is the main socializing agent in the child's life and must therefore bear the brunt of any will-conflicts that arise."

> In Smith's book, ". . . in our study of a large number of agency case records in five large cities, the cruel step-fathers actually outnumber the cruel stepmothers."

> ". . . step-mothers seem no harder to get along with than step-fathers. Thirty-four per cent of respondent step-children did not get along with their step-fathers, while 36 per cent did not get along with their step-mothers," is the finding of *Life Stress and Mental Health,* part of the Midtown Manhattan Study. There were 186 step-child respondents among the 1660 people studied.

Such are the contradictions of undefined measurement; it would be hard to say who is crueler, who more affectionate

until more careful identification is made. Subtleties, over-
looked above, are such important clues that they are fully
discussed in a later chapter. Here, it is not of great moment
whether stepmother or stepfather wins the unpopularity contest. In either case, it is no sinecure for a stepfather to create a
happy family.

"You've got a Daddy-look now, not just a plain-man look."
(BARUCH AND MILLER) This stepchild's banality sorts all adult
males into plain men and fathers; peering closer, the child
of modern marriage comes to know the wrinkled brow and
quizzical expression that is the look of a man confused, concerned, conflicted, a man with a giant-size question mark
flashing against his eyelids, the man who is his stepfather.

Men who marry widows live with her children; men who
marry divorcées live with *her* children (except for the small
percentage whose wives have chosen or are forced to relinquish custody. The few women who disavow conformity to
this extent are not likely to have a daily impact on their
children, except as a memory, their husbands even less so.
Not unusually such stepfathers come *seriatim* and whatever
their intentions, hardly have time to be more than the current
supplier of mother's new name.)* The change in marriage
mores has moved stepmother out of the house but stepfather
is still the living-in stepparent. The change for him is that
there are a great many more of his number, that his new
marriage is an emotional not an economic investment, that
his stepchildren probably have a living part-time father, as
he himself is to his own children if he has any. (As such, he
is married to the remote control stepmother: he is observed with this hat on in the next chapter.) Although the

* "When Billie (stepmother) and Johnnie (mother) appeared before a
judge, he ruled in favor of keeping the children with their stepmother. 'When
the judge heard that I'd been married five times I didn't have a chance,' Johnnie said sadly." This was the situation in a five-page story on second marriages
in the *Ladies Home Journal* of April, 1963. Although it is an example of a
statistically minute fraction of current step family arrangements wherein
children live with their mother and stepfather and stepmother lives elsewhere,
the editors made it part of a *How America Lives* series.

Choosing the unusual to state the case for this subject, so rarely explored
at all by the press, the magazine underlines a speculation now familiar to readers that the living-in stepmother more clearly supports the wicked stepmother
thesis than the modern stepmother who lives out. By thus furthering the
myth, the magazine assumes that its public prefers to keep looking through
the wrong end of the step family telescope.

relationship maze may be temporarily confusing to adults, it
confounds a child;

> Mary's mother has been married three times, stepfather
> twice, father twice. "She plays a game with her young
> stepbrother Jackie," Dr. Despert tells us in *Children
> of Divorce.* "The game is in the form of a quiz. 'What's
> your Daddy's name? Your mummy's name?' she demands
> of Jackie who is not yet three. 'What's your big sister's
> name? Your little brother's name? What's his daddy's
> name? What's your daddy's wife's name?' And so on and
> on until Jackie is in a frantic state and Mary's eyes have
> an unhealthy glitter."

When child, mother and stepfather live together all three
must reshuffle their ideas of getting along in a family. Emily
Post's statement "any man who is kind and decent should
meet with little difficulty in winning . . . [stepchildren's] affections" is a Postian dream. The stepfather needs to be more
than kind and decent in the twentieth century; he has to
care. Caring, he battles anonymity.

Where every motion and emotion of stepmother is scrutinized, stepfather is ignored. Even his wedding was ordered
by his bride's marital status; his was not a consideration although whether divorced or widowed, a former marriage
left as deep a mark on him as on his wife (and perhaps an
even deeper scar, for while she continued some semblance of
family life he switched to the cell-like emptiness of a bachelor
apartment or room at the club). His need for mourning was
forgotten by husband-hunting women whose titillating notes
awaited him on return from the cemetery or divorce court.
He was expected and encouraged to immediately absorb his
departure from home, wife and children and plunge open-
armed toward a new family, or if he had not been married
before, know at once how to manage a ready-made one.
Pressures on his new bride to remarry at all costs propelled
her to disregard his paternal potential and to sell him, herself
and her children the fantasy that "once we are married everything will be all right."

His wife has custody of her children, her ex-husband supports them; neither custom nor law demands anything of a man as a stepfather unless he chooses to act *in loco parentis.* A remarried woman, whether mother or stepmother, is functionally The Mother in the house; a stepfather here parts company from a father and because of him cannot be The Father but rather, while defining a new genus of man, might be known as The Anonymous Presence.

STEPFATHER PROBLEMS

Rich or poor, the stepfather is presented with a threat which has no equal for men in this American culture. Money is the base of his problematic role, money is the key to understanding it. His marriage is an investment in happiness; its balance sheet tallies emotional as well as economic debits and credits. Money speaks for both. The stepfather cannot secure his family relations with the once-familiar assurance of his earning power; in this and what it represents, he faces anonymity.

A man is accustomed to earn and to spend for his family. It is decreed by law that he should; behind the law is custom, behind the custom is physiology, which designates the male as provider for the female, bearer of children. Earning money has come to mean his manliness and in the part of society that counts carats and weighs education by the price of tuition, money means success. Despite the new reality of women's earning capacity and the female contribution to the family budget, neither law nor custom has changed very much. Wives still bask in the golden light of their husband's financial triumph; children regard it their natural right to share in the countinghouse standard father establishes. They ask and get with more than economic need; students of personality say that money means love and a way of showing love, asking for love, being loved is with money. A lonely child steals pennies from his parent's pocket and is comforted; older and more seriously deprived of love, he holds up a man or a bank to get his hands on the precious commodity— money-love. A husband decks his wife in luxuries to show her and the world that he loves her, or doesn't to show that he doesn't. He says "yes" or "no" to children's need for a dollar or a trip to Europe not as much by checking his bank balance as by his desire to give or withhold his love. It is not a new phenomenon:

> In the seventeenth century Milton disinherited "the unkind children I had by her [Mary Powell, his first wife]." After his death these children sued his third wife, Elizabeth, for their "rights," and his will was upset by the Court. (MITFORD, J.) The man who saw his destiny as fighting for rational British rule on divorce took his money (and love?) away from the children he thought were unkind, and they (from avarice or guilt?) begged to get it back again.

For the stepfather, money is not often the simple language of responsibility, manliness, love and affection that it is for most husbands and fathers. It is suddenly full of irregular verbs; even Freud is conjugated differently for him. He cannot finance his family on conventional terms; each act of giving becomes troublesome as well as generous, each parsimony challenges assorted family loyalty. He feels his marriage threatened. He has the fear, guilt, jealousy and hostility that the stepmother has; for him, money expresses these emotions.

He is damned if he does reach his hand into his pocket . . . and damned if he doesn't.

His wife's first husband is in his marriage; his wife's children are there. If he was married before, his former wife and his own children are part of his new marriage too, a Greek chorus of reminder of a life that is finished except for the responsibility thereof which remains. He wants to be as a husband and father to his new family but the crowd that surrounds it prevents him. It may be a simple matter of arithmetic which makes it taxing if not impossible to fulfill his obligations toward the old family and desires toward the new. If wife number one has not remarried, alimony and child-support payments, plus the necessities of life for himself, do not allow wife number two a budget for mink coats and jewels. He finds other ways of saying "I love you." Does it make his new wife happy?

"The trouble with happiness," a cynical remarried woman observed, "is that you can't buy money with it." But if husband number one left her well-off in his will or divorce settlement, husband number two comes face to face with being The Anonymous Presence, a situation unknown before the Married Women's Property Act.

"Gentlemen:" G. Washington wrote to London merchants handling Custis business, "The enclosed is the minister's certificate of my marriage with Mrs. Martha Custis, properly, as I am told, authenticated. You will therefore for the future please to address all your letters which relate to the affairs of the late Daniel Parke Custis Esquire to me as by marriage I am entitled to a third part of that estate . . ." The estate was handsome; more than 17,000 acres, cattle, hogs, sheep, £8958 in slaves, and some 450 books. "Most of these were set aside for Jackie," a biographer tells us, "but in his wife's name Washington took the works on business, agriculture and some of those on history. . . . [He] insisted on getting all that was due him as husband of the former Mrs. Custis." (FREEMAN, D.)

Only the occasional fortune-hunter would brazen such a course today, and he would not find it easy. A modern woman holds on to money accumulated from former husbands or anywhere else; it does not automatically become the unmitigated, uncomplicated blessing to her husband that Martha Custis's was to the Father of Our Country.

On the contrary, it can cause trouble. It is not so much a wife's independence that worries husband number two as its origin; if it comes from her first husband, it comes from the source of his jealousy and his fear. It is another man's money-love that drapes her shoulders and sparkles on her wrist. Husband number two must decide whether he can absorb his emotions while his wife enjoys a bank account and other tangible memories supplied by number one, whether he can ignore his life-long measure of self-respect by not being her bread-winner, or should instead insist that she deprive herself of this other man's wealth so that he can establish his husbandly rights. "I will support you in my fashion" translates in second-marriage language to "I do not want to be reminded of the man who loved you before."

If she is a widow, he treads dangerously hard on the egg-shell delicacy of her loving memories. If she is a divorcée, he reawakens bitterness by his generosity; his wife is reminded of the parsimony of the past marriage, a springboard to recrimination, and the children compare father unfavorably with stepfather. Like Rip Van Winkle, the old hostilities come down from their mountain sleep into the present family to disturb the marriage—and shake awake insecurities in stepchildren.

Their stepfather might want to fulfill a father's economic function as well as a husband's to make the marriage complete. At the same time he resents having to support another man's children, allowing his rival to escape financial responsibility for his children while retaining their loyalty. "Men easily make sacrifices for their own children," sociologist James Bossard comments, but although a man loves his wife he resents the financial drain of her children even though he likes them, because he is "not accustomed to the sacrificial stance for another man's children." It is this intrusion on stepfather's dream of a complete family which brings him full circle to anonymity. One solution is to pretend the problem away:

> "The stepfather who has helped the child have faith in himself and trust in mankind, truly has the right to say 'This is my child,'" states Elizabeth Meier, lecturer at Columbia's School of Social Work. She does not suggest how child or stepfather should dispose of the real father, whose money, memory, or visits, insist that the stepfather who follows her advice indulges in a fabrication.
>
> "Like sex," she comments in magnificent understatement, "money can cause trouble when the family includes children from a former marriage."

Mothers sense stepfather's conflict. Many are afraid that he will give more to his own children than to hers thus to demonstrate that he loves them—and perhaps their mother—better; others make every effort to hide this anxiety. If a remarried mother goes to work to increase the family income, much of which is absorbed by *her* children, or stops working to take care of them, she absolves her guilty worry. At the same time, she sacrifices a state of economic well-being that was hers before; "I gave up my alimony when I married you," one said, "and now I have to work for it!"

Such a comment hardly sets up a man as a proud happy head of the household which his culture tells him he must be to succeed. It makes him feel inadequate, a failure. His wife's insistence on her ex-husband's contributions, earning herself, or otherwise being the mainstay of her child's life leaves little room for help from stepfather. Again he is a shadow; again, he is damned if he does, damned if he doesn't.

A divorced woman of thirty-six with four children married a bachelor. "When she did go out she felt guilty for leaving the children alone and for spending money that might be used to their advantage. The husband soon came to realize and resent the fact that the children always came first. At first the husband tried to take a real interest in the children. However, the mother insisted that they were her responsibility. He finally . . . left them almost completely alone. As the situation developed," the account continues, "the stepfather became an outsider in the actual family circle. He was rather meek and dominated by his wife, who no longer respected him because he had not tried to advance in his work and always acceded to her wishes, showing no initative." (BERNARD, J.)

Another stepfather insists on being a father; the results, which Bernard calls an example of "Mother-and-Son system vs. New Father," are equally disastrous;

Mr. and Mrs. Smith weren't getting along because of nine-year-old Jimmy. Mrs. Smith explained that her husband expected his stepson to "do everything just so, and if Jimmy doesn't, he loses his temper and although he doesn't beat him he stares at him with a mean look," Mrs. Smith added. "My husband and I only have intercourse about twice a month. It isn't that I don't want to have intercourse with him, it's just that when he gets mad at Jimmy I can't love him. Sometimes I can't stand for him to touch me. . . ." (IBID.)

A child who looks too much like his father, acts too much like him, or has too much of his love or money can antagonize a stepfather. "I guess blood's thicker than water," one said angrily. "Ever since last summer when his father stopped to see him, he's been acting up. Like father, like son, I guess. I didn't even know till then that they looked alike." (MEIER, E.) Another stepfather is frustrated by the child's independence made possible by his father. An item in Leonard Lyons' column is to the point:

"Norman Krasna, the playwright, is married to Al Jolson's widow. He has a problem now with his stepson, who just discovered the size of his inheritance from Jolson. 'How can I threaten to cut a boy's allowance when he has millions?' "

The heart of the matter is a wife's love for her child by another man. In the intimacy of today's family, the child's attachment to his own father, whether measured in millions, physiognomy, or mother's possessiveness, may seem to bar stepfather from being anything more than mother's silent husband.

But not for long. As he looks at the marriage he has made, he perceives the new freedom it presents to him. Unshackled from the conventions of The American Male, he can create his family relations in untold variety. He can be the kind of a man he once dimly dreamt of. It was this dream, perhaps, that was unfulfilled in that first young marriage, that encouraged its dissolution, and led him to a new marriage. What he can be to his stepchildren is still a question mark; it entices him to find an answer in his own mind and the children's.

STEPCHILD FEELINGS

The view of mother's new husband, as of father's new wife, depends on the child's age, sex, and stage of emotions at the time be becomes a stepchild. Because mother is more crucial to the child in his early years, a stepfather's coming can be easier then. But at any age, a curious stepfather wonders why the stepchild acts as he does; for him, too, there is THE STEPCHILD PRIMER.

1. THE CHILD WANTS HIS MOTHER. He wants to keep her to himself and had succeeded until stepfather came along.

2. THE CHILD WANTS HIS FATHER, TOO. When father disappeared, the child worried; his secret wishes about father might have caused the departure. Perhaps father doesn't love him any more.

3. MOTHER MAY NOT LOVE THE CHILD. If she does, why did she marry again? He must find out whether she will still be his mother. His research is likely to be less than scholarly.

4. STEPFATHER IS A RIVAL. He is a competitor for mother's love and for the child's notion of his own father. And he is bigger than the stepchild!

5. STEPFATHER BRINGS A NEW SECURITY. The child finds out that it is easier to love his mother and father from a stable family setting. A stepfather who likes him makes it possible.

The child surveys the stepfather through the lens ground by his earliest emotions and his sight is focused by his present relationship with his mother. She is doubly important; important because all mothers are, and because the child in a step family takes his cue from the natural parent who, in this instance, is his mother.

"What's Hecuba to him, or he to Hecuba,
That he should weep for her? What would he do,

Had he the motive and the cue for passion
That I have?"

Many stepchildren have Hamlet's cue for passion if for
different reasons and wonder what their personal Hecuba
will be to them now. No matter how genuine their welcome
of a stepfather, beneath it is concern about the cornerstone
relation with mother. "The funeral bak'd meats/ Did coldly
furnish forth the marriage tables," is Hamlet's reaction and a
twentieth-century stepchild's too. Mother may understand
the bitter indictment but, unable to manage the complex
tearing at her emotions, put the children out of her thoughts
—or the house—until she gets her bearings in her marriage.
Clinic histories are full of examples of children sentenced
to grandparents or boarding school after, as well as before,
the new marriage.

> "Mrs. Myers felt that her seven-year-old son Joseph was
> the 'wrong note' in her remarriage. He has, she said,
> 'the same manners as his father' and she was afraid he'd
> turn out like his father, so she sent him away." (WHITE,
> A.)

> "Walter's mother and stepfather didn't want him in
> their new marriage." He was sent to live with his grand-
> parents. When they died he returned. "As the mother
> related their consternation, the stepfather sat back smok-
> ing his pipe and looking very much like a martyr, and
> quite pleased with himself." (IBID.)

These children resented being sent away and had reactions
extreme enough to require clinical help. More stable youngsters have the same feelings; the real or apparent rejection
boomerangs more often than not:

> "I felt terribly guilty and in the way," writes a step-
> daughter who had the misfortune to get whooping
> cough the day she was scheduled to go to boarding
> school, "because Bill [stepfather] had planned to take
> [mother] abroad with him on a business trip and they

were both bitterly disappointed. Bill urged her to go any-
way. . . . Mother refused to do this, and Bill was hurt
and intimated that he occupied a distinctly secondary
place in her affections." (ANON 5)

Enveloping the child with love and attention does him as
much of a disservice as withdrawing it. With the extra vision
allowed the young, children are quick to see that mother
can, in a sense, be had and be held by them, that she can be
made to put stepfather in the "distinctly secondary place" by
means of such poignant, if uncomfortable, appeals for her
help as the whooping cough (Point 1 in THE STEPCHILD
PRIMER). Stepfather perceives in this super-mothering the
oncoming cloud of anonymity darkening the skies of his
marriage. He may feel martyred like the pipe-smoker, resentful as Bill about his canceled trip, or try, with the "mean
look" or other methods, to take matters into his own hands.

The trap is set for stepfather; if mother withdraws her
attention from the children and he supports her in this,
celebrating victory over assorted young adversaries, he becomes their enemy, failing his admittedly difficult course in
Advanced Stepfatherhood. If he opposes her move, his wife
feels deprived for herself, jealous of his attention to her child;
he is saddled with responsibility for being father to the child
who has a father, and this does not earn him a passing grade
in mental health circles either. On the other hand, if mother
is too engrossed in her children, he is tempted to be stricter
than he might otherwise judge fair and equitable, taking out
his marriage frustrations on the small, although far-from-
innocent persons, which again fails to make him the head
of the house he wants to be. Whichever way he turns, the
trap snaps.

"Too often a stepfather questions his right to be in the
step family," Frances Beatman, director of a family coun-
selling agency tells a visitor. "Most stepfathers in the five
step families under my care just now have more to give,
more they *can* give as an investment in parenthood than the
children's own father; some are more of an asset than the
children's own mothers are." These men, she says, feel they
have failed, partly because their wives consciously or inad-

vertently force them to this conclusion, partly because they try too hard and too fast to make a relationship with their stepchildren. "The child," she concludes, "has to have a good reason to give up old ties for new. It's a slow process at best." Her advice—"Stepfathers . . . relax."

GIRLS

The young female who, with a baleful glance at step-mother, wants Daddy to put her to bed, still wants Daddy to be hers when she lives with mother and stepfather. (Point 2 in THE STEPCHILD PRIMER.) Here mother is the whole of a mother; there is no stepmother close enough to siphon off the evil characteristics all mothers contain for daughters. Mother, not stepmother, is the wicked witch who sent Daddy away; often the girl turns to stepfather who becomes the "love object" in place of her father and her weapon by which to repay mother's villainy.

Stepdaughter is angelically understanding, dear and sweet with her stepfather, *she* makes the martini, fetches and carries for him, and proves she can care for him better than mother, as any girl who wants a father's love might do. The difference, of course, is the crucial one—he is not her father.

This sets another trap for stepfather. There is not a man alive who cannot be coaxed toward it with the bait of a stepdaughter's flattering attention; "Aha, she *likes* me!" one exulted. "Her mother can't do a thing with her but I have no trouble at all," says another. Thus encouraged in his effort to make a happy family, he unknowingly comes closer to disaster. Expensive presents, special treats, exaggerated amounts of attention separate from mother, all with the best stepfatherly intentions (and the money convention), make for danger; "By wooing the mother through the daughter, as many men are apt to do," remarks Dr. Peter Neubauer, psychiatrist, "he supports the stepdaughter's dream that she can have this father for her own."

Should he choose to act like a fatherly father toward his stepdaughter, she is devastated, as she is when he is even an averagely loving husband toward her mother. This is not in her scheme of things; the unexpected violence of her reactions flashes a fast sequence of questions to the puzzled man. He could not have expected nor can he comprehend what Dr. Neubauer calls "reality-testing" (a professional term which describes the effort of an individual to find out what is real in life; the stepdaughter tests to find out if the stepfather is really in love with her mother, really to be trusted). Whether his stepdaughter's fury is expressed in overt hostile acts, in psychosomatic illness, or attempted destruction of the family, school and neighborhood peace, he is alarmed and tempted to retreat. The shelter of The Anonymous Presence now appears a lesser evil.

His benign actions cause reactions that would confound Alice in Wonderland. Since young females as well as old are given to expressing tension by the onset of physical ills, it is even more threatening to stepfather to know that at least part of his stepdaughter's "feeling poorly" is due to his intended kindness. "Weak spots in the body react to anxiety and tension," Dr. Milton Levine, pediatrician, states. "If it's the intestinal tract, there may be diarrhea and heartburn; if it's the respiratory system, asthma; if the nervous system is weak, sleep problems, stammers and stutters, habit spasms such as tics, blinking, and shrugging the shoulders; if the brain is the weak spot, epilepsy may result."

> Both Martha and George Washington often noted that Patsy Custis was "having one of her fits." It is known that Martha was an overindulgent mother; "When either of . . . [her children] was sick she yielded almost frantically to concern," a biographer says. "[It] was a serious state of mind to be encountered by a man who doubtless had grim memories of his mother's efforts to shield him. . . ." Stepfather Washington, too, seemed to have attempted extreme indulgence to the children, having none of his own. Shortly after he had ordered a spinet for Patsy from England "with a good assortment of extra strings," she died, many accounts say, of epilepsy. (FREEMAN, D.)

One step further into the daughter's emotions brings stepfather face to face with father; the stepdaughter endows step-father with feelings she has toward her paternal parent. Resentful jealousy (Points 3 and 4) is one of them.

> " 'Isn't this nice, children? A new Daddy for Christmas,' said my wife. 'I wanted a bike,' said Judy (age 8). I was beginning to feel a little bit like a father when we tucked the children into their beds. . . . Suddenly I heard Judy ask her brothers 'Is he going to sleep in the same room as *my* mother?' I felt like an intruder as I closed the bedroom door." (HALL, P.)

An idealized image is another result. No stepfather, however saintly, can measure up to it; he is bound to disappoint his stepdaughter because he is there, morning and night, real and fallible. Whether he is innocently trying to get along, or guilty of an occasional unpaternal glance or indeed of uncontrolled incestual passion, stepdaughter is enraged.

> "An otherwise most acceptable and promising marriage was on its way to the rocks when we first knew Jose-phine," Dr. James Plant, psychiatrist in a juvenile clinic, reports. ". . . a striking, attractive vivacious girl whose many able talents are stuck as so many barbs in the various tender parts of her amazed and completely baffled stepfather. Even now from the 'safe' distance of a nice boarding school she is carrying on a long-range barrage with fairly accurate aim."
>
> Josephine believed her mother had driven her father away by nagging, "that Josephine alone understood him. She alone will carry his part . . . she alone will make the mother regret those earlier steps and will drive the stepfather to harried retreat. The girl is a miserable failure in school. Only the Devil himself," the doctor concludes, "could conjure the hundreds of ways she can mortify her nice mother and make step-father wonder how he could have ever stepped into this. . . ."

Seymour, Lord High Admiral and officially rejected suitor for the hand of young Princess Elizabeth who was to become England's renowned Virgin Queen, married her most recent stepmother, Catherine Parr, instead. Orphaned Elizabeth, age fourteen, lived with the couple. Stepfather Seymour proceeded to court her assiduously; he "romped boisterously" with her, would "come to her bed-chamber in the mornings in his nightgown, bare-legged." The day Catherine found Elizabeth in her husband's arms, the future Queen was "removed with her establishment." (JENKINS, E.)

Whether Seymour, twenty years older than she, came too close to Elizabeth's memory of her violent attractive father Henry VIII, or shattered her idealized image of the King, can only be guessed at; surely the incident had repercussions in her lifetime of sexual fears.* A fragment of small-girl hope for motherly forgiveness and love is in her letter to Catherine from her new home; ". . . if your Grace had not a good opinion of me, you would not have offered friendship to me. . . ."

Happily, stepfathers today have a powerful ally in a person from whom they may least expect help—the children's father. It is difficult for a girl to cherish a princely paternal dream when father "forgets" to send the promised pocket money or to arrive for an appointed visit, when he seems too engrossed in his new life to care about his daughter's well-being. Conversely a daughter with even a modicum of emotional security is not likely to continue a vendetta with her father (or his representative the stepfather) if over and over again he proves to be a responsible, wise, and fatherly person even from a distance. Whatever he does, father's mere existence can make it possible for stepfather to be openly husband to his wife and his stepdaughter's firm friend.

BOYS

When a man comes along who genuinely loves a boy's mother, a realistic young male takes a long measuring look

---

* Immediately thereafter, her guardian Mrs Ashley recorded that "she became sick." She suffered intermittent ill health in the next years, biographies report. "By the time she was twenty, it was a matter of common rumor . . . that her monthly periods were very few or none."

at his rival and decides that he probably can't beat him so he might as well join him (Points 4 and 5). It's not too bad to have a man in the family again; if the marching emotional troops have fought their battles well enough, a friendship can flourish.

> "Before our marriage the kids had called me Uncle Paul. Now they simply dropped the Uncle. . . . Because I wanted my children to love me I joined them in their games and it became quite common for other young-sters to come knocking at my door to ask my wife if Paul could come out and play stoop ball." (HALL, P.)

Another uncle set off an internal conflict whose drama, like a gigantic magnet, has pulled interest to itself for three centuries. "The central mystery in it . . . has well been called the Sphinx of modern literature," one of its distinguished students, Dr. Ernest Jones, comments. No stepson depths have been more deeply plumbed or more compellingly enunciated than those of the man whose uncle murdered his father and married his mother, the man who when informed of this grievous state of things gave forth what Dr. Jones calls the "almost reflex cry" which heads this chapter . . . "Oh my prophetic soul! Mine Uncle!"

Hamlet, Prince of Denmark, so remarkably rich in insight that it still compels the mind and stirs the soul, contains a catalogue of any boy's emotions when presented with a step-father, albeit without the glorious dramatic trappings of a father's murder, a murdering stepfather-uncle and the tragic ending.* Its particular relevance to the stepson state follows; it is taken from *Hamlet and Oedipus* by Dr. Jones, psychoan-alyst, Freud's biographer and as brilliant an interpreter of the much-interpreted drama as can be found.

Hamlet, Dr. Jones says, is a picture of a strong man tor-tured by some mysterious inhibition against revenging his

---

* It is widely believed that Shakespeare's intuitive knowledge was sharp-ened toward this subject by the death of his own father presumed to be in 1601; *Hamlet* was probably written between 1602 and 1604, according to the late scholar George P. Baker of Harvard.

father's murder. Why didn't Shakespeare identify it? "Strange as it may appear, the answer is probably the same as with Hamlet himself—namely, he could not because he was unaware of its nature."

> "I do not know
> Why yet I live to say, 'This thing's to do'
> Sith I have cause and will and strength and means
> To do't."

With the newly discovered processes of his profession, Dr. Jones interprets the problems Shakespeare expressed. Hamlet's incestual feelings toward his mother cause him a deep depression at her remarriage. "O that this too too solid flesh would melt" is his suicidal wish; he wanted to die himself because the remarriage proved mother's unfaithfulness to father and so to her son. He desperately tries to repress the feelings of desire. "Fraility, thy name is woman! A little month. . . ." is, Dr. Jones tells us, the bitter cry of a small boy building up his defenses against the sexual impulse toward mother.

Hamlet wants to revenge his father's murder; the more urgent the need to do it, the more he must suppress the need because the murderer is his mother's present husband and, to make matters worse, his own uncle. A blood relative has done the two terrible deeds that are buried deep within Hamlet as unacceptable desire; it seems as though he himself has killed father and married mother as Sophocles' *Oedipus Rex* before him. Killing mother's husband is equal to committing original sin himself. The Queen his mother's "markedly sensual nature and passionate fondness for her son" reinforces the conflict. To set it off, Jones remarks, he has chosen a girl whose "naive piety, obedient resignation, simplicity" contrast her to the Queen, as sacred to profane love. Loving Ophelia was another effort to repress his desire for his mother.

Hamlet states the conflict again and again:

> "Thus conscience does make cowards of us all;

And thus the native hue of resolution
Is sicklied o'er with the pale cast of thought."

He would like to sleep, to forget "the thousand natural
shocks that flesh is heir to." Jones lists his symptoms; depression, hopeless in attitude toward the world and the value of
life, dread of death, repeated reference to bad dreams, self-
accusations, desperate efforts to get away from the thought
of his duty, and vain attempts to find an excuse for his
procrastination. "All this points to a tortured conscience . . ."
Jones says, "The call of duty to kill his stepfather cannot be
obeyed because it links itself with the unconscious call of
nature to kill his mother's husband whether it is the first
[his father] or the second." *

Most boys have glimmers of the potent emotion Hamlet expresses; it is easier, with the aid of such scholarship as
Ernest Jones's, to recognize them at the white heat of dramatic tragedy on the stage than in the relatively low temperature of the informed, insightful, modern family at home.
But to some degree, the internal thermometer starts to rise
when a stepfather appears; primitive passions are reawak-
ened, the love, gratitude and admiration for father which
neutralized early rivalries have to build slowly all over again
toward stepfather.

> "He acts liks a lord and master but talks about equal-
> ity in the house," Nelson, sixteen, said of his stepfather
> in a clinic history. The stepfather complained, "Some-
> times during an argument, Nelson would think the
> whole thing very funny and would begin to laugh." It
> made stepfather very angry. The doctor asked Nelson
> why he laughed; the boy answered that he "hoped to

* T. S. Eliot, Jones notes, believed Hamlet's emotions were in excess of
the facts as they appear in real life. Geothe thought Hamlet's character un-
fitted for effective action of any kind. Jones quotes his lines, "To me it is
clear that Shakespeare meant to present a great deed imposed as a duty upon
a soul that is not equal to it." Others theorize that Shakespeare meant Hamlet
to express mental disorder, still others that the task itself was difficult enough
to cause him to hesitate. With precise logic, Jones discusses and discards each
contention.

get stepfather mad enough to hit him so that he could feel justified in hitting back."

"He speaks with considerable nostalgia about his real father, asks his mother questions about him, daydreams about him. When he moved away from the town where he had lived before his parents divorced, he developed asthma and other psychosomatic symptoms." (WHITE, A.)

Hamlet raised every emotion in THE STEPCHILD PRIMER to the Nth degree, every one except the last; he never had a chance to know that stepfather brings a new security, that it is easier to love mother and father from a stable family setting and that a stepfather who likes him makes it possible. Perhaps Nelson will never know it either. But most modern stepsons, given an intelligent, perceptive set of adults, can.

THE RELATIONSHIP

The stepfather finds his route to dignity and contentment in his new marriage off the cemented highways of conventional family life. He winds his way through the tender new growth of step family feelings and its tangled mother-child underbrush, at times baffled, even discouraged. The wilderness may delay but it rarely stops his adventure. Like the mountain to be climbed, it is there, and he, an intellectually vigorous, emotionally well-oriented explorer of modern marriage, finds it if anything more interesting and potentially satisfying than the familiar speedway-to-happiness he has left behind.

He has confronted the apparition of The Anonymous Presence and found it unworthy of a hope he has cherished for some years, a hope enlivened by his conviction that a man might choose his own currency in his closest connections. He aspires to head his family not by fiat but by freedom from it.

He considers it an asset not to possess his stepchildren by paternal right as this enables him to choose the common ground—be it an inch or an acre—that he wants to share with them and they with him. Just because they are not his children, he and they can roam the universe of relationship to find a place to meet in peace and enjoy the meeting. He does not measure himself by the standard requirements of being a good father but prefers the latitude of being a good friend. To this end he encourages the stepchildren to remember father.

In countless ways he demonstrates that there is a place for a father *and* a stepfather in a young person's life; he does not trespass in the private territory that belongs to father and child, compete in the good-father contest, or insist on a paternal title. His reasons are not all altruistic. He has discovered that pretending to be father, saying and believing "this is my child," is a superhighway to anonymity on which his closely-guarded hope for a new kind of family life is sure to meet with grievous collision. Even if wife and children encourage him to believe the fiction a fact for their own reasons, spelled out above, even if he can devise a way around the biological truth that faces him with childish guile at the breakfast table, in the income from father's estate, or in the person of Father himself on a Sunday morning visit, he categorically refuses to be father. He believes it in his own interest to allow father, alive or dead, not only his paternal responsibilities but his firm implacable image—good or bad—to the children. If father is around for the children to desire or deplore as they will, to hold his rightful place in their emotions, stepfather can avoid father-child complexities and be himself to the children.

Trying to be the father he is not makes him a cipher. Insisting on being himself takes a more perilous path, but this way he has an invaluable partner in the children's father. This strangely-harnessed but effective pair plough ground for the new *genus* family man.

His marriage gains. If his wife is defensive about her children, paying too much or too little attention to them, worried about the effects of her former marriage on the present one, doubting now her promise that "once we are married, everything will be all right," he gives her a gift in the currency of confidence in his personal compass and in her ability to share the uncharted adventure with him. He assures his wife that he both acknowledges the existence of her former husband and accepts the fact that another man fathered the children in the house.

With this freedom, the pressure is off; he can more easily share his wife with her children if he doesn't wince at the sight of her embracing a pint-size edition of husband number one. He encourages a stepson's friendship by a casual "You and I are the men of the house and we have to look after mother together" when he means it; the words only stick when he is afraid that that is exactly what will happen. He fields his stepdaughter's seductive smile or stinging attack and is able to remind her that he is not her father, but that because they live together they can, perhaps, come to like each other.

He does what he does because he wants to, not because he has to. His wife and stepchildren discover in him a new measure of man who neither buys nor sells self-respect but enjoys it. He is free to say a firm "No" to P.T.A. meeting or school play without guilt, asserting that he cannot be counted on for such fatherly pursuits, but equally freely administers punishment to fit the crime of the young person who borrows—and wrecks—his car.

He is not anonymous, he simply hasn't been defined yet. His contemporaries do not know what it is to be a stepfather. It is possible that fathers, bent and bowed, find it the better part of valor to remain uninformed. *Genus* modern stepfather might just be the coming family man.

Chapter Twelve

REMOTE CONTROL STEPMOTHERS

"Hast thou named all the birds without a gun;
Loved the wood-rose, and left it on its stalk?"
—EMERSON.

Observe the crowded college green on graduation day. Conspicuous to those sensitized to the stepchild state are the tight knots—two couples—around the central figure in robe and mortar board, clutching his diploma. Polite small-talk, frozen smiles, the women's sidewise measuring glances and men's awkward heartiness encircle the palpitating tassle . . . these are the signs of a stepchild graduating. Whether his diploma certifies his maturity or not depends in large measure on the four people who have surrounded him during at least part of the years before as they do at this moment. The one he knows least is the woman who is his father's new wife.

She is the contemporary stepmother.

She has the name but not the job of the woman who lives with her stepchildren. She has the same emotions but not the same opportunity to resolve them. She can in no sense be mother to the children who live with their mother, yet as father's wife she would like to be as a mother to his children. Like the modern stepfather, she is creating a new kind of stepparent, not a substitute parent but an added adult whose responsibility in undertaking modern marriage is to perceive its new pattern and make it work. It requires more than instinct for this stepmother to find her way, to understand the new relation and discipline her emotions to meet its requirements. But whether or not she has the wisdom Emerson's lines above suggest—to name the birds without a gun, to love the stepchildren in their natural habitat and leave them to grow there undisturbed—she influences them because she is married to their father. By remote control, she plays a part in step family life.

"I'll always be the less important parent to my sons," a divorced father remarks. (ANON 6) "Stevie didn't want me anymore," another says. "Although I loved him more than anything in the world, I let another man have him." (ANON 4) Neither man had remarried, neither intended to; if they had, these sorrowing statements might not have been made. A new wife brings a new look to life and turns a man's eyes ahead. Rejuvenated, revived, rescued from self-pity, he puts his fatherhood into focus with blithe assurance. His children may find him the less important parent but he is important to his wife, and himself now—if he has married the right woman.

If his new wife is an asset to father, they both gain, and the children, even their mother and stepfather, share in the profits. If she is a liability, everyone loses.

The new stepmother might expect to "have the children" for half or all of the year from reading about herself in current literature; stepmother woes, as we know, make better copy if Cinderella is part of everyday life. But the impression is misleading; this remote control stepmother married a divorced man whose children are almost always in their mother's custody. Father's custody or alternating custody between the two parents is rare.*

Typically, her husband has legal rights to visits with his children and is required to support them. Increasingly often both he and their mother have remarried; the crowded graduation indexed the rapid rise of this phenemenon to be seen in Figure 5. If the new stepmother has been married before and has children of her own, father is a stepfather to them and goes to their graduation with still another parent-stepparent couple. For clarity and readers' sanity, the inter-familial tangles that result when his children, her children, and their children mix have been artificially separated into the next chapter. In the spotlight here is the woman the

* A reminder of the changing climate are Jacobson's figures for a recent year; during 1955, 343,000 children had parents whose divorce decree became final, four-fifths were given into mother's custody, one-tenth to father's. "In the relatively few remaining cases, both parents are given custody for part of the time, or the children are awarded to a relative or guardian."

majority of today's stepchildren—and an even larger portion of future stepchildren—know as The Stepmother, father's wife who lives apart from them.

She is not a functional mother, except on weekend and vacation visits, and even then, she is more hostess than mother. Her situation shifts the intensity of stepmother emotions, lessening some, heightening others, and adds its own explosives. Although she is less significant to the child than the classic stepmother, he reacts to her with stepchild feelings. Action and reaction chain stepmother to father, to mother and *her* husband, if she has one, and to the children as certainly as the contagion of the measles.

STEPMOTHER AND FATHER

The character of their modern marriage begins to unfold early in this book's pages. In the small family setting, both man and wife search for happiness. (Witness a recent cartoon; concerned wife to book-engrossed husband "Ralph, are we as happy as we should be?") (SATURDAY REVIEW) If it escapes in the first marriage, that union is dissolved to allow for another try. Despite the child-centered culture, children are generally not a preventive to divorce, in fact the discovery that unhappy parents make unhappy children may encourage it. After some months of experiencing what one lonely father entitled *The Torment Of A Divorced Man,* a man misses home atmosphere more than he enjoys his freedom, and remarries. Both husband and wife bring remnants of former marriages with them.*

* Bernard's study found that both men and women "feigned indifference" toward their own former spouses if divorced. "The reported attitudes of indifference," Bernard tells us, "should probably be taken with a grain of salt. [It] is a culturally imposed attitude for those in the role of divorced persons." Goode's study corroborates hers.
One result—a winter-spring union—is reported by psychiatrist Heilpern. An elderly man remarried a young girl; he was "ashamed to appear before his own child," feeling that he had betrayed his former spouse (who in this instance had died) and thus unsuitably displaced the child's mother. The father, Heilpern reports, felt guilty and on the defensive; the child showed considerable resistance to him, was embarrassed to meet him and his wife, and showed great reserve when with them.

This married pair can concentrate on their search for happiness without the constant company of the children. The convenient, "If it weren't for the children, everything would be all right" is not warranted as their reality brings them no scapegoat but each other. But there is still a serpent in this Eden for the stepmother; the stepchildren are in her husband's thoughts if not in his house. If she is unsure of his love or finds her marriage falling short of expectations, she chafes under the restrictions placed on her by the facts of her life. Stepmother staples—fear, guilt and jealousy—which appear full-strength to the classic stepmother, are diluted, but present. She resents the money her husband spends on his first family (it is often reported that her pressure is his excuse for not meeting support payments) and the money-equivalent, affection, which he gives them on visits. It interferes with her image of herself as a successful second wife.

Like most wives, she intends to make her husband happy. The added goal for a second marriage is to make it happier than the first.

"I would be Mrs. de Winter," the shy, lank-haired, nail-biting successor to Rebecca rejoiced. ". . . we would walk in the garden together, stroll down the path in the valley. . . . And a woman comes in smiling, she is Maxim's sister, and she is saying, 'It's really wonderful how happy you have made him, everyone is so pleased, you are such a success.' " (DuMaurier, D.)

This second wife's fantasy was done in by the superior sound of Rebecca all around her; outside of fiction, women are less likely to admit to their dreams or their jealousy. The stepmother is no exception; when her stepchildren live with her, her jealousy is often transformed into hostile feelings toward them. But when they are remote, it transforms into anxiety; she does not have the knowledge the stepmother who is The Mother gains from the children's constant presence and because of this, anxiety increases. The classic stepmother knows about mother from the children. But the hostess stepmother fights a ghost.

"My stepparents, too, sometimes cross-examine me," a
stepdaughter writes. "But this is rather pathetic, for
each one wants to be told that the second marriage is
a tremendous improvement over the first. The fact that
I may not care about discussing my own parents . . .
seems not to occur to them." (ANON 5)

Stepmother is impelled to give chase to the ghost, to gamble
on being able to sweep wife number one out of her husband's
thoughts, and the children with her. She hopes to whisk away
her anxiousness in the process. The stakes are large, repre-
senting her hopes that this marriage will make her happy.
Her marriage-counseled mind tells her that she will not win
if her husband loses, but if she can make their marriage
sufficiently alluring, she may wean him away from his attentions to the representatives of her rival, source of her disturbance.

Two pressures, particular to the non-resident stepmother,
urge her to bet the other way, to embrace the ghost, not chase
it. The first is her husband's affection for his children, a
matter not easily ignored. He, too, is well-counseled in the
current fashion; the new importance given to fathers in
behavioral circles has filtered through to him. Even the
morning paper encourages his paternal instincts ("Behind
every successful stepmother," *The New York Times* tells him,
"is a father who lends support, encouragement and determination."). He may feel guilty and embarrassed to have
married a young woman, as the man Heilpern describes, or
concerned for the children to like the woman he has chosen
as a wife so that he is truly free to like her too. Their seal
of approval is as necessary for some fathers as the county
clerk's stamp on the marriage license.

The alert new wife senses the tensile quality of her husband's father-love; she knows that she can make it easier for
him to express it and she would like to be part of that expression. It would be a proud day for her to feel approved
as a mother to his children, by them and by their father,
a better mother perhaps than the woman he has divorced. If
given to private candor she may ask herself, "What's in it for
me?" and answer that it would bring her happiness via a

contented husband. It would be, she knows, a socially acceptable choice:

> "Grace's formula for answering invitations for Dad and her, when I was there," is described by a visiting stepdaughter. "She would say, *with more than a hint of nobility,* 'Joan is staying with us now; unless the dear child has some plans of her own, we wouldn't, of course, want to leave her.'" (Italics mine.) (ANON 5)

Another pressure urges stepmother to embrace, not chase, the children; a child's couplet incants it:

> Curiosity killed the cat.
> Satisfaction brought it back.

The power of the new but ancient plague given to the female of the species by some dark spirit is strong in the stepmother, strong enough to determine her approach to the stepchildren. She is curious about the woman who was once her husband's wife; she can most easily satisfy her curiosity through the children. The remote control stepmother places her chips with the finality of the croupier's *"Rien ne va plus!"* The stepchildren, embraced, are what she bets on to satisfy her . . . and bring her happiness back.

STEPMOTHER AND MOTHER

Almost every step family in the modern pattern shares one characteristic, ugly, savage, female, and in its milder form uproarious. It can neither be excised by surgery nor placated by tranquilizers; it can be identified by psychiatry but perhaps even the deepest understanding cannot erase it completely. This is the stepmother-mother competition, surpassing most women's feuds in intensity, and set apart from the usual by the small person of the stepchild.

The child is a spectator at the contest; swiveling from one to the other, he sees a point won here, lost there. He cheers when mother's swiftly delivered "How good of you to be so thoughtful of my children" is a service ace, unreturnable;

when stepmother's caustic birthday present to him—six pairs of underpants "Because we know how much you need them" —scores a bull's-eye. He intercepts the frigid looks at graduation or holiday encounters, the mental measurement of waistline, coiffure, husband. "She does look better now that she's dyed her hair, doesn't she?" will balance, in his tally, the doorway greeting he gets: "How could she bring herself to drive that obvious car!"

With understandable glee the child makes the best possible use of rivalry perceived. A boy whose mother abhors chocolate chip cookies knows he can rely on stepmother to have them always on hand; his sister's weakness for wild Gauguin-print school dresses, denied by stepmother's restraining hand on father's wallet, will arouse mother to compassion and purchase. If mother believes in brisk outdoor exercise, stepmother afternoons by the fire can be counted on for respite; if stepmother is TV-minded, mother cannot understand how any adult could manage its boredom—or allow it to a child.

And so it goes, despite the scoldings of all-knowing experts who sternly warn the warring women:

> "The ex-wife, the husband, and the new wife should be unselfishly united on any decision."

> "Competition between the child's two mothers is a grave error."*

The children are candid:

> "I came back to mother's apartment last fall after spending two months at dad's house," a stepdaughter writes. "I showed her my divine new evening dress, in fact I couldn't resist trying it on, for it's the most becoming one I've ever had. She thought so too; I could see her expression in the mirror. But just as she was about to say so, a suspicious look that I know all too well came over her

---

* Some step family day hence, it is hoped that experts, editors, and authors will consider the facts of life and reconsider their imprecise damaging-to-progress talk about a child with "two mothers," "four parents," etc., etc. And perhaps some greeting card company will soon be the first to print and endorse Stepmother Day greetings, separate from the already profitable establishment of the Sunday in May. It will contribute to peace on stepchild earth.

face. 'Did Grace pick that out?' she demanded. Grace is
dad's wife. 'I should think even Grace would know it's far
too old for a girl of eighteen.' " (Anon 5)

Stepmothers are self-revealing:

"But surely you must want children of your own?" a stepmother says she was asked by "a tactless friend of mine.
Laurie [stepdaughter], who overheard the question, an-
swered for me. 'But she already has children of her own,'
she said, 'she has us.' " (Fancher, B.)

A stepmother ends an exposition of her troubles with a
wish; "The children, as things stand, may quite well have
found an affectionate mother in me and a good friend in
her. Who knows!" (Anon 8)

Grown women can indulge in such feline battle, manage
to lick the superficial scratches inflicted, and fight back with
equal ferocity, aided by husbandly applications of soothing
encouragement. But when it goes deep enough to affect the
children, in fact to use them as weapons, it is no longer amus-
ing but wicked stepmother behaviour that outdoes the
venality even imagined by the spinners of the ancient tales.
It has been seen in the stepmother who lives with the children and insists on being called mother at all costs, who
refuses to allow mother's pictures to be looked at or grave to
be visited, who shocks by seducing stepson or punishing
stepdaughter. The contemporary stepmother, with less reason
for her hostility and less justification, can be equally cruel
by indulging in the war with mother at the cost of the child.

A teen-age girl tells a psychiatrist the story of her trip
abroad with mother shortly after her father's remarriage.
The mother was puzzled when, in each world capital they
visited, her young daughter carefully watched her every
purchase. Whether ski sweater, souvenir, or elegant
leather bag, the girl immediately duplicated the choice,
"with my own money," she explained to mother. "I told

her *I* wanted everything that she chose, too," the girl related, "but *I* knew that *Mother* knew it wasn't true. Why
should I want a French umbrella when I've never even
used an American one?"

Finally, on London's Bond Street, the truth came out:
"I *had* to tell," daughter says, "it was too hard not to."
The truth of the matter was that her new stepmother had
given the girl a goodly number of travelers' checks with
instructions to "buy me everything your mother buys for
herself; you'll be doing me a big favor because I can't go
abroad and you can."

The story, the doctor advises, has every element of destruction for the child. Stepmother, by her avarice, endangered the
mother-daughter relationship during the difficult years of
adolescence, forced the child to live out a lie, challenged
her deep loyalty to mother, let the stepmother appeal of "I
can't go" dizzy her in a guilty conflicted tailspin. "It was not
the unhappy summer," the doctor says, "or the temporary discomfort, but the terrible tearing at the child's already unsettled feelings about mother, father and self that did her in.
She is still working out the results of that incredible international shopping expedition." (SOURCE WITHHELD BY RE-
QUEST)

STEPMOTHER AND STEPFATHER

The connection between father's new wife and mother's
new husband is a long-distance connection with only occasional face-to-face meetings, without the direct contact of
stepmother and father, stepmother and children, or the embattled rivalry of stepmother and mother. But it can make
or break the success of the emerging step family.

The chain of action and reaction links itself into a circle
by the connection between today's stepparents. Stepfather
is attempting to forge a new image of a family man; friendship is his choice over ersatz fatherhood. To achieve it, he
needs a distant partner, the father of the child. If this father
is a reliable, wise, and kindly man he is more help in the

stepfather business, but whatever he is, his presence in the child's life makes it possible for stepfather, clear of father-child confusion, to make his own relationship. Both men make their way toward a new kind of family.

Stepmother has an opportunity to make it possible. It asks considerable wisdom of her. By marrying in the modern manner she has undertaken to puzzle out an unknown, unnamed relationship. If she is anxious, jealous, uncertain of her husband's love because of his children, she is blinded to its potential. Like the stepmother of old, she will interfere, then, with her husband's urge to be a father to his child and ultimately with the possibility of the stepfather's success since he finds it difficult to discover his new role without the father in the picture.

"Why doesn't God make Daddy love me?" a small boy inquired of Dr. Milton Levine, pediatrician, in the course of a talk about his troubles. Aggressive behavior at school and at home had resulted, the doctor comments, from "the father's seeming lack of interest in his son, promises made and not kept, and a truly severe deprivation for the youngster."

One can guess that this small boy might better have appealed to stepmother than to his deity. She has, perhaps, adopted the stance of a wife aggrieved at too many fishing trips or golf games with cronies and applied it to father's attention to his children. They are less easily conquered than the most concentrated stag activities . . . but are more a threat to her security.

She can rationalize by virtue of the respectable wifely patina of her behavior. When her husband is challenged, neglected, or otherwise traumatized by his children, as all fathers are in the course of being fathers, she encourages him; "Of course it's not your fault, dear; those children . . ." Earnestly, perhaps entrancingly, she acts and is the loving wife but with it, because of her fear, comes the penetrating if unspoken message: "Don't be a Father."

The new kind of family life—the weekend life, the vacation visit—is beginning to be understood by many fathers and the

women who share it with them. This contemporary stepmother has a splendid, remarkable chance to be its creative
source. Each time she is tempted to use her wiles in diverting
father from his purpose, she stops progress for stepchild, husband, and the stepfather to whom her behaviour is distantly
but firmly linked. Each time she tries to capture the children
with motherly instinct uncontrolled and unthought-out,
equally she stops progress. If she uses her remote control with
knowledge of herself and the children's needs, with a conviction born of disciplined effort that she can safely be a
good wife to father, a good person to another woman's
children, she helps herself and her opposite—the stepfather—
to achieve the kind of marriage they believe in.

Such a stepmother frees father to be father, mother to be
mother and stepfather to be himself. She finds herself the
richer and may, indeed, find happiness returning without
having had to kill the cat at all.

STEPMOTHER AND CHILDREN

The stepmother who embraces her husband's children
could not imagine herself as the wicked stereotype; her every
action is its obverse. She encourages their visits, plans treats
and entertainment for them, buys lavish presents and carefully, according to the book, labels them "From Father
and . . ." (although it is not beyond her to let it be known
who did the shopping). She shows interest in their lives, affection too. She is gay, permissive, easy and flexible; she
smooths over scenes with father. In her enthusiasm, she dis-
regards the danger signs, forgetting perhaps the second sight
of childhood that perceives what she herself has almost forgotten. The web of loving attention the stepmother weaves
seems benign enough to her; she is being "good to her husband's children," but she overlooks the malignancy in the
problems she creates for them.

The unalterable truth is that she cannot be a mother to
her stepchildren. "If you want to be maternal, get a mother's
satisfactions, love a child as if it was yours, look somewhere

else; you cannot count on your stepchild to fill these needs,"
a candid psychiatrist instructed a stepmother. "But I love
the little girl, I'd like to read her stories, play with her, take
care of her," she answers. Unmoved, the doctor insists that
stepmother-love is tested by its capacity to recognize the
importance of *mother*-love and the ability to let mother-love
flourish unimpaired by rivalrous action. However delightful
the scene stepmother paints, it is, he says, constructed not
by the child's need, but by the woman who wishes to replace
her husband's first wife in the ultimate of becoming her
children's mother. It is for herself that she loves the child
. . . and this, he says, is not true caring.

His words are blunt, their impact hard. But they help the
contemporary stepmother to knowledge. She reviews the
salient points of THE STEPCHILD PRIMER:

> THE CHILD WANTS HIS MOTHER.
> THE CHILD WANTS HIS FATHER.
> THEIR NEW MARRIAGES MAKE HIM FEEL DESERTED.
> STEPMOTHER CAN BE THE ENEMY, OR LOVABLE.
> STEPFATHER CAN BE A RIVAL, OR AN ASSET.

She knows that the child takes his cue from his natural
parent. He will, if he can, come to regard stepmother and
stepfather as a new kind of relative who help him to be
happy with his parents because they help mother and father to
be happy in a new marriage. He can graduate to maturity
with a degree of emotional as well as intellectual accomplish-
ment.

Trouble comes when her own needs and the children's
diverge. If she is driven by anxiety, spiked with curiosity to
enfold the children, she may be unable to temper action with
reason because its base is irrational emotion:

> "A woman of thirty married a divorced doctor whose two
> small children live with their mother," Dr. Robert
> Seely recalls. "This second wife insists on trying to charm
> those youngsters to the degree that they and their own
> mother have become very upset. The stepmother doesn't

want to be hated by anybody, she can't bear it, in fact. She is trying to escape from the hostility she causes but can't stop her chase for these children's love."

Such a stepmother does not deliberately set out to harm the children but is blinded to the results for them by the force of her own desire. If her own needs are uppermost, she has no measurement by which to make rational decisions. "Every child should have one place he calls home. He needs this for his sense of identity and belonging," *Parents Magazine* tells her. ". . . a grave injustice is done to children by second wives who try too hard to turn their visits into one long holiday," says a child specialist in *Good Housekeeping*. She hears the words but is deaf to the message.

Enticing the child closer and closer to her side may temporarily suit the disposition of childish loyalties. The youngster has a certain sympathy for the non-custodial parent, the late sociologist Willard Waller reminds us, and, resenting the ordinary routines imposed by mother, is able to threaten her with an attachment to distant father and stepmother. It is not too difficult for stepmother to promote the threat. "She soon becomes identified in his mind with all the fun in life," *Good Housekeeping* continues, "and [the child] is torn between loyalty to his mother and the greater fascinations of the second home."

The stepchild may encourage her for his own particular need of the moment and so may her husband. His motives are no more child-centered than her own. If, mourning incomplete, he still contains a remainder of bitterness, or its source, desire, toward his first wife, he encourages wife number two in her web-spinning to revenge the hurt and deprivation suffered without having actually to admit to it, even to himself. He can cheer his star player in the rivalry game from the sidelines; his wife's needs and his neatly interlock and reinforce each other. The result has separate but indivisible dangers.

This remote control stepmother behavior appears respectable and responsible to husband, children, friends, and family. It has none of the surface character of the wicked stereotype. When the cruel feelings of every stepmother come out as kindness it is, if anything, more invidious than open hostility. Certainly it is harder to recognize that the core of such action is no different than that which brewed the horrors of the old-time tales. Even this new kind of stepmother herself, suffused with the hope for her own happiness, cannot foretell when her actions will boomerang for the child, because she isn't thinking about him. Her affectionate seduction is self-propelled.

The stepchild may be convinced by her that he has two homes, two mothers, two values . . . and find he has none. Adults, unaware or uncaring, desert him if it suits them. Or, he may make an earnest effort to keep the lines straight only to find them tangled by a too-eager stepmother. Two instances make clear the risks of the new variety of stepmother wickedness:

> Dr. Graham Blaine, psychiatrist, tells of children who are "unintentionally used as pawns in the complicated power struggle." A prep school student came to him for treatment in a deep depression at Christmas time; "His depression turned out to be linked to the fact that . . . neither parent wanted to have him home for Christmas. His mother was going to her second husband's family and his father was planning a honeymoon cruise with his third wife. "He had to face up to the fact," the doctor states, "that he had no one place he could call home."

> A father encouraged his new wife's desire to see his little daughter perform in the school play, which had taken many months to prepare. Eight-year-old Peggy had inadvertently told father and stepmother about it. "I can't come to see you this week," she said, "because we are rehearsing the play." Unable to face the embarrassed agony of their meeting mother there, Peggy's answer to stepmother's request for an invitation was evasive. "The stepmother showed up anyway," Peggy's teacher tells us. "There she sat in the front row, next to Peggy's mother. Peggy forgot every line. She's a courageous child . . . but at the end there were tears. She refused to go near her stepmother." (SOURCE WITHHELD BY REQUEST)

The measure of right and wrong is as various as the situations in each step family. There is no standard for good and bad stepmotherhood except the one hardest to examine—motive. The self-absorbed woman who goes to the play for her gain and her husband's can be a menace to the child; the loving one in the same act could be kind. She might or might not go to the play but she would not *have* to go—motive makes the difference.

If her motive is to try to be mother to the stepchildren from fear, jealousy, rivalry, curiosity, she damages their security. If her motive is to stop father from being Father it is again damaging to the children who need to keep a father in their mind's eye. The reliable motive is only one—and it is the same as for the classic stepmother—the firm belief in the importance of her marriage. This allows her to look straight at the reality of what she is, wife to her husband, friendly companion in his fatherhood.

"Hast thou named all the birds without a gun; loved the wood-rose, and left it on its stalk?" An affirmative answer from the remote control stepmother is an asset to herself, to bird, to rose, in fact to the stepchildren of this day.

Chapter Thirteen

THE COMBINATION FAMILY

"This is the forest primeval."   —LONGFELLOW.

There is no more disunited a nation than the step family which assembles his and her children under one roof. The separate sets of offspring survey the joint endeavor of their parents with the cautious appraisal of cold-war diplomats at the conference table. In secret or openly they prepare for battle. Every stepparent and stepchild problem has intensified, every pretense shows up in new clarity. Parents' instinctive good sense and equitable judgment may bring about disarmament; more difficult to achieve—and more essential—is an unwavering respect for the facts of step family relations. This, they find, is the only way to arrive at a lasting peace.

The natural family presents hazards enough to peaceful co-existence. By its jungle law, every child is catapulted from the marvelous comfort of infancy into the tempestuous give-and-take of a group; here he must fight his first savage battle to survive as an individual amongst his peers. It is hard to be the oldest child, displaced too soon from being The Child, and constantly striving thereafter to hold calendar advantage; hard to be the second child who either chants "me too" or feels forever defeated; the youngest is overindulged; the middle child neither oldest nor youngest; an only child the recipient of undiluted parental attention without the protection of his own generation. Difficulties are less onerous when mother and father are able to be each child's personal resource; the expensive toll of unequal regard may be paid over many years. Miraculously, most children manage well enough to move on into the ever-wider and less-protected groups of the larger society.

Subtract a parent and the struggle is harder. Add a new stepparent, and the intensity is again increased, with mother or father's support at stake. Multiply by the remarriage factor which brings a set of ready-made children into the family sanctum and disturbances go right off the slide rule. Problems cannot be solved by natural family formulas when his and her children's emotions meet those of a wife-mother-stepmother and husband-father-stepfather. Here, indeed, is a family forest primeval.

To survive in this forest, members of the step family have to cultivate a clear definition of who is what to whom and why. The sophisticated manner, the simulation of feelings that are not there, or avoidance of those that are, is not much help where primitive emotions roam free. The mother masquerade is unconvincing for a stepmother in her own children's presence; youngsters are not impressed by her make-believe. On the other hand, if a child observes his mother or father becoming a friendly stepparent to another child and finds such a relationship himself, he can begin to see the strengths in his new kind of family. When honestly regarded, the complications become an asset. There is not much room for fantasy and disappointed dreams in the hardy climate of the "She's *my* mother" "Well, he's *my* father" dialogue. A new kind of peace can happen.

> "At the start, in 1942, we all had other lives and we were seven people thrown together, so many little separate units that could have stayed that way," Jacqueline Kennedy wrote to her mother and stepfather on their tenth wedding anniversary. The couple had combined two teen-age Bouvier sisters with three Auchincloss youngsters, later added two of their own children. "Now we are nine," the letter continues, "and what you've given us and what we've shared has bound us all to each other for the rest of our lives." (THAYER, M.)

Mrs. Kennedy's sentiments would delight a couple who had attempted to make a family of stepbrothers and halfbrothers and sisters. Success in a child's eyes validates their concept of marriage.

Whatever family unity there will be has to absorb the original division, the biological tie of mother and child, father and child. The battle formation is familiar to step families; mother on the sofa with her children, father across the room surrounded by his. There is the poignant, unspoken longing in an enveloping hug that makes the parent the child's exclusive property again, if just for that moment. There are the exaggerated requests for time, for private enterprise, for special assurance of the fact of belonging. There is sabotage neatly executed, flattery, mayhem. Coalitions shift as the marriage and family develops; six possible "cleavage patterns" are identified by Bernard in her study of remarriage. The cleavage may be along original lines as above, or between the parents and the children (who combine resources to battle the mutually untenable fact of their parents' marriage). A third cleavage pits one child against the rest of the family by his own aggression or, as in the case of Cinderella, by theirs. Rare but possible, Bernard states, is the cleavage of one parent against the rest of the family, two or more natural siblings or two or more stepsiblings in combination against the rest.*

Children want to keep their unique relation to parent, brothers and sisters, and simultaneously make relations of a new sort to stepparent and stepsiblings and eventually to the new baby, a half sibling, who is again another kind of relative. This is what the combination family requires of its young members.

---

* This last "cleavage model" occurred, Bernard reports, in one case of "a stepbrother and a stepsister who fell in love and wished to marry, against the strong opposition of their parents." It is a not infrequent dream of young stepsisters presented with intimate closeness to eligible stepbrothers, but usually remains just a dream as it did for the King in *Cymbeline:*
"His daughter, and the heir of's kingdom, whom
He purpos'd to his wife's sole son—a widow
That late he married—hath referr'd herself
Unto a poor but worthy gentleman." Act 1, Scene 1

STEPSIBLINGS

The typical his-and-hers family today combines orphans (his) and children of divorce (hers). Since divorce mores give the mother custody, the divorced father's children live apart from him; when they live with him, he is a widower and his children have one parent and one stepparent alive. Mother's children are likely to have two of each. They live with mother and stepfather and visit father and stepmother. When two bereaved parents marry, the parental equation is even (advancing longevity and the rising divorce rate are decreasing the proportion of stepchildren in this combination).

Mother's children now have the extra advantage of an absentee father who is an asset and a remote control stepmother who may help him so to be. With great good cheer they set off on a Saturday for whatever degree of paternal indulgence father's personality allows, leaving their stepsiblings to pine with only the weekday parent and stepparent to provide weekend excitement. Thus even the best-adjusted combination step family has an inequity for which there is no remedy. It is only reversed if the absentee father and his wife make the children uncomfortable enough with prying question or inattention or both that the stepsibling at home seems the lucky one; then he, quick to catch the despair in "I have to go to Father's house," rejoices in his comparatively old-fashioned family arrangement.

When stepbrothers and stepsisters appear, children bristle at the thought of surrendering their position in the family. Being deposed is assuaged by the assurance one father gave, "You are Daddy's baby; I love Mother's little girl too, in a different way." And it can be a relief to know that there is another, older and wiser, to take the onus of being the first to wear lipstick, drive a car, have a date, or another, smaller and even less qualified to take the trip, see the movie, or enjoy other delights denied the youngest child. For an only child, stepsiblings are harder to accept but relieve pressures of concentrated parenthood.

If there is more than one sibling per category, life is easier. "Children like to discuss their concerns with each other," Dr.

Blaine says. "They need the reassurance which comes from finding that another shares their feelings and they are not alone in experiencing confusion, loneliness, and resentment over what has happened." "There is safety in numbers," Bernard reports, "psychologically as well as sociologically. It is more difficult for a stepmother to 'get away' with cruelty to a child if another child is prepared to protest the mistreatment of his brother or sister. Conversely, it is easier for two siblings than one to 'gang up' against a stepparent and family."

How frequently children join with their own or stepsiblings "against" parents is undetermined. Often an older sister takes the place of mother—sometimes in the fact of household responsibility, sometimes in image—and brother takes on father's attributes, making it easier for younger children so endowed with siblings to quarrel away their resentments of parents. A psychiatrist's educated guess (and it can be, he says, no more than that until research has given it validity) is that stepsiblings employ each other as images of stepmother or stepfather, substituting as natural siblings do, which provides an escape hatch for violent anti-stepparent feelings. Like Cinderella, father's girl regards mother's daughters as wicked and cruel because they are an extension of their mother, her wicked cruel stepmother, (although stepmother, too, as we know, is an extension or representation of the evil qualities of mother.)*

Stepbrothers and sisters may be comrades-in-arms, if divisive forces are not too rampant, against the common enemy . . . their parents' marriage. One instance resulted in a wedding cake the likes of which may never be seen again. The bride's and groom's children together baked their parents' wedding cake. It was unorthodox in more than the fact of being the cake denied by custom to second weddings. They covered its several layers with icing—rose-tinted as a gesture to the

* A fear of interaction, differently expressed, is found in a court decision to disallow the association of two stepsiblings although here there is a one-sided peril. John Bronson, lawyer, reviews the findings in the case: ". . . the young son was not awarded to his mother, whose fitness was not attacked, because in the mother's home was a slightly older stepbrother 'fresh out of reform school.' Fearing the potential danger of the influence of this stepbrother, the court relied on the best-welfare-of-the-child test to excuse itself from permitting this young boy to be in the full care of his mother."

"nothing white" custom—into which were inserted decorations carefully gathered and prepared for the occasion from a nearby beach some weeks before. A spiny circlet of crab shells, jagged black-blue mussel shells alternating with sharp crab claws, climbed the sides of the roseate layers to the cake top where the five-and-dime bride and groom were conventionally entrenched, but without the expected bower. In its place, a menacing scarlet lobster claw, poised to snap, towered over the small black and white figures, which seemed to shiver in their bed of icing under its threat. Satisfied with their creation, the stepsiblings—smiling—presented their mutual feelings to their just-married parents.*

THE NEW BABY—HALFSIBLING

No matter how lovable, the small newcomer stirs sibling rivalries in the stepchild that are those of every child plus particularly painful sensations that have to do with the stepchild state. "The new baby is not just a sibling to the stepchild," Dr. Milton Levine, pediatrician, comments, "he is an evidence of the new marriage."

The frightening fact that the child is desperately trying not to know is now presented by the baby—kicking, smiling, crying evidence of parental sexuality. It revives the emotions of parting from a parent, mourning at death or divorce, concern and conflict at the thought that the new marriage represents unfaithfulness to mother or father, no longer there to defend themselves. The stepchild may decide he must champion the cause of the departed and disallow the baby somehow, or he may be able to extend the affection for mother or father to this new child:

> "I took the little baby in my arms when it was awake and nursed it lovingly. When it was asleep again, I crept close to my mother's side, according to my old custom, broken

---

* This is the author's personal observation, one of the three or four in this book. Because of its extremely powerful character and importance as an example of free expression of valid sentiment, it is included here as a matter of interest to readers and an intended compliment to the step family whose candor in this incident can but be admired.

now a long time, and sat with my arms embracing her waist, and my little red cheek on her shoulder . . . and was very happy indeed." The baby, David Copperfield muses, "was truly dear to me for our mother's sake."

The new baby completes the complement of children. Mother-stepmother and father-stepfather are finally mutual parents of their child. The halfbrother or sister is an increasingly usual relative for stepchildren today; young marriages, young parents, early divorces and consequent young remarriages encourage the couple to want and to have a child together. It was estimated several years ago that about 14 per cent of remarried women have had one or more children born to them; the proportion increases each year as remarriage age gets younger.

There is particular joy in this creation for mother and father. They have been unhappily married parents, single parents, remarried parents, absentee and remote control parents, stepparents singly or together. Now they are parents. From their marriage, undiluted by former marriages, has come their baby. They are apt to invest more than the usual care and affection on the child of their second marriage and do not want to know that the baby represents anything but an unadulterated package of joy to the children in the house—an understandable blind spot in the already multifocal vision of adults in the combination family. They see and report on the delight of the nursery set in wistful purity:

". . . my wife started a campaign to increase the family by one, since 'every man should have a child of his own,' " a stepfather relates. "When Nancy [wife] and Melissa [baby] came home from the hospital, I peered into the other children's faces looking for signs of inner resentment toward the newcomer. . . . Resentment? No! They loved Melissa from the very first look." (HALL, P.)

Four months after the stepchildren arrived, Billie gave birth to a girl, Jeannie, "who finally made us a family." Halfsister Sharon adored the new infant and comments to another, " 'She's more my baby than yours because we have the same father.' Pamela brooded about this until she realized that she and Jeannie shared the same mother." (HOFFMAN, B.)

Children try manfully to overcome the sudden revival of their stepchild terrors; a tender mother's reassurance helps:

> "[She] . . . laid my head down on her bosom near the little creature that was nestling there," David Copperfield tells, "and put its hand up to my lips. I wish I had died, I wish I had died then, with that feeling in my heart! I should have been more fit for Heaven than I have ever been since!"

To latter-day David Copperfields, the baby is an asset in the general sense that parents are increasingly child-oriented and interested because of it.

> "After some years a little sister appeared on the scene, and life was indeed a delight! There was no more loneliness in the nursery and existence became doubly interesting!" a stepchild wrote almost forty years ago. "It meant also that 'mummy' came to our end of the house rather more often than before. . . ." (ANON 8)

Euphoria was short-lived for this stepdaughter who had not known that the stepmother she loved well was not her mother. Told by a nursemaid, she discovered the extra pain a new baby brings to many halfsiblings:

> "Even my little half-sister seemed a thief in my eyes since mummy was hers and not mine—*she* belonged, I didn't!
> 'Aren't you glad she was born?' asked father. All the bottled up injury . . . flashed up in my heart as I said 'No!' Everybody laughed. 'Jealous,' said father as he and mummy went out. . . ." (IBID.)

If father has married a much younger woman, his children are likely to be almost grown—and sometimes new fathers or mothers themselves—when the halfsibling arrives. They regard it with amused tolerance or, with some annoyance and a thought of inheritance, as a different kind of a little thief.* Younger halfsiblings accost the thief and in their child language cry "Help!" "When mother is a bride, and then a new mother," Sylvia Bauman, psychotherapist, says, "the child comes face to face with mother's sexual self." Stepdaughters, and occasionally stepsons, too, are "acting out" their feelings in caring for and coming close to the new baby. It accomplishes unspoken, perhaps unconscious goals; one is to say to parent and stepparent, "You don't know how to take care of the baby," which means, "You don't know how to take care of me; I will give this baby what I wanted and never got."

A psychiatrist recalls an adolescent girl patient whose mother had a new baby and whose father's wife was pregnant. "She continuously talked about her own boy friends," the doctor relates, "trying to tell me and her parents, especially, 'I've got a man of my own.' She threatened, in various ways, to get pregnant herself. It was her way of punishing the parents and stepparents. She really wanted to deny the whole baby business, and would insist, when seeing any sign of mother's tenderness toward the infant, that mother was 'going to spoil that child' and that stepfather's affection for it 'means he is a fag.' She would like," he concluded, "to try to make those parents impotent and sterile so she would not have to face the fact of their marriage."

The visiting stepchild has a particularly virulent brand of sibling rivalry. His home is with his mother, apart from the baby. He cannot guard his interests, hour by hour, day by day, or explode into attention-getting behavior when he feels jealous or left out, or share in the fun of watching the infant grow. From afar, this stepchild must discover

* It is this same glance toward the unopened will that dominates the attitude of adult children toward a parent's remarriage. "[They] favor the remarriage of their parents . . . somewhat less than did dependent children. The relative disapproval of father's remarriages (44 per cent no attitude indifferent, or unfavorable as compared to 35.6 per cent in regard to mother's remarriage) may be . . . for property reasons." (BERNARD, J.)

another way to accept the new halfbrother or sister; he needs the extra sensitivity of both parents, both stepparents, to manage. It asks a good deal of all four adults, none of whom join in the child's special fear and all of whom are experiencing some new and often disturbing sensations themselves. But their competence can make the baby and the child able to share a parent and this, adults will come to know, is a requirement of a contented family life.

Youngsters sure of parental affection, regardless of the variety and number of brothers and sisters in their combination family, can manage to accept the baby if they accept the new marriage itself. Mother, from her uneasy maternal throne, sees that her own children, particularly girls, are likely to show less affection for the baby than do their stepsisters, who may see in it father's gift to themselves.* For all stepchildren the baby must be a mixed blessing; although they feel again displaced and unsure, they learn again the importance of the new marriage and its intent to be a permanent productive relationship. Because parent and stepparent believe in it enough to have a baby, the stepchild can begin anew to believe in it too.

CHILDREN AND PARENTS

Parents report a high-voltage shock when the children they have seen through the rose-tinted glasses of courtship suddenly become their stepchildren. The children, they say, change. It is an old complaint—and a new one.

> 1911 ". . . she was a broken-hearted woman. She herself had remained the same in her love and devotion. 'But,' she said, 'the children are changed beings. They seem entirely to have lost their affection for me. They disregard my wishes, they laugh at my authority, they

---

* Dr. English and Dr. Pearson state that a girl's "intense desire to receive a gift from her father increases her hostility to her mother, whom father really favors and to whom he may in reality have given a baby. . . ." Mother is the villain, not father; for stepdaughters, if mother is absent it is possible to put themselves in her place.

countermand my orders to the servants. . . . I am simply overwhelmed.' " (ANON 10)

1963 "When Mike sat down to a supper of stuffed peppers and remarked, 'Do you expect me to eat this dog food?', Billie [stepmother] was cut to the quick. Little things Billie had tolerated before now annoyed her." (HOFFMAN, B.)

Have children—or adults—really changed? One might suspect that the change is more likely in attitude. The step family rouses the old fears, guilt, jealousy, hostility now familiar to readers; child rejects adult and adult rejects child, or everyone loves each other too much. Felt and quickly hidden, reactions percolate trouble. They begin to insist that the step relation is different from the natural. But parents had consciously agreed that there would be no difference; "I will love them like my own . . ." they had promised each other, deciding to be called, and become, mother and father to the young of either genetic brand. In the combination family, where each is parent *and* stepparent, the insistent difference becomes as plain to both as the proverbial nose on the face.

Setting aside the ephemeral differences in feeling for a moment clears a space for fact. A different house in a different place, change of school, church, and corner store, more money or less money, new people in the house, new friends, new trees, birds, view of sky—this, to a child whose world is still small, means that life is different. His parent wants this new life, the child lacks the adult's motive to make it work; the newness is, in fact, often his simplest explanation for the inability to get along with stepparent and stepsiblings. If his parent has married up or down in the social, cultural or economic scale, or across religious or geographical lines, it is even harder.

"They never go to church like we do—they're bad kids."

"Now I have to go to public school."

"My stepfather hates music; Mama can't play the piano anymore."

"Stepmother is a regular stepmother to me and makes me play in a playground. I like to play in real ground like I did before."

". . . he drinks too much, spends too much money, and we never lived like that. Who wants wall-to-wall carpeting?"

These stepchild comments in clinic histories were often helpful; by separating real from imagined troubles, life was easier. But the realities themselves are not unimportant contributors to the sensation of difference.

Stepparents say the children are different, stepchildren say that life is different. For all, the largest difference is the least perceived—a parent has different feelings about his own child than he does about the stepchild, and so it is too for child in regard to parent and stepparent. In an inner recess, the difference is recorded, but with curious although logical perversity, the attempt to shield the stepchild from the knowledge of this absolute does exactly what it is supposed to prevent—it *forces* the stepchild to feel neglected and desolate. He knows he is not the recipient of the same kind of feelings as his stepsibling, he knows there is a difference. *If he is not respected for himself, not set apart—but to his dying day and despite the most strenuous efforts still not the same—he will have neither the proud right to his own heritage nor the assumed right to someone else's.*

He longs for reassurance that he is what he is. Why, he might ask, do grown people refuse it to him?

Why does father become an assembly-line Santa Claus when his family includes stepchildren? He would not usually give any two of his own children the same Christmas present. Well-instructed member of the child-centered world, he chooses the particular special wonder—bike, book or tropical fish—that has been the individual dream for each, recognizing the small persons in his family as people. But now he is a stepfather, too; "Be fair" is the warning signal from his culture. "Don't show that you feel differently about yours than hers. Treat them all alike." The results are disaster. His own children are sure that he, suddenly insane, has forgotten what they so personally and specially need, or, by duplicating bike, book, or fish for stepchild, has demeaned the importance of gift and child alike. Stepchildren are convinced that he has no regard for them as individuals. It is the obvious, persistent difference that makes such a father feel guilty, a quality incompatible with the character of the jolly saint he annually emulates.

The same guilty uncertainties dominate the ever-troubling problem of discipline. If stepparent is unable to set rules for stepchildren as he does for his own and to justly fit the punishment to the crime, the stepchildren suffer. ". . . many middle-class parents not only tend to refrain from punishing stepchildren but actually seem to be discriminatory in the stepchildren's favor," Bernard comments. "Actually the child may not want this favoritism; he may prefer to be treated in the same way as the other children, for favoritism thus motivated may be interpreted as evidence of his not belonging." The opposite traditional act of superpunishment for the stepchild is recorded in every folk tale and in many modern confessionals.

> "Your reaction to a stepchild's misbehaviour can easily be unfair. You'll find that when a new stepchild is insolent to you, your reaction is apt to be a violent one. The same insolence from your own child you'd take as the naughtiness of a child in anger and deal with it accordingly. Not so your stepchild." So writes Mildred Finch in *Tips for Stepmothers.*

> "The stepmother considered her son a model child who was amiable and easily controlled, while her stepson was quite at the opposite pole and she could not tolerate him," is an example cited in *The Stepchild*. "Paul's father objected to the treatment given the boy, while the stepmother accused him of overindulgence."

"Unless children are rewarded and punished on the basis of merit rather than ancestry," Bernard concludes, "a sense of injustice is likely to develop."

An educated parent does not need lessons in merit.

Each age deserves separate merit; a mother is well able to mop up her toddler's spilt milk with a mild "try not to do it again" and issue a sharp rebuke to the teenager for the same crime. Separate values have separate merit; mother easily shows her genuine interest in one of her children's well-done paintings and her casual disinterest in another's collection of comics. Emotions have their own merit; father does not find it unnatural to take one sibling-rivalry sufferer out for a special treat and leave the sturdier aggressor at home.

Merit is one thing, ancestry another. When expression of love touches the ever-throbbing tie of parenthood, merit has nothing whatsoever to do with the consequences. Ancestry is not lightly given or taken away. The sentiments in the gift, in the discipline or lack of it, in the reaction of person-to-person are different when ancestry is different.

Faced with children and stepchildren both, parents see the truth begin to emerge. They and their children know equality is not possible because it does not exist in fact or in feeling.

Still, promoting equality is a popular pastime of our society. Everywhere, the ancient damaging morality sets the lie as the honorable goal:

> "The stepmother must bend over backward," Emily Post dictates, "to realize the necessity for showing no difference in her love and fairness as between these stepchildren and her own. It is," she continues, "the real test of the greatness of her heart."

Stepparent-parents find bending over backward breaks more than vertebrae; such emotional acrobatics have dangers for them, child and stepchild.

> "I unwisely bestowed, too often, my extra attention upon Mary [stepdaughter] in Patsy's presence. Patsy soon showed us that she was feeling 'pushed aside.' . . . I realized that Pat had every right to object to this overdose of affection her stepsister was getting from me." (FINCH, M.)

When the school nurse would call to say that Sharon

was sick, stepmother Billie "would drive to school, bring Sharon home, tuck her in bed and fuss over her." The teacher says Billie's own daughter Pamela "seems starved for attention." "Billie realized with a sinking heart that in bending over backward to welcome Sharon she had been unwittingly neglecting her own daughter." (HOFF-MAN, B.)

This same mother found it difficult to "balance" her relationship with daughter and stepdaughter, and ultimately tells us why:

> "If I put my arms around Pamela and then look up and see Sharon watching us my impulse is to reach out and include her too. But if I do, Pamela breaks away and runs to shut herself in her room."
>
> "Billie," the report continues, "was also appalled to find herself resenting Sharon when she saw her cuddled in her father's lap." Billie said, "Pamela would stand to one side with her heart in her face, wishing *she* was being loved, and *I did too!*" (IBID.)

There was no escaping her mother-love. It was but temporarily set aside to meet the requirements of bending over backward to "good" stepmotherhood, a maneuver imposed by every spokesman who endorses the prejudices here explored.

It is no wonder that sensations of favoritism—and its opposite, discrimination—flourish, impelling competition and conflict in the stepchild. The source is invariably the same . . . the cruelly misdirected good intention to pretend that the family has not taken the step away from its natural form. The posture, and the step, is backward. It can go forward.

It goes forward when a stepchild knows the new kind of family man, a stepfather who allows that the child has a father of its own and is glad of it, intent as he is on cherishing its mother and becoming his stepchild's warm good friend. And it goes forward in the child whose stepmother does not bribe to be called mother, a woman in love with her husband and interested in making him and his children happy without paying the price for them and herself of fake motherhood.

When there are stepsiblings, parents and children have the challenge extraordinary; mother is mother with one hand, stepmother with the other, and it is the same for father too. It is a step forward to keep the truth clearly in mind. But when two sets of adult-child relations happen simultaneously and under one roof it appears to be a step backward. Guilty conscience and community mores, quick to condemn without knowledge, say that open admission of the difference between the two relationships is *wrong*.

It is wrong, an anxious father says. If he suspected his wife held hostile feelings about his child, he is sure of it when he sees how differently she acts with her own. It is wrong, his wife is convinced. If he gives his children more than hers, that is proof of his undying dedication to the other marriage, the other woman. It is wrong, society insists, wrong to deny stepsibling equality. By this convention it is wrong to allow the stepchild his birthright, wrong to let him cherish the mother and father he remembers. The children know another measure: "She's *my* mother," "Well, he's *my* Daddy," they say, with the truth in mind. The same directness in parents is considered to be wrong.

> "A parent often says to the other, half-joking, half-serious, '*Your* son was bad in school today' or '*My* boy did a fine job,'" Dr. Dora Hartmann, psychoanalyst, comments. "But," she says, "in the natural family the child is a common problem. This division has a unity behind it. Its danger for stepparents is that it is true—the yours *is* yours, mine *is* mine; because the truth is that there is a division, the child divides."

Marriages become battles, husbands despair, women leave home taking their children with them, or fling the impossible challenge "Choose . . . your children or me!"

In this era of brave individualism, with all its round-table talk, endless columns of advice, vast advance in education, and understanding of the human species, the only solution offered to combination families is to make parental attitude —like the packages under the tree—the same for the child of a lifetime and the child in a beginning step relation. Everywhere you look, this is the message. Give no honor to the stepchild's separate heritage, no dignity to conception, birth, nurture of breast and heart for parent or child. Ignore it all. Rationalize away the blood tie for the sake of the stepchild (and for the comfort of adults who shrink from the unpleasant emotions he arouses in them). Forget, if you can, that by this trick the stepchild's personal identity heads for destruction.

In *Remarriage,* the only book extant on the subject, Bernard insists that favoritism, for or against the stepchild, can be conquered if merit, not ancestry, is the measure. Yet on the very same page she makes an observation that has a different logic:

> "Favoritism can and indeed, does exist in families of first marriage. It has been institutionalized in some countries in laws of primogeniture. Even in our own country, among some families in the coal-mining districts of Pennsylvania, for example, it exists in the form of customs which give advantage to the youngest child. . . .
>
> "*But when favoritism is thus sanctioned by law or custom, it is not likely to have serious repercussions on the personalities of those involved.* The least favored do not feel they have been done an injustice, for the favoritism lies in the institution or custom, not in the people who conform to it." (Italics mine.)

Why is it not a custom, firmly institutionalized, to recognize the unalterable fact of ancestry and to hold it in the same high regard in remarriage as in marriage? Why are parents and children not able to sanction the difference in feeling that has only and directly to do with the most cherished productive act on earth? Why should parents, who know so well the differences in their own brood, and are able to discriminate wisely there between need and unreasoned emotion, between oldest and youngest, secure and frightened, gifted and uninspired, suddenly deny perception to the stepchild?

It could be that the stepchild, like any child in the family, can thrive best when rules, embraces and Christmas presents are not the same for all, when difference in relationship is openly reflected in behavior. It could be that allowing the relationship to match its fact and feeling is the only way to integrate child and stepfamily in health.

Society has not dared to admit that there is such a way. It must impose the old conditions on a new frame, keeping parents who divorce and remarry, who challenge the trembling sanctity "until death do us part," under smothering, moldering wraps of prejudice and fear so that they and their children may never look up to see the possibilities of their mutual adventure.

When the family contains his and her children, and theirs, custom could heal the wounds of special separated relationships, as it does in the laws of primogeniture or the habits of coal miners. "You're not my mother," the child insists. The stepmother should be able, *by custom,* to agree. "I'm going to visit my father today," the child informs his stepbrother. "My father lives here," is the reply. Is stepfather to be censured for such an interchange or should it, *by custom,* be an acceptable statement of fact? Feelings can be part of custom too, a custom that insists that the parent relation is one thing, the stepparent relation another. Because the combination family allows no place to hide the differences, it may be here that the deserved recognition will at long last establish the custom that regards the truth.

> It finds an ally in the view of pediatrician Benjamin Spock: "One stepmother will claim that she succeeds because she loves and treats her stepchildren exactly like her own. I've always argued that no parent can treat even two of his children alike, since they are such different characters. I'd explain instead that the good parent keeps all the children feeling secure and relatively unrivalrous by intuitively sensing each one's individual needs and responding to them. In this sense he would recognize the special insecurities of a stepchild and do his best to meet them."

In the good old days of the large, kinship families where the step relationship was less important, less known to founder, Sarah, the second Mrs. Tom Lincoln, who is everywhere said to have made a good home for all the children therein, appears to have had the courage to embrace the doctrine of individual appraisal. For her, it happened to be opposite to the expected stepmother bias, but it was a bias, nevertheless.

Attributed to Sarah Bush Lincoln are these sentences, which have the ring of honesty (although hindsight, under the circumstances, would be understandable): "I had a son John who was raised with Abe. Both were good boys; but I must say, both now being dead, that Abe was the best boy I ever saw, or expect to see."

The informed stepmother chooses to say "My stepchild" with the particular emotion she has for that child. She may or may not feel the tenderness she does for her own; if she does, she is free to demonstrate it, even be biased toward the stepchild as Mrs. Lincoln was. If she does not, she is not impelled to pretend. She hugs her young son without censure from the stepson who knows she is his friend. She enjoys the motherhood she knows and the stepmotherhood she is discovering simultaneously, sometimes together, sometimes separately. Her husband, too, perceives the difference; "favoritism" is not in his vocabulary, "individualism" is. He believes in his abiding love for the young who look and walk and act in his image because their genes and history are his own. While administering gifts and paternal justice with a lifelong knowledge of his children, he is gently exploring his function for the stepchildren. Man and wife look to each other for guidance in understanding the child who is not their own.

A stepchild in this family feels and knows he is different from his stepsibling and might, if given to such expression, say, "So what!" He has a special place, a special relation with parent and stepparent, stepbrother or sister has another, no better, no worse, but different.

Adults and children can civilize the forest primeval, the combination family they live in. In the process, they find it contains a richness the natural family goes out to hunt for when parents and children surround themselves with friends of every age, when, reaching for an enlargement of their own boundaries, they have family vacations and family feasts in conjunction with other families. Step and halfsiblings have potential friends under their own roof, sleeping in the next bed or room, sharing parents, making new kinds of family relations, keeping old family ties intact. Parents are the catalytic agents that can make the experiment work. They can open the family door to his children, her children, and their children with a certainty that there is a place within for each one to live in his own particular dignity and for all to live in a new productive peace.

Chapter Fourteen

THE STEP FAMILY RECONSIDERED

"Beholding the bright countenance of truth . . ." —MILTON.

The step family, product of the new concept of marriage, pioneers its morality against tremendous odds. It is cajoled by the soft sell of conformity to try to fit into the traditional family form. It is threatened by the hard sell of fear and guilt at its evidence of nonconformity. Its unfamiliar, hazardous experiment strains against the bounds of culture, church and state. In the modern family, being for progress and against sin has its difficulties because each facet of society has a different idea of which is which.

The individual ultimately makes his own decision. At the moment, he is torn by opposing pressures which have neither been identified nor evaluated. Only trial and error have helped him to know the truth. He has had no way to measure the validity of public opinion or special pleading, to know what is right and what is wrong or if there is a right and wrong for step family life. "The best test of truth," Oliver Wendell Holmes said, "is the power of the thought to get itself accepted in the competition of the market, and that truth is the only ground upon which [our] wishes can safely be carried out." It is time that the truth of the stepchild state at least makes an appearance in the market. It can well venture the jurist's pragmatic test and be judged in competition with ideas which have, until now, been blindly accepted.

At stake is a morality which extends beyond the immediate unto the next generation and the next.

The stepchild of the '60's is as different from past concept as Jacqueline Kennedy from Cinderella. Some elements of society pressure the step family to belie the change; others encourage and applaud its recognition. As each pressure is identified, it can be measured with reason alert to motive and effect. There are some potent facts available. Until now they have not been put together with the stepchild in mind but were dropped here and there in the tall grasses of research meadows, hidden from each other until this time of harvesting. The measurable observations of the present climate come as close to stating the truth as any study of human behavior, subject always to the personal bias of investigators and the fallibility of their tools. Personality tests, interviews, questionnaires and other methods used to examine how people act and why, have won Gallup, Kinsey and an army of quieter scholars as much notoriety as respect.

But with all their shortcomings, there are some reliable observations of stepchild and stepparent, some concrete statistics, some statements made in interviews for this book which define and delineate the pressures on the step family and their results. Added to the better-documented knowledge of emotions suggested in THE STEPCHILD PRIMER of preceding chapters, they make reassessment of the step family today possible.

THE PRESSURE TO ADOPT

Although nobody has yet demonstrated whether adoption is a help or a hindrance to stepchildren, the present climate makes it popular. The adoption of stepchildren has almost doubled in less than forty years. Figure 6 shows the extraordinary rise in the number of adoptions, now over one hundred thousand children a year. Today, more than 2 per cent of all children are adopted children and an increasing proportion of these are stepchildren.*

People marry, have children, and divorce at a faster pace

---

* There are no figures about adoption before the 1930's; the rapid increase of the past three decades makes it appear that there were few adopted children at the turn of the century, "virtually zero per cent of all children," Jacobson says. There were, of course, fewer stepchildren then, too. Jacobson attributes the current rise in adoptions directly to the rise in adoption of stepchildren by their stepparents.

today, so that the age at which children become stepchildren is becoming progressively younger. Adoption at infancy has traditionally been regarded as optimum, and it is believed that a stepparent more easily takes the place of a natural parent when the child is very young. Since more children are very young at their parents' remarriage than ever, more appear to fit the adoption scheme. They account for part of

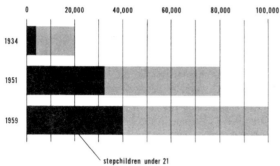

Fig. 6   **THE ADOPTION VOGUE**

The rise in the annual number of adoptions during the past three decades and the increase in the proportion of these which are step-children under 21.

the sharp rise in adoption numbers during the past quarter century.

During these years, illegitimate births have skyrocketed. They have increased a fantastic 453 per cent for mothers in their late twenties, Dr. Clark Vincent of the National Institute of Mental Health states, and an incredible 108 per cent for fifteen- to nineteen-year-olds. These unmarried mothers cannot be stereotyped; investigation shows that they are educated and uneducated, intelligent, dull, rich, poor, from stable and unstable homes. Many subsequently marry; the more stable are likely to choose a responsible husband who will legally become father to the child, whether in fact he is or is not its progenitor. His parenthood is only official and binding when the illegitimate child is legally adopted.

Adoption may be a plus for the very young child of divorce or the occasional orphaned infant, and for the illegitimate baby who is thus presented with a legal father. These adopted children swell the totals of all stepchildren adoptions.* Further facts are even more persuasive that it is the thing to do.

All adoptions are easier today. The waiting period has been reduced, requirements are less rigid. The agencies report that older couples with children are encouraged to apply where once they were almost automatically disqualified. The exploding illegitimate birth rate makes more babies in need of adoption. There are fewer potential adopting couples between the ages of twenty-five and thirty-five today because, the U.S. Children's Bureau states, of the low birth rate during the depression years when they might otherwise have been born in greater numbers, and because of increased fertility which makes it possible for many more of them to have their own babies if they want to.

When stepparents adopt their stepchildren, it is almost always fathers who relinquish parenthood not mothers, and stepfathers who adopt. Reasons most often given for the procedure are to provide a unity for the child in the family, to give him the same name as his mother, step and halfsiblings, and a sense of belonging. Some fathers, engrossed in a new marriage and other children, are pleased to relinquish the necessity to support children of a defunct marriage even at the price of surrendering visits and family name. Others find the process tortuous and conflicting; they search themselves for the knowledge of right and wrong.

> "The severance was complete, I had signed away all rights to my son. Yet, what rights had I ever had? Does a child belong to anyone? The answer I had just given over my signature was that Stevie belonged only to himself. . . .
>
> The adoption papers have been processed and I do not know when my ex-son Stevie and I will meet again. I do know that from a full heart I have made him a free and unconditional gift of my love." (ANON 4)

The well-intentioned gift may be less precious than it has been thought to be; now that there are so many more adopted

---

* Out-of-wedlock babies surrendered by mother for adoption elsewhere are adopted by a new mother and father; not being stepchildren, they are not included in the figures on stepchild adoptions.

children, new research turns up some disturbing proposi-
tions. A current study says that adoption may breed psychiatric problems; children adopted under the age of six months
tend to have these problems more often than those adopted
later.* Whether this is general to all adopted children or specific to the ever-increasing proportion that are stepchildren—
and who may be lending the special problems of stepchild-
hood to the entire adoption scene—is not defined but might
be of intense interest to stepparents and adopting parents
if it were to be investigated.

Twice the proportion of stepchildren are being adopted as
were a short four decades ago, a persuasive figure to the
fathers of many Stevies and a handy sales point for many
mothers urging husbands and ex-husbands to such a decision.
Surely it is a tempting argument to professional advisors of
mother, father and stepfather alike, and to the judiciary in
whose power the final decision rests. Society at large concurs
in encouraging this adoption and makes it easy.

The big news is the increase in numbers; the small print
of facts shows that the everybody's-doing-it argument is not
germaine for all stepparents. The tremendous increase in
adoptions seen in FIGURE 6 is due to the special circumstances
of the moment, the illegitimate child and the very young
child—although the validity here is now being questioned.
And it is due to the relaxation of adoption procedures for
population reasons completely unconnected to the stepchild,
although they affect the ease of his adoption as well as of the
others.

Anguished conflict in a divorced father could be nature's
signal to look at the facts first, a warning not to accept the
apparent message of custom without carefully examining its
source. In his conflict, society's pressure is squarely op-
posed to the essence of dignity in heritage he cherishes for
his child, a dignity which may be more important to the child
than having the same name as everyone else in his house. The

* A child psychiatry team at the Neuropsychiatric Institute, University of
California, are surveying adopted children, who account for 8 to 15 per cent
of all children under psychiatric treatment in Southern California clinical and
private practice. These preliminary results and others are quoted in *Science
News Letter*, 12/1/62.

child might well be given the opportunity to make this major decision for himself.

THE PRESSURE OF RELIGION

Religion has its convictions about the stepchild and applies its particular pressures to stepparents. Official statements on the subject have not been made, to the knowledge of representatives of organized religious faiths who can be presumed to know. Each faith has centralized sources of information which are concerned with the conduct of family life and activities. Comments about the stepchild state by organized religion's family-life experts, although not presuming to represent the opinion of every branch of every denomination, give a general impression of the religious view.

A Catholic view is expressed by the Right Reverend Monsignor George Kelly, Chief of the Family Life Bureau of the Archdiocese of New York, who describes himself as "priest and sociologist."

"Stepparents are bound by the sacrament of matrimony to accept the stepchild as their own. They should think about remarriage more seriously than they do and ask themselves if they are prepared to do it right. If so, wrap it up. Once they have assumed the moral responsibility, they should take it seriously and do their duty."

Reverend Kelly's view of the formation of a Catholic step family: "Children start going steady at thirteen, necking at fifteen, having intercourse at seventeeen. They are caught up in the sport of sex very early and parents are helpless; 'I demand my civil rights,' a boy said to his father. The emotionally unstable and morally weak find each other and go off to Elkton for a civil marriage. Since it is made outside the Church, it can be annulled whether or not there are babies. A second marriage is usually within the Church; they have come to their senses by then and as good Catholics treat the stepchildren no differently than their own. Often they forget which is which."

A Protestant view is expressed by the Reverend William Genne, Director of the Department of Family Life, National Council of the Churches of Christ in the U.S.A.:

> "Those who live in the same household bear a moral responsibility for each other's welfare, for the physical, mental, and spiritual growth of the children. All children should be in as near a natural home as possible. Being a Christian means offering mutual support, forbearance, and all spiritual qualities toward each other.
>
> The goal of remarriage is to establish a meaningful relationship that fulfills the functions of a parent for the children of that marriage. The ideal that we are working toward is that the 'step' will be practically forgotten."

The Constitution of one Protestant sect, the Presbyterian, makes a statement on remarriage:

> "The Church must uphold the Christian home and the permanence of the marriage and at the same time minister sympathetically to any who have failed in this holy relationship. Ministers who are requested to remarry divorced persons shall ascertain whether there is penitence of the past and intention to enter into a marriage of love, honor, and loyalty which shall continue as long as both shall live."

A Jewish view is expressed by Rabbi Bernard Mandelbaum, Director of the Religio-Psychiatric Center of the Jewish Theological Seminary of New York, of Conservative faith, midway between the Reform and the Orthodox Judaic sects:

> "The Talmud says, 'Anyone who brings his friend close to the words of the Torah (ethics), it is as if he had created him.' The words of the Torah stress the idea that education is paramount and if you teach children as if they were your own, you are as their parent. This is the ideal for the stepparent to follow.
>
> The goal for a Jew is to live in a way that will promote the greatest amount of well-being for his fellow-men, be-

ginning with himself. Human dignity, self-respect, integrity and honesty are the qualities to strive for and
these can only be attained in the wholeness of the family."

Rabbi Maurice Bloom, of a Bronx, New York temple, remarks on the Jewish concept of remarriage:

"Judaism believes in making strict marriage laws to safe-
guard marriage, and easy divorce laws to make it possible
to repair mistakes made by the application of those strict
laws. Judaism stresses the sanctity of marriage, and for
that reason it does not condemn people to live together
where strife and incompatability would mar good family
life." (*The New York Times*)

These representatives of the three religious faiths are
unanimous in promoting the idea that the stepchild should
be considered as a natural child and that it is in the best
interests of child, family, and their religion that he be so
considered. They appear to recognize the possibility of error
in a first marriage, of allowable remedy for that error, and
productive remarriage.

But religion's bias *against* recognizing either error or cor-
rection is infinitely more powerful. "Marital stability in our
society is morally approved," Professor William Goode of
Columbia University states. "The roots are in the three major
sects of Judeo-Christian religious tradition. Divorce is judged
as an act of moral failure and few couples divorce without a
guilt component on both sides."

The extremely touchy area of religious attitude toward
divorce exerts powerful pressure on some of its products—
remarried parents, stepparents and stepchildren. The degree
of their religious belief influences their family attitudes and
actions. There is a measurable connection between the degree
of religiousness in parents and the stability of their marriage,
as their children see it.* The more religious the parents, say

* Three thousand university students in eleven separate institutions of
higher education were asked about parents' marriages, religiousness, and their
own attitudes connected to these matters in one of a series of sociological stud-

the children, the more successful their marriage in terms of "permanence and happiness." Children who believe their parents are deeply religious place a higher value on themselves than those from less religiously inclined homes. These young people are more religious, less willing to consider marrying outside their faith or marrying a divorced person or a nonvirgin (both sexes). They credit family religiosity for their self-reported preference to refrain from premarital sex relations. Exceptions to the results of this study "most often occurred among Jews, especially Jewish men and next most often among those of no faith."

Both in the rule and the exception, the current facts presented by religion show that where it is most highly regarded, or most restrictive, or both, it will discourage the formation of a new kind of step family. It encourages the traditional stepchild position should remarriage occur.

PRESSURES OF PREJUDICE ABOUT DIVORCE

Religion is now deep in the marriage counseling business in a variety of forms, all three faiths having agreed that the cause of divorce is lack of knowledge about marriage, the cure, attainment of knowledge. The goal, of course, is to stop the dread tide of divorce. A thorough review, *What Clergymen Tell Young People About Marriage,* reports all denominations watching family breakdown with "anguish" and a new dedication to premarital counseling to prevent it.

Marriage counselors of all descriptions are engaged in the same missionary activity to prevent divorce. The demand has now exceeded the supply of trained—at least to a greater degree than the sympathetic friend—therapists out to hold the family together by increased understanding of its premarital requirements and postmarital strains. Indoctrination starts early; there are "Marriage and Family Life" courses in at least 70 per cent of all colleges in this country and in more than a

ies by Judson T. Landis, University of California. The results are summarized here. Landis' stated hypothesis: ". . . in any culture those who tend to be among the more stable and conventional in society not only subscribe to a religious faith and have more stability in marriage but [transmit it to their children.]"

thousand high schools, a booming trade in light of the fact that the very first such course in the country achieved curriculum status just forty years ago, at Boston University.

"Do not divorce; keep the marriage together," is the marriage counseling credo, a not inconsiderable if indirect pressure on the step family with divorce in its past to try to forget that it has transgressed and pretend to be the same as the natural family.

Another message, increasingly insistent, is available to those who can receive on its frequency; it is a clearly enunciated determination to remove the onus of divorce. Vivian Gentleman, an outspoken authority on matrimonial law, recently stated a view, gaining momentum in many quarters, to stop what she calls *The Real Scandal of Divorce*.

> "Many Americans condemn divorce, believing that marriages are sacrosanct and cannot be dissolved. But there is no reason why other Americans, unhappily married, should be kept in bondage by laws so rigid, unjust and contradictory that they invite dishonesty . . . giving one party an inordinately sharp weapon to use against the other. . . . A Federal divorce law, preserving the marriage relation by eliminating lax and fraudulent practices, and permitting the termination of an unhappy marriage without blackmail, hypocrisy, or perjury, is not only feasible, it is indispensible to the public good."

Robert Drinnan, law school dean, suggests that children of divorce—potential stepchildren—should be taken care of by public assistance if necessary; "We do it for war orphans," he says, "why not for divorce orphans?" Egypt, he points out, which has a higher marriage and divorce rate even than the United States, withholds a small amount of income from each taxpayer to provide social and financial security for the children of divorced parents as a group. Margaret Mead urges public acknowledgment of the fact that divorce may come to any marriage, to remove the stigma of failure. "The end of a marriage should be announced solemnly and responsibly." Like death, she says, it is part of life and there is no reason why newspapers cannot include notice of the termination of a marriage as it does of an engagement . . . or a life. Other opinions and suggestions which, like these, speak out for a new freedom are being spoken and written in the 1960's from many places and by many disciplines. They are not directed to the step family but this family absorbs them as it absorbs the pressures which frown on divorce, the most usual source of its creation. To the degree that the step-father regards divorce as a sin, he cannot choose his role but must act like a father to the stepchildren so to rub out the shady past. The stepmother must be as much like a mother as she can so that the dread word and fact *stepchild* need not weigh on her conscience.

Endorsing the opposite attitude allows a new vision of the step relationship. It appears to be increasing.

PRESSURES OF EDUCATION

While parents struggle in their tumultuous efforts to dis-cover which act is progress and which is sin, the stepchildren in the family are also searching out the new morality. They define their relations with parents, stepparents and assorted siblings and wonder whether to hold them as a source of shame or of pride as they move out into the world. Conflict-ing pressures concern them and affect their ability to do the most important job of every child in today's demanding en-vironment which is to become educated.

The awareness in schools of the stepchild state follows the torrent of new understanding of mental health and its rela-tion to the ability to learn. "If a child is late for school, he no longer gets the black mark 'Late' but the red danger signal 'Trouble at Home.' " Toby Kurzban, a New York City pub-lic school principal, comments. "There has been too much of a rush of amateur psychiatry here; we took on The Whole Child, now we'd like to give part of him back to the com-munity." Guidance counselors in the public school system are a major source of assistance when children do, in reality, have trouble at home. The newly married parent is often the cause of problems which make concentration on learning difficult if not impossible.

The civilized atmosphere of the Dalton Schools, a progressive-minded private school which combines the philosophy of John Dewey with present-day, college-directed educational needs, believes that any assistance it can offer a pupil to permit education to take place to a fuller extent is valid. Here, too, teachers are tempted to "get into the personal things" too often, Jack Kittell, headmaster, says. But with the complicated family life of many pupils (one-fourth to one-third of Dalton's families are in some way broken . . . or mended) the school is aware of emotional disturbance and makes an effort, within bounds, to deal with it when it affects the child's learning potential.

"A parent's remarriage is usually enough of a traumatic process for pupils so that it comes to my desk," Kittell says. "As I put all the instances together, in every part of the school, it is a major consideration here."

The school sees stepchildren stopping study, disrupting classes, unable to do homework, withdrawing from discussions. The degree of disruption depends, it has observed, on parental attitude. Whether difficulties are major or minor, the school takes on "the temporary role the child asks of us" outside of a strictly intellectual discipline. "We cannot be parent-substitutes, become emotionally motivated, and stay a school," Kittell says. "But we can try to build a temporary resting place for the child while he makes the new adjustment. No matter what happens to his idea of mother or father, the teacher image is sustained, and the child is likely to turn to his teacher for more support than knowledge during this period. It usually takes three or four months until he finds his place at home again and can start working again at school."

There is increasingly sophisticated knowledge of childhood emotions in today's teaching profession as it becomes evident that rampant emotional disarray interferes with learning and equally evident that there can be no more important route to sanity and survival in the world than the education of its young. Whether or not a school chooses to give part of the child's care back to the community, it is aware of the whole child and concerned that there be resources some place in his world to help him in becoming and being a stepchild.

THE RESULTS

The wholeness of the unbroken family is different than the broken and mended wholeness of the step family. Many secular and religious pressures urge the step family to try to ignore the lasting evidence of the break, to regard the stepchild as if he were not a stepchild. Some social pioneers, educators, thoughtful professionals, speak out against such pretense and directly or indirectly encourage the step family openly to hold to its realities.

Which direction is progress, which is sin? Only the stepchild himself can expose the truth of the matter. In the 1960's, the modern stepchild and modern methods of observation fuse to make it visible.

Of all the millions of step people in the present U.S.A. culture, only a few thousand have been observed—or at least observed and recorded—by modern behavioral science and these only recently. It is just thirty years since the first study was published here, not yet forty since the first in the modern world appeared in Germany. Until the last few years, court and clinic records were the chief source of information about the stepchild. They deal mostly with children and families in the lowest third of the socio-economic scale who, if brought to court or clinic, are deeply troubled. Here is evidence of the violent reactions, the stealing, delinquency, running away from home, refusal of stepparents or children or both to make any but the most minimal relationship, if that. Wicked stepmothers and stepfathers who whip, deprive and deny are as plentiful as unhappy stepchildren in need of assistance. Whatever attention the stepchild got from researchers was paid to the deprived stepchild in trouble. From this information, generalities were made, conclusions arrived at; it made a stepchild image for all.

The profile of "normal" stepchildren in high school and college differs sharply. It has come fresh from social science laboratories to change impressions of what the stepchild is like and what he thinks about his family. Two studies have been selected to present the new information, both based

on the opinions of the young people themselves. Most recent
and comprehensive is the observation of 2,145 stepchildren
among 29,000 high school students who were all given questionnaires by their classroom teachers. The second is a personality study of 112 stepchildren among 1,053 college students.
The results of both are combined and summarized here.*

Stepchildren of a higher social and economic bracket do not
show the devastation of the lower. Typically, these newly observed youngsters "are not disorganized, unusual, seriously
maladjusted, or emotionally crippled."

Immediately one is impelled to wonder why one group of
stepchildren is greatly disturbed by the new family setting
while another is not. Economic stress—or the lack of it—is the
line of separation, the concept of remarriage its by-product.
Many lower-class parents *must* remarry to acquire a man to
support or a woman to care for the children of a former
marriage. Need demands that these stepparents act like parents. With sufficient resources, a more privileged father can
hire a housekeeper to take care of his young, a mother has an
estate or alimony and child-support payments to finance her
household. They do not have to remarry to survive, and
when they do, the new spouse does not necessarily have to
become a substitute parent to their children. Personal
preference, not economic need, decides. The children's response to a stepparent who does and must act like a parent
and one who does not, demonstrates a reason for the differ-

* The first study is the continuing work of Charles Bowerman and Donald
Irish of the University of North Carolina; the summary here is taken from
their preliminary report on the largest research project ever concerned with
stepchilden. The stepchildren questioned were in several selected high schools
in different parts of the country, all Juniors and Seniors, all white, and predominantly Protestant.

The second study is presented in *Remarriage* as Bernard's evaluation of
middle-class stepchildren. Some of the students were interviewed, all were
given the Bernreuter Personality Inventory tests.

A third set of observations which will enrich future study of stepchildren
and their families, is the scrutiny of the 186 stepchildren among the 1,660 people examined in *Life Stress and Mental Health*, part of the monumental Midtown Manhattan Study. The results, released as this book goes to press, appear
to validate the two pioneer research studies herein described, in most important respects. Because the methods of this new study and its presentation
are complicated in the extreme, they require careful evaluation. The details
therefore are not included here. Authors Langner and Michael's conclusion:
"The practical problem of how to make remarriage into an emotional gain
for the stepchildren rather than have them feel it as a loss deserves our full
consideration."

ence in the children's reaction between one group and the other.

The newly studied stepchildren are not usually disturbed children. However, it is found that the presence of a stepparent diminishes the child's adjustment at home and toward his natural parents as compared to the adjustment of schoolmates who live with both natural parents. The step families have "more stress, ambivalence, and low cohesiveness."

This discovery, which sounds like a negative feature of step family life, paradoxically turns out to be a plus and suggests another reason for the stepchildren's apparent good health. These youngsters *must* be less closely tied to the step family than in a natural family setting if they are keeping their now separate parents both firmly in mind. The questionable logic of comparing step family apples with natural family oranges is apparent. "Ambivalence and low cohesiveness" is weakness in the latter but a strength for the step family's special requirements. It *must* be present if the stepparent is not forced to be a substitute parent, if the child is allowed his own parents in fact or in memory. He is of course ambivalent as he sets off to visit mother's or father's grave, or to spend a weekend with his other parent. He is less closely tied to home . . . and less troubled than if it had to be otherwise.

The particulars of how the stepchild feels about the parent and stepparent in the home he shares with them show that he is less close to the stepparent than to his own parent, feels that the stepparent discriminates against him more; children of both sexes more often believe a stepmother discriminates than a stepfather. They are less sure of being wanted than their fellow students living in the natural family; girls more often feel rejected than do boys. Both boys and girls are less close to their own parents, too, and the father-stepmother home has the least close ties. It is in this environment that investigators asking, "Do you ever wish you were living in a different family?" hear the loudest "Yes."

It is no surprise that children feel less close to stepparent than to parent, or even that they feel less close to their own parent than they would if there was no stepparent rival to interfere. The children studied have a tendency to identify with the parent of their own sex, with whom they share "attitudes, interests and activities of a sub-culture" (male, female cultures—i.e. the ball game vs. the beauty parlor). Both parents and stepparents have more influence with the children of the same sex, the children themselves report. There is a hugely important distinction within these feelings; added to knowledge of present-day statistics it firmly pinpoints the source of trouble.

The final—and crucial—observation is that stepchildren of divorced parents show a higher average adjustment to stepparents in every age-sex combination than children who are orphaned. Their personalities show a "slight edge" of stability over the bereaved.

The logic presented throughout these pages suggests the reason; stepchildren of divorce almost always live with their mother and stepfather, whereas orphans live with whichever parent survives and his new spouse. The father-stepmother home is the difficult one, because the stepparent therein acts more like a parent. It is the more usual home for the orphan who adjusts less well than the child of divorce ensconced in the mother-stepfather setting. The stepparent who children think discriminates most, the one whom they would most like to leave behind, who inspires the least sub-cultural togetherness with girl children is the stepmother. It is she who makes girls feel more rejected, she, because of being the woman in the house, who is functionally closer to being as a parent than the stepfather, she who more often wants to be, and sometimes has to be, like a real mother, she who is less well regarded by stepchildren. The living-in stepmother is less likely to have a living ally in the children's real mother than a stepfather; if mother is alive, the children usually live with her. A stepfather does not often have to be as a parent; the stepmother does.

Deprived stepchildren are more disturbed than the privileged, girls more than boys, orphans more than children of divorce, all for the same reason—so obvious that it is almost unbelievable that it has never before been identified. It is when the stepparent must act like a parent that the trouble comes. Whether he does so from economic need, social function, or emotional necessity, the result is invariably the same.

The observable measurable truth is that when the stepchild is allowed his own parents by stepfather and stepmother, he manages well in his march toward maturity. When this inalienable right is invaded—by reason of one need or another—he falls back to the position of the ancient deprived stereotype. If circumstance allows him to be at once a child of parents and a stepchild of stepparents, there is progress. The child who is one of the thousands of digits assembled in these observations might be the one to say, "Call Me Stepchild!" to the adult whom he is glad, perhaps even proud, but surely not ashamed to identify as his stepparent.

The truth struggles to be known in the market place, where it competes with the impressively spiraling custom of adoption and the persuasions of religious conviction which join in suggesting that the natural family, or a reasonable facsimile thereof, is best. It competes with the pretenses of divorce law, the teaching of counselors, deep, unreasoning prejudice and fear.

The demonstrable truth that the stepchild is better off when honored as a stepchild may not get itself accepted in minds where dogma demands otherwise. But some adults and children find themselves well served by regarding its bright countenance which begins to define the ground where today's stepchildren—and tomorrow's—will flourish.

Chapter Fifteen

THE POTENTIAL

"Ah, but a man's reach should exceed his grasp, or what's a heaven for?" —BROWNING.

The modern stepchild is a new kind of relation. To give him what he needs, the adults around him have to be a new kind of family. The crystal clarity that the stepchild asks of them requires considerable courage, courage enough to believe in the new family they have made and to perceive its potential for the children and themselves. This new family has a lucid reason for being and an absolute logic for success. It is limited only by its prejudices and frightened yearning for old, known relations. If it can overcome them to meet the stepchild's needs, it reaches closer to the potential for the whole family; if not, the child makes grasping, even reaching, difficult for all. He is at once the thorn in the side of the new family and its inspiration.

By his existence, he insists that the shape of families has changed; by his actions, he makes it clear that its emotions are eternal. The message is particularly evident in the modern stepchild's situation, that of the ever-increasing majority of all stepchildren. Parents have chosen to divorce and to marry again; the children live with mother and stepfather, visit father and stepmother. Step and halfbrothers and sisters share the family, each with his own loyalties and separate history. The arrangement can be different but its basic truth remains the same.

The stepchild's passions are those of every child . . . exposed. To make his first vital compromise between self and world, the child needs a mother and a father. Learning to love them and share them with each other, he learns how to

love and be loved. There is no lesson as important or as difficult. Until he is sure of it, the child makes a variety of
efforts to learn, again and again, that mother and father
cherish him in spite of his wishes to get rid of one or the
other. They continue to cherish him, even when they have
to regulate, limit, and deny. There is, as yet, no better design
to turn growth energies toward maturity.

Little Snow White and her friend in the cinders did well
to identify these emotions in the antediluvian days before
the flood of behavioral science. Because they could not say
outright that a parent could both cherish and deny, making
the child feel both loved and neglected, the logical device of
dividing the *corpus parental* into two, said it for them. The
closest parent being the mother, and her most conflicting
relation being with daughters, the result was Cinderella and
the wicked stepmother. For Cinderella, as for Hamlet who
must kill the man who took his mother away, or Don Carlos
who would destroy his father's marriage and so conquer his
rival, a stepparent is the stand-in for parent, evoking the childlike striving to be completely cherished and the misery of its
unfulfillment. What the folk tales delineated, what Shakespeare, Schiller, Dickens, Ibsen saw, were these eternal emotions, laid raw in the step family where a parent's new spouse
provides the effigy of evil in every parent.

The emotions are better understood, now that the great
scientific exploration of the psyche has at least begun. As
knowledge accumulates, the process of growing up is observed
and catalogued. Some results have been noted: millions of
school children whose inner disturbance stops them from
learning; millions of adolescent males who cannot meet the
minimum requirements of emotional stability for armed service; millions of females pregnant in their teens, married or
not; millions of people of all ages flooding psychiatric clinics,
doctors' offices, social agencies and marriage counseling services in need of help.

Did they all have wicked parents?

They have the everlasting emotions of mankind. It is known
now that there is no pain-proof childhood; a motherly
woman and a kindly man, in love with each other, make the
most superior parents as parents go, but at best they must both

give and deny. Too much giving is as detrimental as too little. The overwhelming attention modern society pays to its children's well-being makes it unalterably apparent that when a balance is maintained, children can grow up in health. The modern stepchild is the messenger of this unequivocal truth. Without angelic mien or flaming sword, without the cover of folk tale or fiction, he baldly announces that his safety is in his mother who gives and denies and similarly in his father. He welcomes surcease from the pain they cause him, enjoys new relationships that ease the struggle to accept reality, but his relations with his parents are, nevertheless, his verities for life and he intends to keep them that way. Trespassers, he says, will be prosecuted.

The stepparent who insists on the name and the stance of a parent is a trespasser. The overindulgent or rigid, demanding stepfather invades the child's idea of his own father; the seemingly innocuous efforts of the remote control stepmother to snare the child to her wishfully maternal bosom, or her opposite action to deny him his father, trespasses too. If his own remarrying mother sends him out of her life or makes him too much a part of it, she trespasses on motherhood; if absentee-father becomes too engrossed in his new existence to be a father, he abjures his paternal role. To each trespasser, the child calls "Halt!" Adults whose sensitivity is alerted to the meaning of his behaviour (for he can act more easily than say the words), will begin to enjoy the discovery of the new family.

The stepchild urges them to take a penetrating look at its innovations.

The extraordinary revolutions of the past century have left the family gasping. As it tumbled in the great tides of change, familiar life patterns washed away. Gone are the guides of tradition, the comfortable controls of kin and community, the economic function of the family which divided labors between its men and women and the three or four generations under its roof. Gone the natural parent-substitutes of the large family, the built-in baby sitters. Great waves of technology, emancipation and scientific advance have immersed the traditions of marriage. There is a new topography on the fresh-washed family shore.

It is easier now for man to grasp what he reaches for this side of heaven. He is reaching for happiness, a sense of self-fulfillment and contentment, of cherishing and being cherished. Marriage has always contained this hope; now, stripped of many of its other functions, it concentrates the goal. Instead of asking, "How is he?" friends ask, "Is he happy?" Whatever definition the individual gives it, his personal idea of happiness is what he wants in marriage.

When there is a stepchild in the family, happiness often appears out of reach. "If it weren't for the children, everything would be all right," man and wife say to each other. The stepchild is evidence of the search for happiness and the terrible fear of transgression it engenders. Guilt is caused by each step taken toward the new family, by the torment of admitting that the first marriage did not work, of choosing divorce, fear of the existence as a demarried parent, the anxious search for a new spouse. The second wedding ceremony, the name and stance of stepparents are all affected by the prejudice left over from other-time family values. Pressures to treat the child as though he were not a stepchild, to act as a natural parent, far from the dread stereotype of wicked stepparent—even to the point of adoption whether indicated or not—take the same coloration. It is an effort to pretend that there have been no revolutions, no changes. The terrible unreasoning fear that something precious is slipping away makes society insist that everything is as it once was. Frightened exponents of family conservatism advertise that the pristine step family can, if it tries hard enough, nestle close to the honorable natural family. Then, perhaps, everything will be all right.

The measure of right and wrong is taken on an outmoded scale. When the family was essential to the economic and social survival of its members, breaking it up by choice might have justifiably been considered a wrong, dangerous for its women and children, impossibly selfish of its men. Remarriage after divorce, proof of the sinful motive, was wrong because of it. The tragedy of bereavement could be quickly corrected by another marriage without censure; it was right for the widowed to marry again in a week or a month when the family unit had to be preserved at all costs.

By modern measure right and wrong reverse. If it is right to search for individual fulfillment and happiness in marriage, it is wrong to stay in a marriage that fails to provide either. Divorce is directed toward the accepted goal of the individual in contemporary society. It is better for him, experts say, and better for his children, than continuing an environment of marital strife and unhappiness. It is right, then, for some people to divorce, even more so if they utilize the process to know how they have failed, how they might better succeed in their search for happiness. With this insight, the dash to marry again is wrong; recovery from the breakup of a marriage, whether by death or divorce, takes time to be complete. Pressures that make the demarried parent uncomfortable in his effort to manage alone and impel him, for the sake of his children and himself, toward a quick re-creation of a family setting is as sinful today as it once was essential.

The many pressures from without and within that urge parents toward another marriage have been scrutinized all through these pages, as they are identified by scientific inquiry, literary insight, reportage, or confessional. The same pressures have been seen in the new family; the child still wants the mother that is his mother, the father that is his father. If he is the child of divorce, he has them both, albeit living apart. If he has been orphaned, he is less richly endowed, having only the memory of the parent who has died and the temptation to transform this memory into a less than serviceable ideal. The child still wants to know that his parents have the capacity to cherish and be cherished as parents and people. When they remarry, he has this satisfaction too. He need not fear that he is the center of their world, or feel the burden of guilt upon him. The parent has neither divorced for him, nor married for him, but for the adult's own unique definition of happiness and this makes the child safe again, and sure.

But even if a parent has logically, slowly come to the creation of a new family through difficult months, even years, of acquiring wisdom enough and courage enough to pioneer its wilderness, there are pressures. The census-taker rings the doorbell but does not identify stepchildren because asking relationships might embarrass or answers not be known. In more ways than this, society does not count stepchildren. Stepmothers are afraid of the difference from natural children. Stepfathers buy everyone identical Christmas presents from the same fear and they compete with the financially responsible visiting fathers or capitulate to them and retire to anonymity. Mother-stepmother rivalry damages with more then feline scratches when it hits at the tender center of the child's world. The very best stepparents—in the eyes of the uninformed segments of present culture—are the ones who allow this damage. These are the stepparents who know no difference between real and make-believe parenthood and because of this ignorance, will never be able to know what the stepchild needs from them.

From many high places they are encouraged in their pretense; the urging is from outside the window, from inside the mirror on the wall. But the child of modern marriage, product of modern revolutions, is wiser. In one way or another, he lets the adults in the family know his needs.

The stepparent who is free to look and listen, understands. He reads the stepchild's message, which concerns the one and only essential of every child's family life—the need to know that his mother and father love and cherish him in their fashion. For this he rebels, begs, fights, steals, becomes delinquent, asthmatic, neurotic, epileptic. For this, he runs away from home, threatens suicide. For this, he will not be forced to say "mother or "father" to stepparents, unknown and undetermined quantities in his emotions. To know his own mother's and father's caring is his need and his desire.

If it does not interfere with these primary primitive feelings, he can communicate what the stepparent might be to him. His age, sex, and circumstance determine needs, his actions say what they are. He may need a stepmother who is an almost complete mother-substitute to care for his body and soul and provide the tender hands and capacious lap of a maternal person. Or he may need a pleasant friend who is father's good wife and packs a good picnic lunch, a welcoming, companionable, receptive woman who knows what motherhood and fatherhood are about and respects both from an impeccably-regarded distance. He may need complete understanding and support from a stepfather and lean heavily on his shoulder, or he may skirt the reality of mother's husband with as polite and distant a relation as he can manage. He may want to say "mother" or "father" to the stepparent; he may not. But no one knows better than he that he is the child of his parents, stepchild of his stepparents. Because this is what he is, this is what he wants to be. It frees him to make the step relationship an asset.

Childhood is a little time of life but what happens in it shapes the rest. Parent and stepparent can afford the small sacrifices of ego and the large lessons of the pioneer life they have chosen to make childhood right and sound for the stepchildren. They have taken bold steps toward the new way of a family in their determination to find their own fulfillment. It lies ahead of them in certain exhilarating freshness; turning back in fear and pretense denies the good life to the stepchild as he in turn will deny it to adults around him. But happiness in the family is up to them.

It comes swiftly to some, very slowly to others. Doctors, laywers, social workers, counselors to the human spirit of many sorts and disciplines, all caution the new family to take time in finding its way to live. If the instinct is to send the child away, get a divorce, stop trying to make a relationship, don't do it, the advisors chorus, until some understanding of self has been achieved. If the step relation makes trouble after months of effort (some say three months, some say a year, even two) it is recommended that the adults get professional guidance, not for the child in the first instance, but for themselves. Knowing themselves, man and wife can come to look and listen to the insistent if at times unintelligible message of the child's need and, perhaps, meet it.

The great adventure of the stepchild in the family is being discovered every day. The woman who is a stepmother finds it in the satisfying sensations of the extra dimension in her marriage, her husband's children. She does not have to reject or embrace these small replicas of the man she has married; they have a special enchantment for her because they help to make her husband happy. Since it is to his fulfillment and her own that she devotes her talents, she is able to help him toward satisfying fatherhood and toward their mutual happiness goal. The stepfather, too, pioneers as he becomes the sort of family man he sometimes had imagined. His new relation with the stepchild is free, directed only by his wish and the child's. They can make it what they will. If friendship happens, it comes from the heart, as good a friendship as either man or child may know. It is welcomed by wife and mother. Although she and her husband do not have an equivalent relation with each other's children, the fear this might once have engendered is replaced by the steady joy of discovering the potential of the new kind of family.

The stepchild in the family can be its inspiration. His dignity lies in being exactly what he is. In his every act, he urges respect for modern marriage. He will not be forced to the indignity of its pretenses; he wants wisdom around him which honors its absolute truth. To this, he devotes the most valiant battle of his life.

BIBLIOGRAPHY

Adcock, Ruth H., "A Study of Inharmony and Its Effects upon Children." Unpublished Master's thesis, Columbia University School of Social Work, 1945.

Aichorn, August, *Wayward Youth*. New York: The Viking Press, 1938.

Anonymous (1), "A Brief Manual for Stepmothers." *Good Housekeeping,* March 1943.

———— (2), "Can Divorce Be Successful?" *Harper's Magazine,* February 1938.

———— (3), "Frequent Divorce in New England." *American Quarterly Church Review,* Vol. 20, July 1868.

———— (4) (as told to Terry Morris), "I Gave My Son Away." *McCall's Magazine,* June 1957.

———— (5), "I Have Four Parents." *Saturday Evening Post,* 6 February 1937.

———— (6) (as told to Judith Krantz), "I'm an Uncle to My Sons." *Coronet,* May 1958.

———— (7), "I'm a Stepparent—But Not an Ogre." *Better Homes and Gardens,* March 1952.

———— (8), "Other Women's Children." *Harper's Magazine,* July 1927.

———— (9), "The New Father." *Forum and Century,* c. 1938.

———— (10), "When a Bride Becomes a Stepmother." *Ladies' Home Journal,* 15 April 1911.

Ariès, Philippe, *Centuries of Childhood.* Translated by Robert Baldick. New York: Alfred A. Knopf, Inc., 1962.

Arnstein, Helene, in cooperation with The Child Study Association of America, *What to Tell Your Child.* New York: The Bobbs-Merrill Company, Inc., 1962.

Aubrey, Edwin E., "The Protestant Point of View on Sex, Marriage and Divorce," in *Man and Wife,* edited by Emily Hartshorne Mudd and Aaron Krich. New York: W. W. Norton & Company, Inc., 1957.

Austen, Jane, *Emma.* London: J. M. Dent & Co., 1898.

Baber, R. E., *Marriage and the Family.* New York: McGraw-Hill Book Company, 1939.

Bacal, J., and Sloane, L., "Are Second Marriages Better?" *Look,* 25 November 1947.

Baker, George P., Preface to *Hamlet* (The Tudor Shakespeare). New York: The Macmillan Company, 1922.

Barclay, Dorothy, "Double Role of the Single Parent." *The New York Times,* 13 October 1957.

Barton, William E., *The Women Lincoln Loved*. New York: The Bobbs-Merrill Company, Inc., 1927.

Baruch, Dorothy W., and Miller, Hyman, "A Second Marriage Means a Second Chance." *Parents' Magazine,* April 1962.

Beatman, Frances, "When a Child Gets a New Parent." *The New York Times,* 29 January 1961.

Becker, Howard, "The Sorrow of Bereavement." *Journal of Abnormal and Social Psychology,* XXVII, 1933.

Becker, Howard, and Hill, Reuben (eds.), *Family, Marriage and Parenthood.* Boston: D. C. Heath & Company, 1948.

Belloc, Hilaire, *Napoleon.* Philadelphia: J. B. Lippincott Co., 1932.

Benedict, Ruth, "Folklore." *Encyclopedia of the Social Sciences.* New York: The Macmillan Company, 1937.

Beres, David, and Obers, Samuel, "The Effects of Extreme Deprivation in Infancy on Psychic Structure." *Psychoanalytic Study of the Child,* Vol. 5, 1950.

Bergler, Edmund, *Divorce Won't Help.* New York: Harper & Brothers, 1948.

Bernard, Jessie, *Remarriage: A Study of Marriage.* New York: The Dryden Press, 1956.

Bernert, Eleanor H., *America's Children.* New York: John Wiley & Sons, Inc., 1958.

Blaine, Graham B., Jr., "The Children of Divorce." *Atlantic Monthly,* March 1963.

Blake, Nelson Manfred, *The Road to Reno.* New York: The Macmillan Company, 1962.

Bossard, James H. S., "Divorce, Some Selected Repercussions," in *Man and Wife,* edited by Emily Hartshorne Mudd and Aaron Krich. New York: W. W. Norton & Company, Inc., 1957.

————, *Family Situations.* Philadelphia: University of Pennsylvania Press, 1943.

————, *Marriage and the Child.* Philadelphia: University of Pennsylvania Press, 1940.

————, *Parent and Child.* Philadelphia: University of Pennsylvania Press, 1953.

Bossard, James H. S., and Boll, Eleanor S., *The Sociology of Child Development.* New York: Harper & Brothers, 1960.

Bowerman, Charles E., and Irish, Donald P., "Some Relationships of Stepchildren to Their Parents." *Marriage and Family Living,* Vol. 24, No. 2, May 1962.

Bride's Magazine Editors, *The Bride's Book of Etiquette.* New York: Grosset & Dunlap, 1948.

Bromley, Dorothy Dunbar (ed.), *A Decade of Progress* (Report to New York State Committee for 1960 White House Conference). Distributed by New York State Youth Commission.

Bronson, John W., "Custody on Appeal." *Law and Contemporary Problems,* Vol. X, No. 5, 1944.

Brown, Helen Gurley, *Sex and the Single Girl.* New York: Bernard Geis Associates, 1962.

Brunner, Edmund de S., "Education as a Factor in Divorce." *Teacher's College Record,* No. 49, 1948.

Burgess, Ernest W., "The Family in a Changing Society." *American Journal of Sociology,* No. 53, 1948.

Burgess, Ernest W., and Cottrell, L. S., *Predicting Success or Failure in Marriage.* New York: Prentice-Hall, Inc., 1939.

Burgess, Helen S., "Stepmothers Can Be Nice." *Public Affairs Pamphlet No. 198,* June 1953.

Campbell, Joseph, "Folkloristic Commentary," in Grimm Brothers' *Fairy Tales.* New York: Pantheon Books, Inc., 1944.

Carter, Hugh, "Improving National Marriage and Divorce Statistics." *Journal of the American Statistical Association,* No. 48, 1953.

Clemens, A. H., "The Catholic Point of View on Sex, Marriage and Divorce," in *Man and Wife,* edited by Emily Hartshorne Mudd and Aaron Krich. New York: W. W. Norton & Company, Inc., 1957.

Cochrane, A. L., "A Little Widow Is a Dangerous Thing." *International Journal of Psychoanalysis,* Vol. XVII, 1936.

Cohen, Dorothy H., "Children of Divorce." *Parents' Magazine,* August 1960.

Collier, Mary J., "The Psychological Appeal in the Cinderella Theme." *American Imago,* No. 18, 1961.

Colum, Padraic, Introduction to Grimm Brothers' *Fairy Tales.* New York: Pantheon Books, Inc., 1944.

Corpus Jurus Secundum. Vol. 2, 1936; Vol. 67, 1950; Vol. 26a, 1956; Supplement, 1962. American Law Book Co. (Brooklyn) and West Publishing Co. (St. Paul).

Cox, Marion R., *Cinderella: Three Hundred and Forty-five Variants.* London: Folk Lore Society, 1893.

Davis, Kingsley, "A Sociological and Statistical Analysis." *Law and Contemporary Problems,* Vol. X, No. 5 (Children of Divorced Parents), Summer 1944.

————, "Statistical Perspective on Divorce." *Annals of the American Academy of Political and Social Sciences,* No. 272, 1950.

Decter, Midge, "The Young Divorcée." *Harper's Magazine,* October 1962.

Despert, J. Louise, *Children of Divorce.* New York: Doubleday & Company, Inc., 1953.

Deutsch, Helene, *The Psychology of Women.* New York: Grune & Stratton, Inc., 1944.

Dickens, Charles, *David Copperfield* (Great Illustrated Classics). New York: Dodd, Mead and Company.

Drinnan, Robert F., "America's Half Orphans." *Vital Speeches,* No. 28, 1 November 1961.

Dublin, Louis I., and Spiegelman, M., *Facts of Life from Birth to Death.* New York: The Macmillan Company, 1951.

249

Du Maurier, Daphne, *Rebecca*. New York: Doubleday, Doran & Co., 1938.

Duvall, Evelyn M., and Hill, Reuben, *When You Marry*. Boston: D. C. Heath & Company, 1953.

Earle, Alice M., *Customs and Fashions in Old New England*. New York: Charles Scribner's Sons, 1894.

Egleson, Jim, and Egleson, Janet Frank, *Parents Without Partners*. New York: E. P. Dutton & Co., Inc., 1961.

Eisendorfer, Arnold, "The Clinical Significance of the Single Parent Relationship in Women." *Psychoanalytic Quarterly*, Vol. XII, No. 2, 1943.

Eliot, Thomas D., "The Bereaved Family." *Annals of the American Academy of Political and Social Sciences*, Vol. 160, March 1932.

————, "Bereavement: Inevitable but Not Insurmountable," in *Family, Marriage and Parenthood*, edited by Howard Becker and Reuben Hill. Boston: D. C. Heath & Company, 1948.

"Elizabeth." *Encyclopaedia Britannica*, Fourteenth Edition, 1929.

Engel, Tinka D., "Adoption Agencies Adapt." *The New York Times*, 28 October 1962.

English, O. Spurgeon, and Foster, Constance J., *Fathers Are Parents, Too*. New York: G. P. Putnam's Sons, 1951.

English, O. Spurgeon, and Pearson, Gerald H. J., *Common Neuroses of Children and Adults*. New York: W. W. Norton & Company, Inc., 1937.

Ernst, Morris, "The Case of the Pretty Widow." *Harper's Magazine*, May 1957.

Ernst, Morris, and Loth, D. G., *For Better or Worse*. New York: Harper & Brothers, 1951.

Estrin, Anne E., "The Child and the Stepmother." Unpublished Master's thesis, Columbia University School of Social Work, 1944.

Faegre, Marion L., "The 'Cruel' Stepmother." *Ladies' Home Journal*, February 1935.

Families with Children (Parents' Magazine Data Book No. 4). New York: Parents' Institute, Inc., 1960.

Fancher, Betsy H., "I was an 'Instant' Mother." *Redbook*, March 1962.

Fenichel, Otto, *The Psychoanalytic Theory of Neurosis*. New York: W. W. Norton & Company, Inc., 1945.

Fielding, William J., *Strange Customs of Courtship and Marriage*. New York: Doubleday & Company, Inc., 1960.

Finch, Mildred S., "Tips for Stepmothers." *Parents' Magazine*, January 1951.

Fletcher, Ronald, *Britain in the Sixties: The Family and Marriage*. Baltimore: Penguin Books, Inc., 1962.

Flügel, J. C., *Psychoanalytic Study of the Family*. London: Hogarth Press, 1935.

Fortes, A. N., "Terrorization of the Libido and Snow-White." *Psychoanalytic Review*, Vol. 2, No. 27, 1940.

Franzblau, Rose, "Sloppy Stepdaughter." *New York Post,* 20 September 1962.
————, "Stepchild's Expenses." *New York Post,* 5 November 1962.
Freeman, Douglas S., *George Washington.* New York: Charles Scribner's Sons, 1951.
Freud, Sigmund, *A General Introduction to Psychoanalysis.* Translated by Joan Riviere. New York: Garden City Publishing Co., 1948.
————, "The Interpretation of Dreams." *The Basic Writings of Sigmund Freud,* edited by A. A. Brill. New York: Random House, Inc., 1938.
————, "The Occurrence in Dreams of Material from Fairy Tales." *Collected Papers,* Vol. IV. London: Hogarth Press, 1924.
————, "The Theme of the Three Caskets." *Collected Papers,* Vol. IV. London: Hogarth Press, 1924.
————, *Totem and Taboo.* Translated by A. A. Brill. New York: Moffat, Yard & Co., 1918.
————, "The 'Uncanny.' " *Collected Papers,* Vol. IV. London: Hogarth Press, 1924.
Friedan, Betty, *The Feminine Mystique.* New York: W. W. Norton & Company, Inc., 1963.
Fromm, Erich, *The Forgotten Language.* New York: Rinehart & Co., Inc., 1951.
————, *Man for Himself.* New York: Rinehart & Co., Inc., 1947.
Gentleman, Vivian F., "The Real Scandal of Divorce." *Saturday Evening Post,* 15 December 1962.
Gesell, Arnold, and Ilg, Frances, *Infant and Child in the Culture of Today.* New York: Harper & Brothers, 1943.
Glick, Paul C., *American Families.* New York: John Wiley & Sons, Inc., 1957.
————, "First Marriages and Remarriages." *American Sociological Review,* No. 14, 1949.
Goode, William J., *After Divorce.* Glencoe: The Free Press, 1956.
————, "Problems in Postdivorce Adjustment." *American Sociological Review,* No. 14, 1949.
Goodman, David, "The Torment of the Divorced Man." *Coronet,* June 1961.
Goodman, Paul, *Growing Up Absurd.* New York: Random House, Inc., 1960.
"Gretchen," "I'll Take My Parents Separately." *Harper's Magazine.* March 1938.
Grimm, Wilhelm, and Grimm, Jacob, *Fairy Tales.* New York: Pantheon Books, Inc., 1944.
————, *Household Tales,* Vol. 2. Translated by Margaret Hunt. London, 1884.
Hall, Paul, "They Didn't *Have* to Love Me!" *Coronet,* February 1961.
Halliday, William H., "Folklore." *Encyclopaedia Britannica,* Fourteenth Edition, 1929.

Hammet, Marion, "Are You a Readymade Parent?" *American Home,* November 1950.

"Happily Ever After?" *Psychiatric Quarterly Supplement,* Vol. 22, 1948.

Haussamen, Florence, and Guitar, Mary Anne, *The Divorce Handbook.* New York: G. P. Putnam's Sons, 1960.

Havemann, Ernest, *Men, Women and Marriage.* New York: Doubleday & Company, Inc., 1962.

Heilpern, Else P., "Psychological Problems of Stepchildren." *Psychoanalytic Review,* No. 30, April 1943.

Hoffmann, Betty H., "Second Marriages." *Ladies' Home Journal,* April 1963.

Hollingshead, August B., "Marital Status and Wedding Behaviour." *Marriage and Family Living,* Vol. 14, November 1952.

Hollingshead, August B., and Redlich, Frederick C., *Social Class and Mental Illness.* New York: John Wiley & Sons, Inc., 1958.

Howard, George E., *A History of Matrimonial Institutions.* Chicago: University of Chicago Press, 1904.

Hutzler, Ellen B., "Our Children Can Tell Us." *Parents Without Partners Journal,* September 1962.

Ibsen, Henrik, *When We Dead Awaken and Three Other Plays.* Translated by Michael Meyer. New York: Anchor Books (Doubleday & Company, Inc.), 1960.

Ilg, Frances L., and Ames, Louise B., *Parents Ask.* New York: Harper & Brothers, 1962.

Ilgenfritz, M. P., "Mothers on Their Own—Widows and Divorcées." *Marriage and Family Living,* Vol. 23, February 1961.

Isaacs, Susan, *Childhood and After.* London: Routledge & Kegan Paul, Ltd., 1948.

————, *The Nursery Years.* New York: The Vanguard Press, 1929.

Jacobson, Paul H., *American Marriage and Divorce.* New York: Rinehart & Company, 1959.

————, Special study for *Stepchild in the Family.*

Jenkins, Elizabeth, *Elizabeth the Great.* New York: Coward-McCann, Inc., 1959.

Jones, Ernest, *Hamlet and Oedipus.* New York: W. W. Norton & Company, Inc., 1949.

Jung, C. G., *Memories, Dreams, Reflections.* Recorded and edited by Aniela Jaffé. New York: Pantheon Books, Inc., 1963.

Kaplan, R., "A Woman Without a Man." *Coronet,* October 1960.

Kellogg, Rhoda, *Babies Need Fathers Too.* New York: Comet Press, Inc., 1953.

Kubie, Lawrence S., *Neurotic Distortion of the Creative Process.* Lawrence: University of Kansas Press, 1958.

Landis, Judson T., "A Comparison of Children from Divorced and Nondivorced Unhappy Marriages." *The Family Life Coordinator,* Vol. XI, No. 3, 1962.

————, "The Pattern of Divorce in Three Generations." *Social Forces,* Vol. XXXIV, No. 3, March 1956.

————, "Religiousness, Family Relationships, and Family Values in Protestant, Catholic and Jewish Families." *Marriage and Family Living*, Vol. 22, No. 4. November 1960.

————, "Social Correlates of Divorce or Nondivorce among the Unhappily Married." *Marriage and Family Living*, Vol. 25, March 1963.

————, "The Trauma of Children When Parents Divorce." *Marriage and Family Living*, Vol. 22, No. 1, February 1960.

Landis, Judson T., and Landis, Mary (eds.), *Readings in Marriage and the Family*. New York: Prentice-Hall, Inc., 1952.

Landis, Paul, "Sequential Marriage." *Journal of Home Economics*, No. 42, 1950.

Lang, Andrew, Introduction to *Cinderella: Three Hundred and Forty-five Variants* (Cox, Marion R.). London: Folk Lore Society, 1893.

Langman (now Simon), Anne W., "When Parents Remarry." *McCall's Magazine*, May 1962.

Langner, Thomas S., and Michael, Stanley T., *Life Stress and Mental Health* (Vol. 2 of *The Midtown Manhattan Study*). New York: The Free Press of Glencoe, 1963.

Lederer, Anne R., "How Remarriage Works." *Parents Without Partners Journal*, December 1962.

Lemasters, E. E., *Modern Courtship and Marriage*. New York: The Macmillan Company, 1957.

Lerner, Max, *America as a Civilization*. New York: Simon & Schuster, Inc., 1957.

Lewin, S. A., and Gilmore, John, *Sex After Forty*. New York: Dell Publishing Co., Inc., 1952.

Locke, Harvey J., *Predicting Happiness or Divorce in Marriage*. Henry Holt & Co., Inc., 1951.

Locke, Harvey J., and Klausner, Wm. J., "Marital Adjustment of Divorced Persons in Subsequent Marriages." *Sociology and Social Research*, No. 33, 1948.

Lorand, Sandor, "Fairy Tales and Neurosis." *Psychoanalytic Quarterly*, No. 4, 1935.

Ludwig, Emil, *Napoleon*. Translated by Eden and Cedar Paul. New York: Boni & Liveright, 1926.

Lyons, Leonard, "The Lyons Den." *New York Post*, 27 March 1963.

Mace, David R., "Plight of the Lone Parent." *McCall's Magazine*, August 1962.

Maisel, Albert Q., "Divorce Is Going Out of Style." *Reader's Digest*, August 1957.

Mann, Thomas, *The Magic Mountain*. Translated by H. T. Lowe-Porter. New York: Alfred A. Knopf, Inc., 1927.

Marcus, Donald M. "The Cinderella Motif: Fairy Tale and Defense." *American Imago*, Vol. 20, No. 1, Spring 1963.

Mead, Margaret, *Beyond the Nuclear Family*. Speech to Child Study Association of America, March 1963.

——, *Male and Female.* New York: William Morrow & Co., 1949.
Meier, Elizabeth G., "Is There a Stepfather in the House?" *Parents'
Magazine,* August 1961.
Meriam, Adele S., *The Stepfather in the Family.* Chicago: University of
Chicago Press, 1940.
Metropolitan Life Insurance Company Statistical Bulletin.
"American Marriages in 1962." Vol. 44, May 1963.
"America's Children." Vol. 37, August 1956.
"Family Disruption by Death." Vol. 38, June 1957.
"Family Responsibility Increasing." Vol. 40, April 1959.
"Mortality Lowest in Married Population." Vol. 38, February 1957.
"Population Gains in the United States and Canada." Vol. 44,
January 1963.
"The American Widow." Vol. 43, November 1962.
"The Frequency of Remarriage." Vol. 30, January 1949.
"Young Widows and Their Dependents." Vol. 37, March 1956.
Milton, John, *The Works of John Milton.* Boston: C. C. Little and
J. Brown, 1851.
Mitford, Rev. John, "Life of John Milton," in *The Works of John
Milton.* Boston: C. C. Little and J. Brown, 1851.
Monahan, Thomas P., "Changing Nature and Instability of Remar-
riages." *Eugenics Quarterly,* Vol. 5, No. 2, 1958.
——, "How Stable Are Remarriages?" *American Journal of Sociology,*
No. 58, 1952.
Morris, Terry, "What Clergymen Tell Young People About Marriage."
Redbook, March 1963.
Mowrer, Ernest R., "Divorce and Readjustment." *Annals of the Ameri-
can Academy of Political and Social Sciences,* Vol. 160, 1932.
Mudd, Emily Hartshorne, "Marriage Counseling: A Philosophy and
Method," in *Man and Wife,* edited by Emily Hartshorne Mudd
and Aaron Krich. New York: W. W. Norton & Company, Inc., 1957.
——, "The Special Task of Premarital Counseling," *ibid.*
Mullahy, Patrick, *Oedipus, Myth and Complex.* New York: Hermitage
House, 1948.
National Office of Vital Statistics, *Annual Report,* 1959.
Neubauer, Peter B., "The One-Parent Child and His Oedipal Devel-
opment." *The Psychoanalytic Study of the Child,* Vol. XV, 1960.
New York Post, "Will Rocky Wed Mrs. Murphy?" 20 April 1963.
New York Times, The, "Divorce Reform Urged by Rabbi." 26 May 1963.
——, "Early Marriage Is Assessed." 3 November 1962.
——, "Minister Reproved." 9 May 1963.
——, "Punishment for Miracle Makers." 27 November 1962.
Nimkoff, Mayer F., "Occupational Factors and Marriage." *American
Journal of Sociology,* No. 49, 1943.
Nye, Ivan, "Child Adjustment in Broken and in Unhappy Unbroken
Homes." *Marriage and Family Living,* No. 19, November 1957.
Ogburn, William, "The Changing Functions of the Family." *Journal
of Home Economics,* No. 25, 1933.

O'Neill, Eugene, *Desire Under the Elms*. New York: Random House, Inc., 1924.

Ostrovsky, Everett S., *Father to the Child*. New York: G. P. Putnam's Sons, 1959.

Palmer, Gretta, "My Husband's Children." *Good Housekeeping*, February 1941.

Paulsen, Monrad G., "Support Rights and Duties Between Husband and Wife." *Vanderbilt Law Review*, Vol. 9, 1956.

Pfleger, Janet, "The 'Wicked Stepmother' in a Child Guidance Clinic." *Smith College Studies in Social Work*, Vol. XVII, No. 3, March 1947.

Pickering, Gov. William, quoted in Vannest, Charles G., *Lincoln the Hoosier*. Eden Publishing House, 1928.

Pilpel, Harriet F., and Zavin, Theodora, *Your Marriage and the Law*. New York: Rinehart & Company, 1952.

Plant, James S., "The Psychiatrist Views Children of Divorced Parents." *Law and Contemporary Problems*, Vol. X, No. 5 (Children of Divorced Parents), Summer 1944.

Podolsky, Edward, "The Emotional Problems of the Stepchild." *Mental Hygiene*, Vol. XXXIX, January 1955.

Popenoe, Paul, "Divorce and Remarriage from a Eugenic Point of View." *Social Forces*, No. 12, October 1933.

————, *Modern Marriage*. New York: The Macmillan Company, 1943.

————, *Modern Marriage Handbook for Men*. New York: The Macmillan Company, 1947.

————, "Remarriage of Divorcees to Each Other." *American Sociological Review*, Vol. 3, No. 5, October 1938.

Post, Emily, *Children Are People*. New York: Funk & Wagnalls Co., revised 1959.

————, *Etiquette*. New York: Funk & Wagnalls Co., revised 1960.

Reston, James, "The Presidential Ideal and Rockefeller's Remarriage." *The New York Times*, 8 May 1963.

Ricklin, Franz, *Wish Fulfillment and Symbolism in Fairy Tales*. Translated by William A. White. New York: The Nervous and Mental Disease Publishing Co., 1915.

Riesman, David, *Individualism Reconsidered*. Glencoe: The Free Press, 1954.

Rochford, Elbrun, *Mothers on Their Own*. New York: Harper & Brothers, 1953.

Rogers, Donald I., *Teach Your Wife to Be a Widow*. New York: Henry Holt & Co., 1953.

Roheim, Geza, "Myth and Folktale." *American Imago*, Vol. 2, No. 3, 1940.

Roosevelt, Eleanor, *Book of Common Sense Etiquette*. New York: The Macmillan Company, 1962.

Rosebery, Lord, *Napoleon, the Last Phase*. New York: Harper & Brothers, 1900.

Roulston, Marjorie Hillis, "How to Choose a Second Husband." *Cosmopolitan*, April 1951.

————, *You Can Start All Over*. New York: Harper & Brothers, 1951.

Rutledge, Aaron L., "Marriage Problems and Divorce," in *Children and Youth in the 1960s*. Golden Anniversary White House Conference on Children and Youth, Inc., 1960.

Sandburg, Carl, *Abraham Lincoln*. New York: Harcourt Brace & Co., Inc., 1926.

Saturday Review. Cartoon, 1 June 1963.

————. Classified advertisment, 4 April 1963.

Schiller, Friedrich von, *Don Carlos*. Translated by Charles E. Passage. New York: Frederick Ungar Publishing Co., 1959.

Science News Letter. "Adoption May Trigger Psychiatric Problems." 1 December 1962.

Sevigné, Madame de, *Letters*. Translated by Violet Hammersley. London: Secker & Warburg, 1955.

Shakespeare, William, *Cymbeline* (The Tudor Shakespeare, edited by W. A. Neilson and A. H. Thorndike). New York: The Macmillan Company, 1922.

————, *Hamlet. Ibid.*

————, *King Henry IV, Part 2. Ibid.*

Shaw, George Bernard, *Man and Superman*. New York: Bantam Books, 1959.

Shultz, Gladys D., *Widows: Wise and Otherwise*. Philadelphia: J. B. Lippincott Co., 1949.

Smith, Wiliam C., *The Stepchild*. Chicago: University of Chicago Press, 1953.

————, "The Stepmother." *Sociology and Social Research*, Vol. XXXIII, 5-6, 1941.

Sophocles, *Oedipus, King of Thebes*. Translated by Gilbert Murray. New York: Oxford University Press, 1911.

Spock, Benjamin, *Baby and Child Care*. New York: Pocket Books, Inc., 1957.

————, "The Stepchild." *Ladies' Home Journal*, November 1962.

Steinbeck, John, *East of Eden*. New York: The Viking Press, 1952.

Stoddard, William O., *Abraham Lincoln: The True Story of a Great Life*. New York: Fords, Howard & Hulbut, 1885.

"T. M. H.," "Don't Be Afraid of a Stepchild." *Woman's Home Companion*, July 1949.

Tarbell, Ida M. *The Early Life of Abraham Lincoln*. New York: S. S. McClure, 1896.

Taylor, Harold, *The American Family as an Educational Institution*. Speech to the Child Study Association of America, March 1963.

Terman, Lewis M., *Psychological Factors in Marital Happiness*. New York: McGraw-Hill Book Company, 1938.

Thayer, Mary van Rensselaer, *Jacqueline Bouvier Kennedy*. New York: Doubleday & Co., Inc., 1961.

Thompson, Stith, *The Folk Tale*. New York: The Dryden Press, 1946.
————, *Motif-Index of Folk Literature*. Bloomington: Indiana University Press, 1957.
Tolchin, Martin, "Age Gap in a Marriage." *The New York Times*, 17 October 1962.
————, "Second Marriage Can Succeed." *The New York Times*, 15 April 1963.
————, "Stepmother's Role Is a Difficult One." *The New York Times*, 12 November 1962.
Townsend, Elizabeth, "An Encyclopedic Approach to Finding a Second Husband." *McCall's Magazine*, July 1960.
Vernier, Chester G., *American Family Laws*, Vol. IV. Stanford: Stanford University Press, 1936.
Vincent, Clark E., *Unmarried Mothers*. New York: The Free Press of Glencoe, 1961.
Waller, Willard W., *The Family*, revised by Reuben Hill. New York: The Dryden Press, 1951.
Webster's New International Dictionary of the English Language, second edition. Springfield: G. & C. Merriam Company, 1959.
Wertenbaker, William, "A Problem of Identity." *The New Yorker*, 1 December 1962.
Westermarck, Edward, *The History of Human Marriage*. New York: The Macmillan Company, 1921.
White, Annie M., "Factors Making for Difficulty in the Step Relationship." Unpublished Master's thesis, Smith College School of Social Work, 1943.
Whitman, Arthur, "The Mystery of Lincoln." *Philadelphia Inquirer*, 10 February 1963.
Wice, David H., "The Jewish Point of View on Sex, Marriage and Divorce," in *Man and Wife*, edited by Emily Hartshorne Mudd and Aaron Krich. New York: W. W. Norton & Company, Inc., 1957.
Wittels, Fritz, *Set the Children Free*. London: G. Allen & Unwin, 1932.
Wittman, Robert, "A Pampered Child and His Stepmother." *International Journal of Individual Psychology*, Fourth Quarter, 1936.
Wolf, Anna W. M., and Stein, Lucille, "The One Parent Family." *Public Affairs Pamphlet FL 287*, August 1959.
Woman's Home Companion Survey, LXIV, September 1937.
Zimmerman, Carle C., *The Family of Tomorrow*. New York: Harper & Brothers, 1949.

Curculation   016.3

M 667

Augsburg College
George Sverdrup Library
Minneapolis, Minnesota 55404